Children's Voices in Surrogacy Law

About the Authors

Katherine Wade is a Senior Lecturer in Law at the University of Bristol Law School. Her research areas are in family law, medical law and children's rights. Her research examines issues in assisted reproduction from a children's rights perspective, with a focus on surrogacy and donor conception.

Kirsty Horsey is a Professor of Law at Loughborough University. Her research interests lie primarily in the regulation of surrogacy and other forms of assisted human reproduction. She is particularly interested in where these areas overlap and intersect with issues in family law, especially the concept of legal parenthood.

Zaina Mahmoud is a Senior Lecturer in Law in the School of Law and Social Justice at the University of Liverpool. She has a keen interest in (assisted) reproduction and gestation. As a socio-legal scholar, she takes an empirical approach to enhancing the legal analytical component of her research.

Acknowledgements

Our biggest thanks go to the 54 children and young people who gave up their time to participate in this research. Thank you also to their parents and carers for agreeing to their participation and facilitating the interviews.

We also thank all the non-profit surrogacy organisations who helped us recruit many of the participants who have lived experience of surrogacy and the schools that recruited the participants in Phase Two and facilitated the interviews in their schools.

Thank you also to other organisations, groups and individuals who published or shared our call for participants.

Thank you to the Law Commission of England and Wales and the Scottish Law Commission for inviting us to present the preliminary findings of Phase One of this research and for encouraging us to undertake Phase Two, thereby making the project even more ambitious than we had envisaged.

Thank you to all those who gave up their time to give us input and advice, or to read drafts of one or more chapters of this book at various stages of the writing process, including Professor Lois Bibbings, Dr Nicolás Brando, Professor Mandy Burton, Dr Louise Forde, Dr Leah Gilman, Professor Emily Grabham, Professor Rosemary Hunter, and Professor Dawn Watkins.

We would like to also give special thanks to Dr Charlotte Mills, our research assistant on Phase One of this project, who was instrumental in its initiation in terms of recruitment, logistical planning and in the co-design of the methodology and methods.

This book is for everyone born through, or to be born through, surrogacy.

HFE Act	Human Fertilisation and Embryology Act (1990 or 2008).
HFEA	The Human Fertilisation and Embryology Authority.
Intended parent/s	A person who uses a surrogacy arrangement to have a child, and who intends to raise that child from birth. Intended parent/s may or may not be genetically related to the child.
International surrogacy	A surrogacy arrangement undertaken in a different jurisdiction from the one in which the intended parent/s live (sometimes referred to as cross-border or transnational surrogacy).
IVF	In-vitro fertilisation.
Origin information	Information (both non-identifying and identifying) about surrogates, gamete or embryo donors, and intended parents (with or without a genetic relationship to a child).
Parental order	A court order removing legal parenthood from the surrogate (and her spouse/partner where appropriate) and granting it to the intended parent/s.
Regulated Surrogacy Organisation (RSO)	A proposed State regulated non-profit surrogacy support organisation.
Regulated Surrogacy Statement (RSS)	A proposed official document setting out the details of a surrogacy arrangement signed by all parties to it.
SAA	Surrogacy Arrangements Act 1985.
Surrogacy arrangement	An arrangement in which a surrogate agrees to carry and give birth to a child that will be raised by its intended parent/s.
Surrogacy expenses	Out-of-pocket expenses incurred by a surrogate in preparation for, during or connected to the surrogacy process.
Surrogacy Register	A proposed Register to collect information about surrogates, gamete donors and intended parents that the surrogate-born person could access.
Surrogate	A person who agrees to carry and give birth to a child that will be raised by its intended parent/s.

Traditional surrogacy	Where the surrogate carries a child genetically related to her on behalf of the intended parent/s. This could be following the transfer of an embryo created using her own egg (as a donor), or via her insemination in either a clinical setting or at home.
UNCRC	United Nations Convention on the Rights of the Child 1989.

Introduction

This book explores findings from the Children's Voices in Surrogacy Law (CVSL) project.[1] The project involved 54 children and young people and gathered and analysed their views about surrogacy law and reform proposals in the United Kingdom.[2] The data were collected through (a) interviews, which allowed for the collection of rich insights through in-depth discussion and (b) artwork, which allowed for exploration of children's experiences and perception of surrogacy in the United Kingdom. The book's aim is twofold: first, to present and analyse children's views on surrogacy and surrogacy *law* for the first time for use in academic, legal and policy debates. In it, we detail our findings, while making some policy arguments about how the law should (or should not) be changed. Second, we present a novel method for the inclusion of children in consultation on law reform, especially when legislating for matters which directly concern them.

The book presents the first insights into children's views on surrogacy law, at a time when surrogacy and its regulation is the subject of ethical and legal debate in many parts of the world. We hope that the insights from this project can influence law and policy debates in these jurisdictions, contribute to the research on surrogacy law reform from children's perspectives and contribute a new methodology for involving children in law reform by researchers, reform bodies and policymakers. As will become apparent, this study was conducted within what may be termed a partially permissive 'tolerant' legal framework (Scherpe et al., 2019) in the United Kingdom in which commercial surrogacy activity is

[1]The research was funded by the Institute of Medical Ethics Research Funding (2021), Research England participatory research grant (University of Leicester (2023), University of Bristol (2023)).
[2]There is a distinction in terminology between children and young people in terms of age and maturity. However, the term 'children' will be used throughout for ease of reading.

Children's Voices in Surrogacy Law, 1–25

doi:10.1108/978-1-83549-642-820261001

prohibited but surrogacy is recognised as a legitimate form of family-building by the State and supported by the activities of several non-profit organisations.[3]

This research is timely, given current domestic and global debates on surrogacy, as well as ongoing law reform agendas. In March 2023, the Law Commission of England and Wales and Scottish Law Commission published joint recommendations on surrogacy law reform alongside draft new surrogacy legislation (Law Commissions, 2023). Their five-year project (re)ignited academic, public and parliamentary interest in surrogacy. There are also surrogacy law reform projects happening in other jurisdictions, most notably (due to their similarity) Ireland, Australia and New Zealand, and there are transnational attempts to formulate or influence global policy on surrogacy (Declaration of Casablanca for the Universal Abolition of Surrogacy, 2023; Child Identity Protection, 2026a, 2026b; HCCH Working Group on Parentage/Surrogacy, 2025; International Social Service General Secretariat, 2021; United Nations Special Rapporteur on violence against women and girls, its causes and consequences, 2025). As these illustrate, surrogacy can be a divisive topic, and there is no global consensus on how it should be regulated. Some advocate prohibition (Declaration of Casablanca for the Universal Abolition of Surrogacy, 2023; United Nations Special Rapporteur on violence against women and girls, its causes and consequences, 2025), while others call for implementation of minimum universal standards of protection (HCCH Working Group on Parentage/Surrogacy, 2025; International Social Service– General Secretariat, 2021; Surrogacy360, 2023). At national levels, 'it is possible to encounter the absence of special legislation, a complete ban on surrogacy or some sort of legalization of the procedure' (Valc, 2025, pp. 3–4), though there are almost constant shifts in the formation or amendment of existing national laws (Horsey, 2024). This book therefore provides an original and essential contribution to such policy debates.

The project adopts a predominantly qualitative approach, with quantitative elements.[4] We adopt a socio-legal approach, exploring the social, political and economic contexts in which law develops and how these impact the law (Economic and Social Science Research Council, 2023). This was necessary to answer our central research questions, which sought to explore how children perceive and experience surrogacy and their perspectives on surrogacy law and potential law reform. Our work is interdisciplinary: in seeking to examine the law as a social phenomenon, it draws on other disciplines, including sociology, social policy, social work, social psychology and childhood studies. As is the case with the research underpinning this book, a socio-legal approach may also adopt empirical research methods to examine the operation and impact of law and policy in practice. Our findings are situated amidst this wider literature: as such, this book should appeal to those researching or studying surrogacy (or related family-making techniques) in disciplines beyond law and at any level, as well as

---

[3]Some of these were involved in the recruitment of participants for this study: see Chapter 1, p. 48.

[4]See Chapter 1 for a full explanation of the methodology.

those supporting surrogacy, including inter alia legal practitioners, counsellors, advocates and regulatory bodies. This book is also policy-orientated, as its insights can be used to inform policymakers in an evidence-based way (Cownie & Bradney, 2017, p. 52).

There is a growing literature on the lived experiences of those seeking to have a child through surrogacy ('intended parents') and parents through surrogacy (Horsey et al., 2025; Jadva et al., 2003, 2012; Jones et al., 2023), surrogates (Blyth, 1993, 1994; Horsey, 2025a, 2025b, 2025c; Horsey et al., 2022; Jadva et al., 2003, 2012, 2015; Lamba et al., 2018; Mahmoud, 2023, 2025a, 2025b), as well as gamete donors (Gilman et al., 2025; Gilman & Nordqvist, 2022; Imrie et al., 2019; Imrie & Golombok, 2018; Nordqvist & Gilman, 2024), and there is increased engagement from law and policymakers with these groups (Law Commissions, 2019a, 2023). Empirical studies have also focused on experiences of surrogacy in other countries, including India (Pande, 2014; Saravanan, 2013), Canada (Gruben et al., 2018; White, 2018; Yee et al., 2019), the United States (Mahmoud, 2023; Martínez-López & Munuera-Gómez, 2024) and Denmark (Tanderup et al., 2023, 2025), among others. Some systematic reviews also provide further data (Kneebone et al., 2022; Söderström-Anttila et al., 2016). Other work has considered experiences of particular groups of intended parents, including same-sex male couples (Carone, 2017a; Nebeling Petersen, 2018; Smietana, 2017), solo intended parents (Carone, 2017b) or those who engage in surrogacy outside their home country (international surrogacy) (Jackson et al., 2017; Jadva et al., 2018).[5] Such studies make it possible to understand more about who undertakes surrogacy and why (either as a potential parent or as a surrogate), and their experiences of the process. However, to date, *children* have not been included in the legal and ethical debates around surrogacy regulation, despite the fact that many of the contentious issues in debates on surrogacy relate to children.[6]

This book also fits within a wider and growing literature on children's rights theory and child participation in research (Groundwater-Smith et al., 2015; Križ & Petersen, 2023; Parkes, 2013; Percy-Smith et al., 2023; Schrama et al., 2021; Tisdall, 2014, 2017). Much of the United Kingdom's current regulatory framework for surrogacy is shaped by the interests of adults and underpinned by assumptions of what is in the best interests of children. We explore children's views on core legal issues in surrogacy and their experiences of surrogacy, and consider what this might mean for law and policy in the United Kingdom, rather than exploring adults' reflections on their childhood experiences (Wade & Mills, 2025). This chapter situates the book within wider literature, including core

---

[5]Though such arrangements are sometimes referred to as 'transnational' or 'cross-border' surrogacy, we use the term 'international surrogacy' throughout, reflecting the Law Commissions' choice to use the term in their public consultation (2019a, para. 3.100) and Final Report (2023, para. 16.2).

[6]There has been limited engagement from *adults* born from surrogacy, which reflects either positivity (see e.g. Annelo, 2026; Hardach, 2022) or late discovery of their birth story through surrogacy in less-than-optimal ways (see e.g. Maurel, 2026).

findings from longitudinal research which examined the psychological adjustment and well-being of children born through surrogacy (Golombok et al., 2004, 2006a, 2006b, 2011, 2013, 2018; Jadva et al., 2012, 2015, 2023, 2026; Zadeh et al., 2018). Our data complements this research, by focusing on what children think about issues in surrogacy that the law regulates and their experience of surrogacy under the UK regulatory framework, as opposed to their psychological development.

This introductory chapter provides the legal background and context for the CVSL project and for the analysis in the subsequent chapters. It concludes by setting out the importance of including children's views in law reform.

The History of Surrogacy in the United Kingdom

Some forms of surrogacy have occurred through history and across different cultures. Surrogacy is a form of third party assisted reproduction whereby a person (the surrogate) carries a pregnancy and gives birth to a child intended to be raised by another person/people (the intended parent/s). In 'traditional' surrogacy (also called genetic/partial/straight/low-tech surrogacy), the surrogate's own egg is used, meaning that they are genetically related to the child born.[7] In gestational surrogacy (also called full/host/IVF/high-tech surrogacy), embryo(s) created by in vitro fertilisation (IVF) are transferred to the surrogate's uterus; as a result, the surrogate usually has no genetic connection to the child.[8] Embryos may be created by gametes from both intended parents, from one of them and an egg or sperm donor or, rarely, from neither (using both donor egg and sperm, or a donated embryo). Intended parents may be couples (heterosexual, same-sex or otherwise),[9] or a single person.

In the United Kingdom, all gestational surrogacy, and some traditional surrogacy, occurs within a clinical setting. Fertility clinics are licensed by the Human Fertilisation and Embryology Authority (HFEA) and must operate

---

[7]We acknowledge that not everyone who gives birth may define themselves as a woman. However, the term will be used as a factual description of what the law says, or in using quotes.

[8]There are rare instances where a surrogate may also be a known egg donor, with egg retrieval taking place in a clinic, before being fertilised by IVF and (re)implanted into the same woman acting as a surrogate (Horsey, 2025a; Horsey et al., 2022).

[9]Intended parents could also be in polyamorous relationships in the *factual* sense, but in the *legal* sense, a maximum of two intended parents can be recognised under UK law. This is not the case everywhere: in September 2025 a New York court ruled that a child born through assisted reproduction can have three parents named on their birth certificate, where all were involved biologically and intentionally in the child's conception (*In the Matter of Baby D.K.N.* (2025 NY Slip Op 25,202)). A similar provision exists in British Columbia (Canada) under the Family Law Act 2013 (Kelly, 2014). An internet search reveals that at least 14 US states/districts have laws that allow for more than two legal parents. In late 2022, Cuba promulgated a new Family Code (Ley No. 156 Código de las Familias), recognising multiple parents in certain situations on an intention-based model (Pelegrino Toraño, 2025).

under its Code of Practice (2023a). The HFEA records that over 77,500 IVF cycles were performed in 2023, with about 20,700 babies born as a result (HFEA, 2025). IVF now accounts for around one in 32 births per year, though only a small proportion of these involve surrogacy: 233 surrogates received IVF treatment in 2023 (HFEA, 2025). It is hard to gauge an accurate number of children born through surrogacy; one way to estimate this is through court data on the number of parental orders granted, whereby intended parents become legal parents of surrogate-born children through a court order. These show a gradual increase in the number of orders granted each year since records began in 2011. In 2011, 117 parental orders were issued, rising to 543 in 2025 (Ministry of Justice, 2026),[10] though it should be noted that these capture children born through surrogacy in the United Kingdom *and overseas*.[11] This is a small proportion of the number of children born each year: by contrast, 594,677 births were registered in England and Wales in 2024 (Office for National Statistics, 2025). Surrogacy is not a common way of having children; it is an option sought by people who have, for example, been unsuccessful in using IVF or other fertility treatments, are unable to carry a baby for medical reasons such as cancer or a congenital condition, or who cannot conceive by 'natural' means, such as same-sex male couples or single men.

Surrogacy has been regulated since 1985 by the Surrogacy Arrangements Act (SAA 1985), alongside certain provisions of the Human Fertilisation and Embryology Acts 1990/2008 (HFE Acts 1990, 2008), some secondary legislation and a sizeable body of case law. This section traces the development of, and policy behind, the United Kingdom's surrogacy law over the last 40 years. It has a particular focus on three aspects, as these formed the basis for our data collection: legal parenthood, payments/contributions to surrogates and access to origin information.

The Warnock Report and the SAA 1985

In 1958, the government established the Feversham Committee to enquire 'into the existing practice of human artificial insemination and its legal consequences and to consider whether, taking account of the interests of individuals involved

---

[10]Scotland records parental orders separately. In 2022, 17 orders were granted; 27 in 2023 and 20 in 2024 (Scotland National Records Office, 2025).

[11]A response from the Child and Family Court Advisory and Support Service (Cafcass) to a Freedom of Information inquiry from Kirsty Horsey (ref Gov/CAF23-31530, 28.11.23) shows that 51% of surrogate births between 2016 and 2023 to UK-based parents occurred outside the United Kingdom. Note also, the number of parental orders granted may not accurately represent the number of surrogate *births* in any given year, not only due to the lag in granting orders once an application is made (so the birth may have in fact occurred in a previous year) but also because some intended parents may not apply for one, particularly perhaps if they are issued a foreign birth certificate with their names on it. Additionally, some (though few) who have children via surrogacy will achieve parenthood via adoption.

and of society as a whole, any change in the law is necessary or desirable' (Committee on Human Artificial Insemination, 1960, p. 1). The Feversham Report described sperm donation as 'an activity which might be expected to attract more than the usual proportion of psychopaths' and sought to discourage the practice (Annual Report of Council, 1973, p. 59).

Twenty years later, the birth of Louise Brown via IVF was lauded as a success story of science helping 'married heterosexual couples have "ordinary" families,' and realising (infertile) women's '"innate" and natural desire to have genetically related children' (Dow, 2018, p. 317). Notwithstanding doubt expressed by some prominent scientists (Tranfield-Thomas, 2024), early media narratives were generally positive, locating IVF within the boundaries of '"respectable" heterosexual family formation' (Dow, 2019, p. 191). This chimed with a fundamental tenet of Thatcherism, the dominant political outlook of the time: promotion and defence of the traditional/nuclear family, understood restrictively as married heterosexual couples and their biologically related children (David, 2014; Fineman, 1995; Lewis & Cannell, 1986).

Another feature of Thatcherism was enthusiasm for increased surveillance and scrutiny of professional actions, and the promise of transparency and accountability borne by external oversight (Wilson, 2011, pp. 131–132). Reflecting this ethos and responding to growing public calls for oversight of assisted reproductive technologies (ART), in 1982 the government established a Committee of Inquiry into Human Fertilisation and Embryology (Warnock Committee). Chaired by moral philosopher Mary Warnock, it was charged with developing practical proposals for regulating IVF and related science before 'the swift developments in embryology go much further' (Warnock, 1985, p. 521), ensuring that debate and potential regulation of ART would occur 'not in the private, but in the public sphere' (Warnock, 1983, p. 249).

The Warnock Report was published in 1984, recommending regulation of ART based on an assumed 'common moral position' on the importance of promoting the nuclear family (Department of Health & Social Security, 1984, p. 3). It emphasised the urgent need for external regulatory oversight, recommending the creation of a state regulator for ART and embryology. The Warnock Committee viewed ART as an acceptable, albeit extraordinary technology assisting 'ordinary' (traditional/nuclear) families, reflected by its recommendations regarding donation. Where donor eggs were used, which was rare at this time, the woman who gave birth was recognised as the legal mother, in line with the principle *mater est quam gestatio demonstrat*[12] (1984, paras. 4.17, 4.25, 6.8). Where donor sperm was used, the husband of the woman receiving treatment would be the child's legal father, in line with the principle *pater est quem nuptiae demonstrant*,[13] thereby replicating the nuclear family and, crucially perhaps, establishing a culture of secrecy in relation to donor insemination that was reflected inter alia in the policy, existing until 2005, of allowing anonymous

[12]Maternity is demonstrated by gestation.
[13]Paternity is demonstrated by marriage.

donation (Gilman & Nordqvist, 2022, pp. 9–10; Speirs, 2012). This recommendation was reflected in the Family Law Reform Act (FLRA) 1987 which allowed the husband of the woman receiving treatment using donor sperm to be entered on the birth certificate as the legal father (FLRA 1987, s. 27). The Warnock Committee considered that the same principles should apply to embryo donation, so that 'an embryo once transferred should be regarded for all purposes as that of the carrying mother' (1984, para. 7.6). The Committee recommended donor anonymity, as it considered this provided protection from potential 'emotional difficulties' and minimised 'invasion of the third party into the family' (1984, paras. 4.22, 6.6, 7.7). Anonymity was thought necessary to protect the donor from parental responsibility and to allow the husband parental rights (Dewar, 1989). However, the Committee also recommended that children should have access to 'basic information about [their] donor's ethnic origin and genetic health' when they turned 18 (1984, paras. 3.2, 4.21, 4.22).

The Warnock Committee also considered surrogacy. The Committee's response to surrogacy appears to be an inevitable consequence of the timing. Media coverage of surrogacy at that time was generally not positively framed, utilising terms such as 'rentawomb', 'procreation for profit' and 'prostitution of motherhood' (see discussion in Mahmoud, 2026a). Much of this was influenced by the (mis)perception of surrogacy as inevitably commercial, and by feminist critiques of the practice – particularly emerging from the United States – framed it as involving the commodification of women/children or the alienation of women's reproductive capacity (Allen, 1990; Corea, 1985; Lee & Morgan, 2001; Overall, 1987; Pateman, 1988; Shanley, 1995).[14] Other feminist arguments against (commercial) surrogacy include questions about whether surrogates can give true consent, or whether coercion (financial or otherwise) makes this impossible (Anderson, 2000). Others argue that surrogacy 'contributes to and perpetuates gender inequality' (Hill, 2024, p. 703; Satz, 2010). There are also concerns about undertaking the physical and psychological risks of pregnancy for someone else (Warnock Report, para. 8.12; Levron et al., 2014; McCoy et al., 2024; Parker, 1983; Reame & Parker, 1990; Yadav et al., 2018), as well as welfare concerns for children separated from their birth or 'true' mother (Okin, 1990). Though these concerns achieved prominence in the 1980s and 1990s, divergent feminist perspectives remain today, some of which reflect those earlier anxieties. For example, some argue that commercial (or even all) surrogacy is inherently exploitative and the practice should be abolished (Declaration of Casablanca for the Universal Abolition of Surrogacy, 2023; United Nations Special Rapporteur on violence against women and girls, its causes and consequences, 2025). Others, however, view surrogacy as a legitimate choice for women, allowing them to express their reproductive/bodily autonomy (and even financial autonomy)

---

[14]US commercial surrogacy agencies began to emerge in the early 1980s, prompting these concerns. The strength of the US feminist backlash against surrogacy increased following the infamous 1986 *Baby M* case, where Mary Beth Whitehead, a traditional surrogate, changed her mind and fled with the baby (*In re Baby M* 109 NJ 396 (NJ 1988) leading to several trials, appeals and ultimately the recognition of Whitehead's legal parentage.

where informed consent is present (Robertson, 1983; Walker & van Zyl, 2017a, 2017b; Wilkinson, 2016). Rather than prohibit the practice, many in the latter group would advocate for regulation to facilitate 'ethical' surrogacy that prioritises the welfare of women and children (Fischer et al., 2024; Hill, 2024).

The Warnock Report appears to be influenced by views of surrogacy that had developed in the 1970s and 1980s, and 'exceptionalised' surrogacy from other ART, describing it as 'the wrong way to approach pregnancy' (1984, paras. 8.10, 8.17). A surrogate's contribution was considered 'greater, more intimate and personal than the contribution of a semen donor' (para. 8.10). Following donor-assisted conception, social policy to promote the nuclear family meant allocating legal parenthood to the person who gave birth and their partner – if applicable – as opposed to following genetics. Therefore, in surrogacy, the view was that the surrogate should be recognised as the legal mother (paras. 8.8, 8.20).

The Warnock Committee deemed surrogacy 'inconsistent with human dignity', causing public concern by enabling a person's use 'as a means to [an] end' (1984, paras. 8.11, 8.17). It believed that paying for surrogacy rendered it 'positively exploitative,' as well as damaging and 'degrading to the child [. . .] since, for all practical purposes, the child will have been bought for money' (paras. 8.11, 8.17). Despite its opposition to surrogacy the Committee recommended a legal framework strongly discouraging surrogacy; recognising complete prohibition as impossible and criminalisation undesirable, the recommendations aimed to thwart surrogacy's growth (Horsey, 2016).[15] Mary Warnock later explained how concerns with surrogacy arose 'largely because of possible consequences for the child' given its disruption of the nuclear family (Warnock, 1985, p. xii). Later still, she said that she thought the Committee 'could have done better' in respect of its recommendations about surrogacy, explaining that meeting representatives from American surrogacy agencies and thinking about how she herself would be unable to hand a baby she had carried to someone else 'made her (and the majority of the committee) averse to surrogacy as a whole' (Horsey & Avery, 2016).

Shortly after the Warnock Report was published, Kim Cotton gave birth to the United Kingdom's first (publicised) baby through commercial surrogacy organised by an American agency, for which she received £6,500. After Kim Cotton left the hospital, the local authority applied to have the baby made a ward of court. Latey J later ruled that the baby could leave the jurisdiction with the Swedish intended parents as 'at the heart of the prerogative jurisdiction in wardship, is what is best for the child or children concerned' (*Re C (Wardship)* [1985] FLR 846). At this time, surrogacy arrangements were occurring in a predominantly private and secretive manner, using rudimentary methods of self-insemination, with sparse and sporadic media coverage (Mahmoud, 2026a). However, *Baby Cotton*, viewed as a 'baby-for-cash' deal (BBC, 1985), became 'synonymous with discourses relating to surrogacy' generating forceful

[15]A dissenting minority recognised the practice would continue and suggested therefore that it should be regulated (Warnock Report, 1983; Expression of Dissent).

emotional, ideological and political responses (Blyth, 2003, p. 226; Feasey, 2019, p. 107; Mahmoud, 2023). Public concern was magnified, with the markedly negative and critical media focus on Kim Cotton increasing the amount of moralisation (Mahmoud, 2026b). As anticipated by the Warnock Committee, the British press was outraged by the perceived condoning of the 'purchase' of a child. The threat posed by surrogacy, disturbing 'the calm waters of personal integrity, family life and national security,' was supposedly clear and required swift legislative action (Morgan, 1986, p. 358). Envisioned as an interim measure to deal with 'the most repugnant manifestation of surrogacy' (Priest, 1988, p. 545) with the government intending 'comprehensive legislation as soon as practicable' (HC Deb 15 April 1985, vol 77 (Surrogacy Arrangements Bill)), Parliament implemented the Warnock Committee's recommendations hastily and partially through the SAA 1985.

The SAA 1985 established the legal landscape for surrogacy: the practice was to be reluctantly tolerated, and its perceived objectionable nature underscored, such that it was neither accepted nor outright prohibited. The Act comprised only five sections. It sought to ban commercial surrogacy outright while also pursuing two further goals: discouraging surrogacy as a practice and protecting (presumed vulnerable) women and children (Jackson, 2001, p. 262). The SAA 1985 criminalised third-party involvement in surrogacy undertaken 'on a commercial basis', defined as receiving payment for making, negotiating or facilitating surrogacy arrangements (s. 2(3)). Prohibited commercial activities were distinguished from compensatory payments to surrogates (which were not covered within the statute) to ensure children would not be born 'under the taint of criminality' (Warnock Report, 1984; para. 8.19; Expression of Dissent at 4).[16] Adding to the deterrence of commerciality, s. 3 prohibited advertising for or as a surrogate.

The SAA 1985 left many critical legal issues outstanding including, inter alia, the legal status of surrogate-born children and the acceptability or otherwise of payments to surrogates for the material costs associated with carrying and giving birth; these issues were later (imperfectly) addressed in the HFE Act 1990.

The HFE Acts 1990 & 2008 and the Brazier Review

The HFE Act 1990 was a legislative response to ART and related embryo research which reflected the remainder of the Warnock Committee's recommendations. It followed six years of ethical and legal deliberation inside and outside of Parliament, and provided 'a legislative precedent, an ethical foundation, and a moral framework for the UK to build on' (Mahmoud, 2023). ART

[16]Commercial surrogacy could be described as taking place within a framework which involves third parties making profit from organising and facilitating surrogacy arrangements. Paying surrogates (beyond expenses) for 'gestational services' (sometimes known as 'compensated surrogacy') is different, though is often one feature of a commercial model. For a breakdown of different models, see Horsey, 2018b, pp. 16–19. See also Law Commissions, 2023, para. 12.5.

was 'singled out as special, as a part of medicine of such particular social concern and significance that the state should have a direct stake in its evolution' (Brazier, 1999, p. 166). The Act has been termed the 'gold standard' for other jurisdictions, as an extensive and detailed legal framework for ART (Blank, 2004, p. 120; Franklin & Roberts, 2006, p. 40). Implementing the Warnock Committee's recommendation, it created the HFEA, a statutory regulatory body, which was and remains responsible for, inter alia, the licensing of fertility treatment centres and research involving the creation and use of embryos. Crucial to the development of the law on surrogacy, it also introduced the 'parental order', a court order that facilitates the transfer of legal parenthood to intended parents, where certain criteria are met (HC Deb vol. 170, col. 945, 1990).[17] Central to this system was that the intended parents were husband and wife, the gametes of at least one of them were used, the order was applied for within six months and the surrogate gave her consent. In addition, the court needed to be satisfied that no money or other benefit (other than expenses reasonably incurred) had been exchanged (s. 30 HFE Act 1990). The HFE Act 1990 also inserted s. 1A into the SAA 1985, rendering all surrogacy arrangements unenforceable by or against any of the parties.

However, in the decade following the passage of the HFE Act 1990, high-profile and controversial surrogacy cases began to cast 'doubt on the ability of the current [law] to meet society's legitimate concerns about such cases' (Brazier et al., 1998; paras. 1.9, 3.26–3.27; Golombok, 2020b, p. 107). Among these, Karen Roche was a surrogate who was paid £12,000 and who reneged on the agreement. She claimed to have terminated the pregnancy, before announcing to the media that she and her husband would keep the baby (Watson-Smyth, 1997). This case prompted then-Health Minister Tessa Jowell to commission the Surrogacy Review, chaired by Professor Margaret Brazier in 1998. The other members of the Review panel were Professors Susan Golombok and Alastair Campbell. Its limited Terms of Reference included consideration of whether payment, including expenses, should be allowed and what changes were needed to the SAA 1985; HFE Act 1990 s. 30 (Brazier et al., 1998; para. 1.2). Golombok later stated that the lack of empirical evidence before the review panel about either children born through surrogacy or surrogates' own experiences are what prompted her subsequent longitudinal study with families and further study on the experience of surrogates post-birth (2020b, p. 108). Despite recognising that (at the time) 'very little is known about the consequences for children of being born as a result of a surrogacy arrangement' and that any concerns about the risks to surrogate-born children were 'purely speculative', the Brazier Review maintained that paying surrogates would be 'psychologically damaging' for children (para. 5.18). Furthermore, it was thought to be 'not necessarily in children's best interests to learn that their surrogate mother benefitted financially from their birth or from giving

[17]See discussion in Chapter 2, pp. 54–55.

them away to the commissioning couple' (paras. 5.18–5.19).[18] It was thought this may have a damaging effect on family relationships and the child's development of a 'secure sense of identity and positive self-esteem' (para. 4.14). Recognising that surrogacy could have an impact on children's development, the Review also concluded that:

> It is not known . . . how a child will feel about having been created for the purpose of being given away to other parents or, if the surrogate mother remains in contact with the family, what the impact of two mothers will be on his or her social, emotional and identity development through childhood and into adult life, particularly in families where the surrogate mother is also the genetic mother of the child (para. 4.11).

The Brazier Review also identified that 'the child born in consequence of a particular surrogacy arrangement is often not the only child at risk of psychological harm' (para. 4.15), going on to discuss the potential emotional impact on children of surrogates in seeing their mother 'give up a sibling... in some instances on more than one occasion'. This led the panel to have 'concerns regarding the psychological consequences of surrogacy for the surrogate mother's own children' (para. 5.20). It also highlighted concerns about the potential 'distress' to children caused by maintaining contact with the surrogate (para. 4.13) or in learning that the surrogate who gave birth to them had also given birth to other surrogate children for other families (para. 4.14).

The HFE Act 2008 was an amending statute, merely 'tinkering at the margins' (Fox, 2009, p. 333) while leaving much of the 'regulatory architecture' intact (Jackson, 2008, p. 429). While it did more in relation to the regulation of embryology, it did not pay as close attention to ART or surrogacy (see Horsey (ed.), 2015). In respect of ART and surrogacy, it extended the ability to become legal parents to civil partners and those living in enduring family relationships, which included same sex couples. This was largely inevitable in the light of other social changes such as the legislative recognition of same sex partnerships in the Civil Partnerships Act 2004. What was left, therefore, were slightly expanded categories of those who were eligible to apply for a parental order following surrogacy, within the framework created by the SAA 1985; HFE Act 1990 (s. 54 HFE Act 2008). The 2008 reforms to the HFE Act also partially lifted the ban on advertising in the SAA 1985 and allowed non-profit surrogacy organisations to receive payment to cover their costs for certain services (s. 3(1A) SAA 1985 as inserted by s. 59(7) HFE Act 2008).

[18]Note that the terminology of 'intended' rather than 'commissioning' parents (or couple) is usually preferred, other than by those who oppose surrogacy.

Moving Towards Domestic Law Reform

The 'tolerant' regulatory framework in the United Kingdom allowed a form of domestic (altruistic) surrogacy to quietly flourish (Golombok, 2020b, p. 107). Pockets of good practice developed in which intended parents and surrogates are supported by non-profit groups, which are backed by their depth of knowledge and experience, including *Childlessness Overcome Through Surrogacy* (COTS),[19] *SurrogacyUK*, *Brilliant Beginnings* and *My Surrogacy Journey* (Gamble, 2025; Horsey, 2025c, pp. 18–19; Pott & White, 2025; Prosser & Gamble, 2016; Smith, 2016). Each has its own organisational model and principles, but these organisations have become an important part of the UK surrogacy landscape. However, the law on paper, over the forty-plus years since its inception, is increasingly not reflective of the ethos of this praxis, nor is it congruent with government support of surrogacy as a legitimate form of family formation.

In 2018, the Department of Health and Social Care (DHSC) published two sets of guidance on surrogacy: one for those going through the process, outlining 'good practice' and what can/should be expected based in part on the work of non-profit organisations, and one for those who provide care and support for surrogates and intended parents, clinical or otherwise (DHSC, 2018a; 2018b; 2018c). Produced in collaboration with several non-profit surrogacy organisations, Cafcass and other stakeholders, the guidance provides practical public information, which aims to assist surrogates, intended parents and professionals through the surrogacy process. It demonstrates a significant shift from state disapproval to acceptance of surrogacy as a form of family-building and non-traditional families. It endorses existing non-profit organisations, recognising their important role. However, while the HFEA oversees all licensed fertility clinics, no such regulatory oversight has been present for the non-profit organisations, notwithstanding calls for appropriate regulation (Brazier et al., 1998; para. 4.44; Horsey, 2018b, p. 45; Percy, 2020).

The social landscape has changed considerably since the Warnock Report was published. However, the legal framework has failed to accommodate 'significant changes to our understanding of family, parenthood and the creation of life itself' (Pascoe, 2018), as its development proceeded 'in a haphazard fashion through piecemeal changes' (Freeman, 1989, p. 165). The law is no longer (if it ever was) fit for purpose, neither reflecting lived experience, nor operating in the best interests of those involved, including children (Horsey, 2015; Percy, 2020). It is 'simply an empty shell that sets out clear principles, but is of little benefit in practice' (Fenton-Glynn, 2019, p. 117) and exhibits 'a kind of "putting up" with surrogacy falling short of genuine respect' (Mahmoud, 2026a). In the meantime, surrogacy continues with or without facilitating legislation and the difficulties that have developed with the existing framework can be seen to operate to the

[19]Established by Kim Cotton in 1998, COTS was the longest-running non-profit surrogacy organisation until its closure in September 2025. The HFEA recommends the organisations listed in the DHSC guidance (see below), alongside one other (*Nappy Endings*), on its public-facing website.

detriment of children and families in some cases. This can be illustrated through cases emerging since international surrogacy arrangements became more commonplace in the first decade of this millennium. Whereas such arrangements accounted for 2% of parental order applications in 2008, by 2024, this was over 50% (Fischer et al., 2024). These arrangements occurred in 'surrohubs', loosely regulated or unregulated reproductive tourism destinations that emerge and subside over time (Horsey, 2024). Various factors have motivated this practice, including the uncertainty relating to legal parenthood,[20] financial costs of surrogacy,[21] difficulties in finding a surrogate and the unenforceability of surrogacy agreements. At the same time, the growth of the internet and social media services made it easier to access information about practices, clinics and agencies in other countries.

Increasingly, these and other issues led to calls for reform from academics (Alghrani & Griffiths, 2017; Horsey, 2016; Horsey & Sheldon, 2012), practitioners (Prosser & Gamble, 2016), the judiciary (Bowcott, 2015), parliamentarians (HC Deb 7 February 2017, vol 621; HC Deb 14 October 2014, vol 586, col 2WG; HC Deb 21 Jan 2020 vol 670, col 69WH; HL Deb 14 December 2016, vol 777, col 1317), surrogacy organisations (Horsey, 2015, 2018b, 2025c; Pott & White, 2025; Prosser & Gamble, 2016; Smith, 2016) and even by Mary Warnock herself (Warnock, 2016). Notably, a campaign led by SurrogacyUK's (SUK's) Working Group on Law Reform resulted in the publication of two reports (Horsey, 2015; 2018b) which aimed to address ongoing 'surrogacy myths' and argued for a complete review and overhaul of the law to better reflect the intentions of the parties involved and the lived realities of modern-day surrogacy. These reports were endorsed by Dame Mary Warnock and Professors Margaret Brazier and Susan Golombok (in Horsey, 2015, foreword p. 5; Horsey, 2018b, foreword, p. 6). The reports included results from the largest ever surveys of surrogates, intended parents and other interested parties: in 2015, 434 responses, including 111 surrogates and 206 intended parents; in 2018, 510 responses, including 103 surrogates and 209 intended parents. The ongoing campaign had several impacts. All but three of the 20 recommendations made in the 2015 and 2018 reports were adopted,[22] partially adopted, or were proposed in the Law Commissions' 2019 public consultation. Additionally, the 10 recommendations later made by the All-Party Parliamentary Group (APPG) on Surrogacy (Percy, 2020) mirrored those in the SUK reports.

Influenced by the increasing calls for reform, the Law Commission of England and Wales and the Scottish Law Commission (the Law Commissions) undertook a joint project on surrogacy law reform, recognising that key aspects of UK surrogacy law had failed to keep pace with social changes. This was also inspired by the significant number of responses received to their pre-consultation from surrogates, intended parents and parents through surrogacy (Law Commissions,

---

[20]See further Chapter 2.
[21]See further Chapter 4.
[22]This included the creation of the DHSC Guidelines in 2018.

2019a; para. 1.40). Their reform project included an open public consultation, which ran from June-October 2019 and received over 680 responses, including from many of these interest-holders (Akl et al., 2024), as well as those working in a non-profit or professional capacity to support surrogacy arrangements. In a Westminster Hall parliamentary debate on surrogacy in 2021, the Law Commissions were credited with ensuring that 'lived experience [was] front and centre of all the proposals' (HC Deb 21 Jan 2020 vol 670, col WH72). Phase One of the CVSL project was completed in time to include the views of children born through surrogacy and children whose mothers had been surrogates in the evidence considered by the Law Commissions (CVSL, 2023a). According to the Law Commissions, this 'informed [their] understanding of how reform might be perceived by the children it affects' (2023, para. 1.115).

The Proposed Reforms

The Law Commissions' final Report, *Building Families through Surrogacy: A New Law*, and a draft Surrogacy Bill were published in March 2023 (Law Commissions, 2023). The Report outlines proposals for a new regulatory scheme, including a new route for legal parenthood in domestic surrogacy, which would recognise intended parents as legal parents *from birth* in some situations. Further proposed reforms include State regulation of non-profit organisations as 'Regulated Surrogacy Organisations (RSOs)', the introduction of a Surrogacy Register to record information about children's genetic and gestational origins and a new system of 'permitted payments' for surrogates (see Horsey et al., 2025). At the time of writing, a full Government response has not been published, though an interim response suggests that law reform is not stalled forever (DHSC, 2023, 2025), meaning that this research will be well placed to inform the shaping of a new legal framework for surrogacy when legislative time allows.

In the following sections, we introduce the aspects of the proposed reforms on which we collected data in the CVSL project: legal parenthood, permitted and prohibited payments in surrogacy, and the proposed Surrogacy Register. Each topic is discussed later in depth in the relevant substantive chapter of this book.

Legal Parenthood

In their final Report, the Law Commissions recognised that the current approach to legal parenthood does not always reflect the best interests of the child, or others, in part because surrogates neither view themselves as parents nor have any intention of parenting the children they carry (Horsey, 2015, 2022; Mahmoud, 2023). Further, children born through surrogacy are usually cared for by their intended parents from the point of birth or soon thereafter. Legal parenthood (and parental responsibility) resting with the surrogate (and often her spouse/partner, as described earlier) means typically that those people caring for the child lack parental responsibility and therefore legal decision-making authority, including in relation to medical care, unless other court orders are granted. Meanwhile the surrogate, who by this time is not caring for the child, does hold decision-making authority.[23]

The Law Commissions outlined a new 'Pathway to Parenthood' which would lead to legal recognition of intended parents as parents from birth, without the need to apply for a parental order.[24] The pathway would be overseen by RSOs, non-profit surrogacy support organisations that would be regulated by the state, likely by an extension of the HFEA. They would guide surrogates and intended parents through the surrogacy process, culminating in the creation of a Regulated Surrogacy Statement (RSS) and the obligation for the RSO to pass details of the arrangement to the Surrogacy Register. The new pathway would ensure that safeguarding, medical and criminal checks, independent legal advice and implications counselling for all parties would occur prior to conception being attempted.[25] If all requisite steps are taken, the intended parents would become legal parents at birth, subject to the surrogate having the right to withdraw her consent to this until six weeks after the birth (with differing effects depending on whether consent is withdrawn before or after birth). Intended parents who choose to pursue surrogacy in the United Kingdom outside of the pathway would need to follow a (modernised) parental order procedure, as in this situation the surrogate would remain the legal mother at birth. The same would be true for intended parents pursuing international surrogacy. The Commissions acknowledge that international surrogacy arrangements will continue to occur, while expressing the hope that reliance on such arrangements will diminish as safe and ethical domestic options improve (Law Commissions, 2023; para. 8.247).

Permitted and Prohibited Payments

As mentioned earlier, the Warnock Committee viewed the introduction of money into surrogacy arrangements as damaging and degrading to the child (1984, paras. 8.11, 8.17), though excluded surrogates and intended parents from criminalisation if/when money changed hands, to ensure children were not born 'subject to the taint of criminality' (paras. 8.18–8.19). The Brazier Review also deemed criminal sanctions for these parties inappropriate (1998, para. 5.22). The Brazier Review noted the 'fudging' undertaken by courts due to the opacity surrounding payments to surrogates, and argued that 'without intervention,

---

[23]This is before considering still important but typically more future concerns such as inheritance and succession rights.

[24]Applicants for parental orders must meet the requirements under s. 54 HFE Act 2008 if they are a couple. Since 2019, solo applicants have also been allowed, with the Human Fertilisation and Embryology Act 2008 (Remedial) Order 2018 inserting s. 54A into the HFE Act 2008.

[25]The court has recognised that this is good practice and that agreements made in such a way, with all parties receiving accurate advice and support, are less likely to result in breakdown of the surrogacy arrangement (see *Re Z (Surrogacy: Step-parent Adoption)* [2024] EWFC 20, [208]–[211]).

payments disguised as expenses are in any case likely to rise. Undefined and unregulated disputes about expenses add to the perils of surrogacy arrangements' (para. 4.43). It also stated that there could be negative effects on a child from 'learning that the woman who bore him or her was paid to do so' (para. 4.14).

It is a common misperception that it is illegal to pay a surrogate in the United Kingdom; this is not a feature of the law. Some of the confusion stems from the requirement that the court must be satisfied that no money or other benefit (other than expenses reasonably incurred) has been exchanged ((ss. 54(8)) and 54A(7) HFE Act 2008) (Horsey & Sheldon, 2012). However, there is no definition of 'reasonable expenses' (Brown, 2021) and the courts can and do authorise payments that go beyond reasonable expenses under ss. 54(8)) and 54A (7) HFE Act (2008). Also, as identified by Gamble (2019), 'some UK surrogates do choose to receive, and some intended parents do choose to pay, a financial acknowledgement (beyond pure out-of-pocket expenses) of the enormous commitment a surrogate and her family makes'. This may include, for example, paying for a family holiday for the surrogate, something that is not an 'expense' per se, but has been regularly authorised by the courts.[26] While high payments are not common in domestic surrogacy (Horsey, 2015; 2018b; 2025c), the courts authorise sums that go beyond reasonable expenses and have authorised large sums of money in international surrogacy cases, where commercial payments are often the norm (*Re X (Children) (Parental Order: Foreign Surrogacy)* [2008] EWHC 3030 (Fam)). In this regard, Hedley J found that given that the court is bound by the welfare of the child principle,[27] it would only be in the 'clearest case of the abuse of public policy' that a parental order would not be granted (*Re L (Commercial Surrogacy)* [2010] EWHC 3146 (Fam), [10]).[28]

The current approach regarding payments was criticised by the Law Commissions. In their Consultation Paper, the Law Commissions asked for consultees' opinions on different categories of payments (2019a, p. 18).[29] Based on the responses received, the Law Commissions adopted a different approach in their Final Report (2023), detailing what they proposed would be permitted payments intended parents may make to surrogates, including preparatory costs relating to the decision to enter a surrogacy arrangement, costs of screening and safeguarding for entry onto the new pathway, medical, insurance, dietary and related costs, travel and accommodation and lost earnings (para. 12.119).[30] Generally, 'permitted payments' include the type of 'expenses' that have been legitimated by the courts in parental order hearings, including e.g. a modest

[26]See further, the discussion in Chapter 3, pp. 101–103.
[27]Human Fertilisation and Embryology (Parental Orders) Regulations 2010.
[28]In *A & B* v *C & D* [2026] EWHC 972 (Fam), Williams J found that public policy breaches were not *by themselves* enough to deny a parental order, but have relevance in assessing the lifelong welfare of the child, which must be the court's paramount consideration (at [78]).
[29]See infographic in Appendix 3.
[30]While there is no move towards commercial surrogacy proposed, the change of language from 'reasonable expenses' to 'permitted *payments*' is deliberate and reflects a commitment to transparency and clarity surrounding payments.

recuperative holiday for the surrogate after the birth, gifts or tokens of appreciation (Horsey, 2018b; Mahmoud, 2023; *Re A, B and C (expenses)* [2016] EWFC 33). Additionally, the Law Commissions outlined payments that intended parents should be *prohibited* from making, which are payments for the surrogate's gestational services, compensation for pain and inconvenience, general living expenses and 'unspecified costs' (para. 12.110).

The Surrogacy Register

A central registry for surrogacy arrangements, akin to the HFEA's donor-conceived register, was proposed by SUK's Working Group on Law Reform (Horsey, 2015; 2018b) and endorsed by the APPG on Surrogacy (Percy, 2020). The Law Commissions' Final Report recommends a new Surrogacy Register, to record information about intended parents, gamete donors and the surrogate, including whether or not the surrogate is genetically related to the child (2023, para. 13.156). The Report recommends that children born through surrogacy in England and Wales should be able to access non-identifying information about surrogates and donors at age 16 and identifying information at age 18 as a matter of course, or at age 16–17 following assessment of whether they lacked capacity under the Mental Capacity Act 2005. It is further suggested that access to identifying and non-identifying information should be permitted under the age of 16 if children are Gillick competent.[31] Due to different law on capacity in Scotland, the Report proposes access to both identifying and non-identifying information at age 16 and access to information under 16, where the young person meets the test for legal capacity under the Adults with Incapacity (Scotland) Act 2000. This proposal demonstrates a commitment to children's identity rights under Articles 7 and 8 of the United Nations Convention on the Rights of the Child (UNCRC). It seeks to protect the interests children have in accessing information for establishing contact and for health reasons, and reflects research on the value of openness and identity formation (Brown & Wade, 2024; Nordqvist, 2017; Wade, 2020, 2025; Wallbank, 2004).

The International Landscape

As well as being a current topic of debate domestically, surrogacy is debated internationally.[32] Several other jurisdictions are considering implementing or reforming law on surrogacy, including in the Majority World, such as Mexico, Chile and Nigeria (Centre for Health Ethics Law and Development, 2024; Grupo

---

[31]i.e., if they have 'achieve[d] a sufficient understanding and intelligence to enable [them] to understand fully what is proposed' (*Gillick* v *West Norfolk and Wisbech Area Health Authority* [1986] 1 FLR 229).

[32]For discussion of the legal and social position of surrogacy in other jurisdictions, see inter alia Espejo-Yaksic et al., 2024; Scherpe et al., 2019; Sills, E. S., 2016; Trimmings et al., 2025; Vidalis & Kriari, 2026.

de Información en Reproducción Elegida AC, 2017; Nardi et al., 2025; Olajoku, 2026). It is important that the international position is considered, as it is true that there are places where surrogacy occurs in suboptimal situations, and bad practice exists. There is a greater risk of exploitation of women and intended parents where surrogacy is unregulated and/or performed unethically (Fischer et al., 2024; Just Futures Collaborative, 2025; Women Deliver, 2025). Such surrogacy practices paint a very negative picture, causing some to oppose it in its entirety. As described earlier, this can lead to overlooking ethical practices of surrogacy that support the creation of families and the best interests of all parties, including children.

Various inter/transnational organisations have taken stances on surrogacy, particularly international arrangements. These are seen as raising human rights concerns, especially for children in relation to securing citizenship and identity rights and access to origins information (Brown & Wade, 2022). There is also often concern about removal of the child from the surrogate, enforceability of pre-birth agreements (and the impact of these on the surrogate's consent), as well as concerns of baby selling or child trafficking. The European Parliament has addressed surrogacy in the context of human trafficking and exploitation. In a series of resolutions, including its 2014 Resolution on Sexual Exploitation and Prostitution and its 2016 Resolution on Trafficking in Human Beings, it characterised international commercial surrogacy as a practice that may contribute to the trafficking of women and children, calling on Member States to discourage the practice and to ensure that children born through surrogacy are protected from human rights violations (Directive (EU) 2024/1712). In 2016, the Parliamentary Assembly of the Council of Europe released a report on children's rights related to surrogacy and produced 'European guidelines to safeguard children's rights in relation to surrogacy arrangements' (Committee on Social Affairs, Health and Sustainable Development, 2016). Drawing on the UNCRC, it proposed banning for-profit surrogacy, but the proposal was rejected. In 2019, the UN Special Rapporteur on the Sale and Sexual Exploitation of Children released a thematic report to the General Assembly of the UN on safeguards for the protection of the rights of children born through surrogacy arrangements. It concluded that altruistic surrogacy would not amount to the sale of children, if payments are reasonable and itemised (para. 76). It also stated that commercial surrogacy would not amount to the sale of children under certain conditions, including that the surrogate must be the mother at birth, payments must be made post-transfer of the child, the surrogate is not obliged to relinquish parental status and both pre-birth screening of parents and post-birth best interests assessments are conducted (paras. 72–75). In 2025, the UN Special Rapporteur on Violence Against Women and Girls (VAWG) released a separate report to the General Assembly. It took a less tolerant approach, calling for global abolition of surrogacy, stating that no form of regulation can eradicate surrogacy's connection to VAWG.[33]

[33]This report has been widely criticised: see e.g. Horsey, 2025b; Jefford, 2025; Page, 2025.

There have been some attempts internationally to regulate issues to do with legal recognition of parenthood, including in international surrogacy. In 2010, the Hague Private International Law Conference (HCCH), with an advisory group made up of representatives of 92 countries, was tasked with developing an international instrument on legal parentage in cross-border situations, including ART, international surrogacy and adoption. It published its final report in November 2025, containing a draft Convention, which is concerned with a system for the recognition of judgements on legal parentage across Contracting States provided certain conditions are met (HCCH Working Group on Parentage/Surrogacy, 2025). However, the Report noted that due to divergent national policies and views on legal parenthood and appropriate safeguards in surrogacy and other areas of ART, there are feasibility challenges in advancing the Convention to the next stage (Special Commission) (para. 45).[34] In 2022, however, the European Commission adopted a proposal for a Council regulation to establish European Certificates of Parenthood, which would allow for recognition of parenthood across European Union (EU) Member States (European Commission, 2022). A majority of members of the European Parliament voted in favour of the legislation and the next stage is for EU governments to decide on the final version of the rules (European Parliament, 2023). It should also be noted that the European Court of Human Rights has held that Council of Europe Member States must recognise the legal parenthood of biological intended fathers established in another jurisdiction after an international arrangement and must provide a mechanism for parenthood to be established with a non-biological intended mothers where they were also on the birth certificate issued in the country of birth (*Mennesson* v *France*, Application No. 65192/11, 26 June 2014; European Court of Human Rights, 2019; see also Bracken, 2021; Iliadou, 2025a, 2025b).[35]

In addition, international non-Governmental bodies have developed non-binding instruments focusing on children's rights in surrogacy. These draw on Article 2 UNCRC (non-discrimination), Article 3 (best interests) and rights relating to birth registration, nationality and care by parents (Article 7) and the right to preservation of identity (Article 8). The International Social Service (ISS), following consultations with relevant organisations and individuals around the world (including those with lived experience), published the *Verona Principles for the Protection of the Rights of the Child Born through Surrogacy* (International Social Service–General Secretariat, 2021). These are good practice guidelines for lawmakers that articulate minimum standards for the protection of children's rights before, during and after surrogacy arrangements, with

---

[34]This was considered by the HCCH Council on General Affairs and Policy (CGAP) in March 2026, at which it was decided not to take forward a Convention at this stage, with the understanding that this decision may be revisited. Instead, CGAP tasked the Permanent Bureau to monitor legal and practical developments, and to report them to CGAP in advance of its 2028 meeting.

[35]It is not clear whether this also extends to a non-biological intended father who achieves joint legal parenthood with the biological intended father in the country of birth.

particular emphasis on legal identity, family life, access to origins information and protection from exploitation. In certain contexts, they accept that pre-birth allocation of parenthood is acceptable.

It is notable that the international developments detailed in this section are based around abstract legal interpretation of children's rights and there is a sustained lack of engagement with children and young people. Against the international and domestic legal backdrop, the importance of empirical research that centres the lived experiences of those directly affected by surrogacy arrangements – especially children – becomes clear. Legal and policy instruments invoke abstract principles such as the 'best interests of the child' and respect for identity and family life, yet these cannot be meaningfully interpreted without grounding in the voices and opinions of children with experience of surrogacy. Lived experience research provides critical insights into how surrogacy arrangements and family relationships are experienced, revealing gaps between legal standards and reality. Such research also responds directly to the UNCRC's emphasis on the child's right to be heard, offering a way for children's perspectives to inform assessments of their best interests when law and policy is being developed. Empirical research on lived experience serves an essential function, enabling more nuanced, child-centred and rights-respecting law and policy development.

The Value of Lived Experience

People interact with law and legal institutions in various ways and in different social settings, leading to different experiences of law. Exploring lived experiences allows for an understanding of various phenomena and the meanings and interpretations that people attribute to them. To be effective, law must be empirically examined in the real world and insights gleaned should inform lawmakers through feedback mechanisms (Nielsen, 2010, p. 972). Empirical evidence challenges underlying assumptions and intuitions, thereby contributing to relevant legal and policy debates (Goldberg, 2006, pp. 1989–1992). To shed clarity on some contentious dilemmas from the perspective of children involved in surrogacy arrangements, the CVSL project focused on children's lived experiences of surrogacy and their ideas about these contentious issues and how they should be regulated. Gathering such data is very important, as there has been a trend among anti-surrogacy campaigners of using arguments about harm to children that are not based on empirical research. Several anti-surrogacy campaigns exist, often calling for global prohibition of the practice, or criticising law reform proposals as 'liberalising' the law. Some of these groups were instrumental in flooding the Law Commissions' consultation with template responses calling for an outright ban on surrogacy (Nordic Model Now, 2019a; see Wade & Mills, 2025) and criticising the initial proposals as contravening principles of international law that protect children (Law Commissions, 2023; para. 3.3). Others came into existence *because of* the Law Commissions' work (Stop Surrogacy Now UK, 2025b; Surrogacy Concern, n.d.) and are vocal in campaigning against reform, especially on social media. Such campaigns are based on arguments that children will be harmed by knowing their surrogate was paid (Nordic Model Now, 2019a) and could experience serious lifelong mental health and emotional problems from being separated from the surrogate (Nordic Model Now, 2019b). While adoption research is drawn upon, their arguments do not engage with children born through surrogacy.

What Is Known About Children's Experiences of Surrogacy?

Previous studies of children born from surrogacy in the United Kingdom emerge primarily from the field of social psychology. An important longitudinal study was run by the Centre for Child, Adolescent and Family Research at the University of Cambridge, led by Professor Susan Golombok. The *UK Longitudinal Study of Assisted Reproduction Families* compared four groups of families: those created using egg donation, sperm donation and surrogacy, and a comparison group of natural conception families, all of whom had two heterosexual parents when the study began. At the outset, 50 sperm donation families, 51 egg donation families, 42 surrogacy families and 80 natural conception families were included. The researchers assessed parent-child relationships and the psychological adjustment of the children as they developed using in-home observational methods. Overall, the study showed that families created by donor conception and surrogacy (including those with lesbian mothers, gay fathers or solo parents by choice), are 'as likely to flourish as traditional families, and sometimes more so' (Golombok, 2020a). The researchers found that the quality of family relationships and the wider social circumstances in which they grow up have a greater impact on children's psychological well-being than the way a family is created, including the biological relatedness or otherwise of their parents (an accessible summary of the findings is in Golombok, 2020b).

The families created by surrogacy in the study were followed from the year 2000, when the children were babies, into adulthood. The research team visited the families at seven stages during the children's development up to adulthood. They found that, when the children were aged one, their parents showed greater 'warmth and engagement' compared to parents in the study who had conceived naturally (Golombok et al., 2004). When the children were two, it was observed that the mothers in the surrogacy families 'took greater pleasure' in their children (Golombok et al., 2006a), and when they were three, the mothers were comparably 'more affectionate' and had greater interaction with their children than in other family types (Golombok et al., 2006b). The children were next visited at age seven, by which time most of them had been told how they were born. At this point, despite good ongoing family relationships, the children were not doing 'better' than naturally conceived children and there were indications of psychological problems in some of them (Golombok et al., 2011). However, these issues were not seen when the families were next visited, when the children were aged 10 (Golombok et al., 2013). Such a pattern (of early psychological difficulties which disappear as children get older) has also been seen in adopted children, and Golombok surmises that the reasons for this will be similar, in that the surrogacy-born (and adopted) children were 'faced with issues relating to their identity at a younger age than most children' (Golombok, 2020a; Ilioi et al., 2017), and dealt with these.

The children seen at age 14 were 'flourishing' (Imrie & Golombok, 2018). At this stage, the children were asked about how they felt about having been born through surrogacy, with some seeing this as an 'advantage', the majority being largely ambivalent about it and only one expressing any kind of unhappiness (Zadeh et al., 2018). The last report on this cohort came when they had reached 20 years old, with the researchers finding that, even with an 'adult understanding of what it means to lack a genetic and/or gestational connection to their parents', the young adults remained psychologically well-adjusted and family relationships were happy (Jadva et al., 2023). The researchers surmised that this was because the children had been 'raised from the start by parents who see them as their own children, and who went to great lengths to have them, often experiencing years of infertility, and failed fertility treatment, beforehand' (Jadva et al., 2023).

The Cambridge team also interviewed 36 children of surrogates (Jadva & Imrie, 2014a, 2014b) – one of our main cohorts in Phase One of CVSL. They sought to establish what psychological or developmental impact surrogacy might have on surrogates' own children. They found that such children do not experience any negative consequences as a result of their mother being a surrogate, whether or not she also used her own egg.

The data presented in this book complements this body of social psychology research, as well as existing socio-legal research on surrogacy, through its focus on children's views on the law and potential law reform.

The Importance of Including Children's Views in Policy and Law Reform

As mentioned earlier, during their consultation, the Law Commissions heard from various interest-holders, including surrogates and intended parents, to ensure that 'lived experience [was] front and centre of all the proposals' (HC Deb 21 Jan 2020 vol 670, col 71). However, what was missing from research were *children's* views and their lived experiences. Without children's participation on issues concerning them and impacting their lives, any reform may not reflect their realities and diverse experiences. Indeed, in many respects, children's direct involvement should guide research concerning children's lives and experiences (Alderson, 2001; Christensen & James, 2008, 2017; Franks, 2011; Graham et al., 2017). However, a significant gap between the principle and practice of children's participation remains (Fitzgerald & Graham, 2011). The importance of including children's views was recognised by the Law Commissions at a late stage in their project, leading to an invitation to present the findings of Phase One of the CVSL project, and a suggestion to seek and compare the views of children with no direct experience of surrogacy.

Children's views in other areas of research and in policymaking are increasingly valued. Calls have been made to include and respect the views and interests of children in several aspects of public life, including data-driven healthcare policy (Bessant, 2022; Bessant & Allsopp, 2024; Lundy et al., 2021), climate change policy (Parsons et al., 2025), youth justice decision-making (Case et al., 2024) and experiences (Kilkelly et al., 2021; Kilkelly & Forde, 2020; Forde & Kilkelly, 2023), family court proceedings (Barlow et al., 2026; Children and Family Court Advisory and Support Service, 2023; Hargreaves et al., 2024; Jones et al., 2026) and family justice more widely (Dimopoulos et al., 2025), child-inclusive mediation when parents separate (Barlow & Ewing, 2024) and the views of LGBTQ+ young people in family law matters (Wray, 2025). Further, research hubs focused on ensuring children's participation in research and shaping policy debates have been created (Institute for Children's Futures, 2024; Lundy et al., 2021) and there is consultation with children on general government policies affecting children (Children's Commissioner, 2025; Government Office for Science, 2025; Lundy et al., 2021).

As an example of the inclusion of children's views in policy, Bessant (2022) conducted research on children's views about governmental use of their data during the COVID-19 pandemic. It was found that children expected and wanted the government to consider their views on how their data was used and a model was proposed for involving children in data policy development. There is also work on involving children in family law contexts. For example, Jones et al. (2026) conducted a pilot which offered structured, judge-led meetings with children. This was found to be beneficial to children, but there were variations in practice in allowing children to meet judges. It was suggested that practical challenges could be addressed through guidance and training, that meetings with judges should be integrated into existing processes and meeting tools should be co-designed with young people. Barlow and Ewing's research (2024) led to recommendations for a universal offer of child-inclusive mediation to families, provision of child-friendly information and enhanced mediator training, facilitated by a change in culture in the mediation community. Youth justice is another area where there has been engagement with children. Case et al.'s (2024) qualitative research exploring children's collaboration in decision-making in the Youth Justice System revealed children's desire to be listened to about ideas for improvement of *Child First* (the Youth Justice Board's practice framework), to have child-friendly environments/power imbalances broken down, to be continually informed by youth justice agencies and to be involved in decision-making to improve the system.[36] Increasingly, there are also calls to better communicate law and its impacts *to* children (Foster, 2025; President of the Family Division, 2025; see also *Mother* v *Father* [2024] EWFC 252). Perhaps the closest study for our purposes is a project seeking the views of young adults

[36]Similarly, in Ireland, Kilkelly et al. (2021) conducted studies involving young people exploring their pathways into and experiences of the youth justice system; other studies focused on young people's experiences of being interviewed by the police (Kilkelly & Forde, 2020; Forde & Kilkelly, 2023) and the impact of arts-based interventions with young people (Forde, 2026).

(though not children) conceived through egg or sperm donation or surrogacy (Jadva et al., 2023), though this did not focus on legal issues.

There is also a growing body of research on children's legal capability and human rights education with children. Watkins et al. (2018) carried out research on children's legal capability, which refers to 'the abilities that a person needs to be able to deal effectively with law-related issues' (Jones, 2009, p. 1 as cited in Watkins et al., 2018). They found high levels of competence regarding gender equality and consumer rights but low levels of awareness of children's rights under the UNCRC and low expectations concerning their capacity to participate in decision-making in schools/policies. However, it was also found that children demonstrated the ability to think meaningfully about law and welcomed the opportunity to do so. Drawing from this, Watkins et al. (2025) proposed a framework of legal capability which 'decentres' the law and legal institutions and places the learner and their needs at the centre. They introduce the concept of 'baseline' legal capability, which envisages that children can identify situations as problems and know how the UNCRC applies to these situations. Struther's research focuses on human rights education and has found that children of primary school age can learn about human rights and that it is beneficial to them (Struthers, 2016, 2017). However, there is often reluctance to provide human rights education to this age group, as it is seen as too controversial, abstract or biased and that, therefore, a cultural shift is needed in education and improved teacher training (Struthers, 2016).

Involving children in research generates new data and perspectives on children's lives, expanding insight into their experiences. It requires 'providing opportunities for meaningful participation and creating capacity for children to undertake research' (Kellett, 2011, p. 209). Such insights are most accurately captured by exploring children's views during childhood, as they have 'a unique "insider" perspective critical to our understanding of their worlds' (Kellett, 2010, p. 195). Recognising this, the CVSL project explored children's perspectives on surrogacy from those with and without direct lived experience of surrogacy. Conducted in three phases, CVSL involved 54 children aged 8–18. Phase One involved children with lived experience of surrogacy; these were surrogate-born children, children of surrogates and a child who had a cousin born through surrogacy. Phase Two involved children with no experience of surrogacy, allowing for insights and perceptions of surrogacy from children without direct experience or knowledge. Phase Three involved children living in the United Kingdom who were born through international commercial surrogacy arrangements that took place in the United States.

Conclusion

This chapter contextualised CVSL within the broader social, historical and policy landscape of surrogacy in the United Kingdom, with a particular focus on the issues that affect children. It considered how law and policy has responded to these issues in the development of surrogacy law in the United Kingdom and internationally. After tracing the development of surrogacy law, it introduced relevant proposals for law reform recommended by the Law Commissions. The chapter discussed the clear need to engage more critically with the lived realities of surrogacy arrangements by listening to all interest-holders – including children. It underscored the value of lived experience in shaping law and policy, particularly the perspectives of children, who are the least consulted interest-holders in surrogacy debates. This is also important in countering anti-surrogacy narratives. While previous research has focused on the psychological well-being of surrogate-born children, CVSL is the first project to centre children's views on the legal frameworks that govern their lives. In doing so, it fills a critical gap in both academic literature and policy discourse.

The chapters that follow detail the methodology of the project and explore the findings from the data analysis. Chapter 1 sets out the theoretical justification for the research, the methodology and the methods used, including the data analysis method. Chapter 2 explores children's views on legal issues relating to legal parenthood in surrogacy. Chapter 3 explores children's views on appropriate and inappropriate (financial) contributions to surrogates from intended parents. Chapter 4 considers children's views on being told about surrogacy and access to origin information about surrogates and donors. Chapter 5 analyses how children understand, perceive and navigate surrogacy and the relationships formed from surrogacy in their social worlds. The final chapter, Conclusions, brings together the main insights for law and policy and reflects on the methodology used to listen to children's views.

Chapter 1

Methodology: Hearing Children's Voices in Research on Law and Law Reform

'Thank you for being respectfull (sic) and listening to us'.[1]

Introduction

This chapter presents the methodology and methods of this project. There is immense value in consulting with children on law and law reform. Such consultation seeks to ensure that law and policy that affects children is based on their experiences and that future law meets the needs of those it will impact. However, engaging with children about law and law reform raises practical and ethical issues, and consideration needs to be given to the methods used. Drawing on the Lundy model of participation (Lundy, 2007) and the Mosaic approach (Clark, 2017), we undertook qualitative research, using semi-structured interviews with games and artwork elements. This chapter presents the theoretical justifications for undertaking such research. The methodology is grounded on the premise from international children's rights law and sociology of childhood that children should participate in decision-making that affects them and in the development of law and policy. Thereafter, the details of the data collection methods are set out, followed by the data analysis approach and limitations of the research. The chapter presents an innovative method to capture not only children's views on the ethical issues that law regulates, but also their experiences of law in their everyday lives. Such a method could be adapted for use in any area of law and policy where consultation with children is being considered.

---

[1]This was written on a note given to the interviewer after group interview 5 with Aoife, (10), Lilly, (9) and Valeria, (9), all children of surrogates. This is included in Appendix 4, Fig. 1.

Children's Voices in Surrogacy Law, 27–50

doi:10.1108/978-1-83549-642-820261002

Data Collection: An Overview

The project had three overarching research questions. These were addressed by different qualitative research tools, as follows:

- what do children think of the current law and law reform on surrogacy? The semi-structured interviews aimed to address this research question.
- what are children's experiences and perceptions of surrogacy in the United Kingdom? This was explored through the structured interviews and the art-work element.
- what do these insights mean for current and future law and policy?

To address the first research question, we undertook semi-structured group and one-on-one interviews. When working with groups of children, we undertook semi-structured group interviews, whereby the mechanics of a one-on-one interview were replicated in a group setting; the moderator controlled the discussion by asking the same questions of each participant (Parker & Tritter, 2006).[2] This did not mean complete lack of open-ended discussion. After set questions, there were open-ended questions, such as 'Is there anything else you would like to add?', and participants were asked if they had any questions for the researchers. In some group interviews, discussion ensued between participants, and this was supported and encouraged by the researchers. The reason for choosing group interviews was that younger children tend to engage more easily in small groups or pairs; groups are good for generating discussion and can be more fun (Greig et al., 2013, p. 1). In past studies, children have reported feeling more comfortable with peers (Borland et al., 2001) and groups can help to dilute power dynamics compared with one-on-one interviews (Hill, 2006). Since children may need time to formulate responses (Clark, 2017; Kellet & Ding, 2004), the group setting allowed individual children the option to speak either during the discussion or at the end. It also provided a clear structure, which was important in order for children to stay focused on the research questions. Group numbers ranged from two to six, and there was no more than a three-year age range in each group, to seek to ensure there was not an imbalance in abilities (Hennessy & Heary, 2005; Hill et al., 1996). It is acknowledged that this structured design means that researchers' questions and interests are dominant and set the agenda for discussion (Morgan, 2001, p. 147). Our positionality is explained below. However, this method fitted with the aim of the project, which was to explore children's views on ethical issues in surrogacy, which were under discussion by the Law Commission of England and Wales and the Scottish Law Commission (the Law Commissions) in their project on law reform. The aim was to produce data that could feed into this law reform project, based around some of the main issues from the consultation (Law

[2] This is in contrast to focus groups, the latter of which involves interaction of participants with the researcher taking on a more peripheral role (Parker & Tritter, 2006; Smithson, 2000). The distinction is not fully agreed upon. Another way of conceptualising this is a 'structured focus group'. See Morgan (2001).

Commissions, 2019a), which reflect the main ethical tensions that have been the subject of discussion in surrogacy in the United Kingdom and globally.

In line with this, the three planned topics in the interviews were parenthood, contributions to surrogates and origin information. These reflected the main areas examined by the Law Commissions that had most relevance to children. While international surrogacy raises important issues relating to citizenship and immigration law, this was not chosen as a topic. Compared with the other topics, concepts such as citizenship and nationality, particularly when involving international elements, were considered overly complex for our age range and UK-based cohort. Research with children needs to be carefully designed to ensure that they understand the issues discussed, are not overburdened and do not lose focus (Kellett & Ding, 2004). In line with this, interviews were limited to 1.5 hours and choices had to be made about which topics could realistically be included to fit with this timeframe.

The first research question was complemented by the second, which is about children's *experiences* of surrogacy in the United Kingdom. To address this question, we asked children a series of questions about surrogacy in their lives, as explored in Chapter 5: Surrogacy in Children's Social Worlds. Data were collected through artwork on the themes 'What surrogacy means to me' (Phases One and Three) and 'What I learned about surrogacy' (Phase Two). These different themes were set because participants in Phases One and Three had lived experiences of surrogacy and those in Phase Two did not. The aim was to explore children's experiences of and feelings about surrogacy (Phase One) and their knowledge/perceptions of surrogacy (Phase Two) and how law, policy and practice shape these experiences. Artwork allowed for the exploration to go beyond the interests and issues deemed important by law and policymakers and to get insights into what children deem important. In this regard, artwork supports subjective narrative storytelling about children's personal perspectives and feelings (Brooks, 2009), as well as physical and abstract elements of their social worlds (Literat, 2013). A thematic analysis of artwork from Phases One and Three was conducted (Wade & Mills, 2025). The artwork allowed us to see the kind of experiences the current law in the United Kingdom facilitates for children. It gave insights into the extent to which the status quo should be maintained and/or reform measures should be introduced. A full exploration of this artwork is outside the scope of this book. However, where the findings in the following chapters align with those from the artwork, these are set out. The artwork is available to view on the project's website.[3]

This project therefore used qualitative research methods (Savin-Baden & Major, 2013). Following the constructivist approach, we recognise that social practices are constructed through people's interactions (Robson & McCartan, 2016, p. 23). Children, more specifically, are seen as relational, dynamic beings who construct meaning with their carers (Greig et al., 2013, p. 65). This meaning is

[3]Art from Phases One and Three is available to view on the project website: https://childrensvoices.bristol.ac.uk/childrens-artwork/. Phase Two artwork was not analysed with these phases since the research question was different: 'What I learned about surrogacy today'.

also shaped by cultural and historical practices (Greig et al., 2013, p. 65). Therefore, the data and the knowledge gained have been constructed by us, the researchers, alongside the participants. In addition, we also recognise the reflexive nature of this research, and that our positions affect the interpretation of the data (Hennink et al., 2020, p. 17). In this respect, all three researchers have independently researched the issue of surrogacy and hold various stances on the topics outlined above (Brown & Wade, 2022, 2024; Horsey, 2010, 2016, 2018a, 2024, 2025a, 2026; Horsey et al., 2025; Mahmoud, 2023, 2024, 2025a, 2025b, 2026a, 2026b; Wade, 2020, 2025). All three authors are of the view that ethical regulation of surrogacy is possible. One of the researchers, Horsey, has been actively involved in movements with SurrogacyUK (SUK) and the All-Party Parliamentary Group (APPG) on Surrogacy to reform the law on surrogacy since 2014. Therefore, the questions we asked and the data we produced are shaped by our own research and stances on surrogacy. We acknowledge that the questions we asked were deliberately shaped by those in the Law Commissions' consultation paper (Law Commissions, 2019a). This means the research took place within a particular social and political context, as it is answering questions deemed important by adult stakeholders, such as non-profit surrogacy organisations which lobbied the Law Commissions and government for change.[4] How we took this positionality into account is set out below in the data analysis section.

There are also some quantitative elements in this project. In this respect, '[m]any qualitative studies include some data that can be counted and analysed using traditional quantitative methods' (Greig et al., 2013, p. 171). The reason for using quantitative elements was twofold. First, the quantitative element was an inclusive and fun aspect of the group interviews. The games described below involved a polling element – children were asked to vote and choose different options. This was an engaging way to ascertain participants' instinctive reactions to normative questions. Participants enjoyed seeing each other's answers and comparing them with their own. It also provided an activity from which open-ended questions could flow (Grieg et al., 2013, p. 119). Second, the project follows the consultation approach to law and policy undertaken by the Law Commissions which sought views on what the law's stance should be on ethical issues. The aim is to see the themes and trends in response to ethical dilemmas, which often involves taking a stance on these issues. The polling element was used as a tool to capture these general trends, before exploring participants' reasons for their stances. While it can be argued that this polling type activity is a very legalistic approach, in most questions the option of 'not sure' and/or 'maybe' was available, to allow participants to give multifaceted answers to the questions or to avoid taking definitive stances.

The Participants

The Children's Voices in Surrogacy Law (CVSL) project was carried out in three Phases and involved 54 children. For ease of reference, the term 'child' or

[4] See Introduction, p. 13.

'children' will be used to refer to all children up to the age of 18, in line with the definition in the Convention on the Rights of the Child (UNCRC) (United Nations, 1989, p. 4). Phase One involved children aged between 8 and 17 who had experience of surrogacy in the United Kingdom. Phase Two involved 24 school pupils, aged between 8 and 18 who did not have experience of surrogacy. Phase Three involved five children, aged between 9 and 14 who were born through international surrogacy in the United States.[5] An overview of participants is in Table 1.

Children were involved in the research based on their informed consent and the informed consent of a person with parental responsibility.[6] The approach taken was that where children have sufficient maturity and understanding to make their own decision, consent was obtained, and where children are not able to make their own decision, they were involved in the decision as much as possible (Alderson & Morrow, 2020, p. 137; Nuffield Council on Bioethics, 2015, p. 148). In all cases, the

Table 1. Overview of Participants.

Phase	Number of Participants	Breakdown of Participants
Phase One	25	7 – born through surrogacy (six gestational surrogacy; one traditional surrogacy) 17 – children of surrogates 1 – cousin of a child born through surrogacy
Phase Two	24	School pupils from two primary and two secondary schools.
Phase Three	5	All were born through US gestational surrogacy involving egg donation.

[5]A table of participants' individual details is in Appendix 1. Throughout the book, when we use quotes from or refer to the participants, we will do so in the following way:
Phase One: pseudonym, age, connection to surrogacy ('child of surrogate' or 'born through traditional/gestational surrogacy');
Phase Two: pseudonym, age;
Phase Three: pseudonym, age and either 'born through US gestational surrogacy and egg donation' (Chapter 4 (Origins)) or 'born through US gestational surrogacy' (all other chapters).

[6]Informed consent refers to informed and voluntary agreement to partake in the research, from a person with capacity to consent. It is specific, applying to each aspect of the research and ongoing, i.e., subject to withdrawal at any time (See World Medical Association (2024), paras. 25–28). Ethical approval for Phases One and Two was obtained from the University of Leicester Ethics Committee, and for Phase Three from the Kent Law School Research Ethics Advisory Group.

consent of a person with parental responsibility was obtained. Those parents/carers who expressed interest were sent a child-friendly information sheet, a parent/carer information sheet and a consent form for both the child and parent/carer to sign.[7]

The child-friendly forms were designed with simple language, phrasing and layout (Alderson & Morrow, 2020, p. 119), explaining who the team was, why the research was taking place and how it would be conducted (Alderson & Morrow, 2020, p. 111). The forms were returned to the project's email address or given to the team at the group interviews. At the start of the interviews, participants' assent was obtained, meaning we established their ongoing willingness to participate (Mills et al., 2026).[8] The project was explained verbally and supported with a 'code of conduct' card. The aim of the research and the interview process, based on the information sheet, was explained (Alderson & Morrow, 2020, p. 106). Participants were reminded they could skip any question they did not want to answer by saying this or by holding up a 'not sure' card, and they were told they could withdraw at any time.[9] We asked them to give themselves a pseudonym, and explained that this was to be used for the interview and would be used afterwards in any published research.[10] Children were given a project branded tote bag, card deck, pen, badge and a £20.00 voucher as a token of appreciation.[11]

The next section provides the justification for doing research on law and policy reform with children, drawing on sociology of childhood and children's rights.

---

[7]We relied on parents/carers to inform their children of the research and share the information with their children. The process of informing participants and reminding them of their right to withdraw was then reiterated in the interviews between the researcher and the participants. In Phase Two, information sheets and consent forms were sent via the school to parents/carers. Written agreement was also obtained from a representative from the schools.

[8]There is significant debate, outside the scope of this chapter, about the definition and role of assent (Parsons, 2018) and whether it is a replacement for consent for younger children or a complementary process for all children (Alderson & Morrow, 2020; Mills et al., 2026; Spriggs, 2023).

[9]Phone numbers of parents/carers were taken and they were asked to stay nearby in case of participant withdrawal. We did not have any children withdraw from the interviews, but did have (very minimal) instances where children disengaged from activities, either by not answering a question or not following the artwork prompt. In such cases, children would play with other cards or make general art. Having multiple team members at groups helped to manage this, as the team could engage children in another activity and check their ongoing agreement to participate.

[10]For the first four group interviews, we chose the pseudonyms. We allowed children to choose their own from this point onwards as they found it a fun activity. We also asked them not to give real names for other people, like surrogates/intended parents, if they mentioned them.

[11]The information forms stated the voucher was a way to say 'thank you'. The amount was considered not too high to be an incentive, but sufficient to acknowledge the children's participation. The additional items were seen as keepsakes for children to feel part of a research project and possibly as providing a means to share their experience with their parents and others.

Involving Children in Law and Policy Reform

Children as Agents and Rights-Holders

Movements in both sociology and law have led to a reconceptualisation of the child and childhood in society. Sociology of childhood began to emerge in the 1980s, viewing childhood as socially constructed rather than static, universal and immutable (Hendricks, 1997). Children are not seen as passive recipients of socialisation, but as agents who are actively participating in the construction of knowledge (Christensen & Prout, 2002a, 2002b; Clark & Statham, 2005; James, 2001; Mayall, 1994, 2002, p. 22). This signalled a move away from the conception of childhood in developmental psychology, which focused on the trajectory of childhood towards adulthood; children were seen as 'becomings' not beings (Uprichard, 2008). Under developmental psychology approaches, childhood was also seen as a natural stage, as opposed to a socially constructed one (Quennerstedt & Quennerstedt, 2014). As James (1999) notes, in the sociology of childhood:

> Children were no longer simply to be judged as non-adult by reference to the idealized standards of adult rationality. They were not to be labelled as *"pre-operational"* or *"pre-moral" or pre-*anything else. Children were just different ... what children meant was what they said ... nor was it a problem that these meanings might not be congruent with those of the adult world. (p. 239)

Another major development in how children and childhood were viewed was the conception of children as rights-holders. In 1989, the United Nations (UN) General Assembly adopted the UNCRC, which views children as independent rights-holders at an international level. Setting out a range of civil, political, economic, social and cultural rights, the UNCRC places legal obligations on ratifying States Parties to undertake all appropriate legislative, administrative and other measures to implement the rights in the Convention (UNCRC, Art. 4). In 1992, the United Kingdom ratified the UNCRC, meaning it is legally bound by the treaty under the rules of international law.[12] The Committee on the Rights of the Child, an expert body which monitors the treaty's implementation, has interpreted Article 4 of the UNCRC to mean that States Parties are required to adopt both legal and non-legal measures to implement the Convention (Committee on the Rights of the Child, 2003). However, due to a lack of incorporation of the Treaty, the UNCRC lacks binding authority in domestic law in England.[13]

---

[12]Article 26, Vienna Convention on the Law of Treaties.

[13]This can be contrasted with approaches in Scotland which incorporated the Convention through the UNCRC (Incorporation) (Scotland) Act 2004). See also the Rights of Children and Young Persons (Wales) Measure 2011, which requires Welsh ministers to have due regard to the Convention when exercising their functions. See, further, Kilkelly et al. (2021).

One of the most influential provisions of the Convention, and one which has particular relevance for this research, is Article 12 which concerns respect for children's views (Lundy et al., 2019). Article 12 states:

> States Parties shall assure to the child who is capable of forming his or her own views the right to express those views freely in all matters affecting the child, the views of the child being given due weight in accordance with the age and maturity of the child.

This inclusion of Article 12 represented a shift in the perception of children as passive objects in need of protection to individuals with evolving capacity who can express views and be involved in decision-making that affect them (Lundy et al., 2019). The significance of Article 12 is also reflected in the fact that the Committee on the Rights of the Child identified it as a guiding principle of the UNCRC, meaning it is crucial in the implementation of all other Convention rights (Committee on the Rights of the Child, 1991). Such rights include, for example, Article 2 (non-discrimination), Article 3 (best interests), Article 5 (right to guidance), Article 13 (right to seek, receive and impart information) and Article 19 (protection from abuse) (Lundy, 2007, p. 933). Article 12 links closely with Article 13, which recognises a right to information in ways which children can understand. It states:

> The child shall have the right to freedom of expression; this right shall include freedom to seek, receive and impart information and ideas of all kinds, regardless of frontiers, either orally, in writing or in print, in the form of art, or through any other media of the child's choice.

The Committee is clear that these rights apply to children of all ages, even the very young, noting that children make choices and communicate feelings in numerous ways before they are able to communicate these verbally (Committee on the Rights of the Child, 2009; para. 21). In this respect, full implementation of Article 12 requires respect for non-verbal communication, such as play, body language, facial expression, drawing and painting through which very young children demonstrate understanding choices and preferences (Committee on the Rights of the Child, 2009; para. 21). The Committee also stresses that participation is a form of ongoing dialogue. The Committee's General Comment on Article 12 (Committee on the Rights of the Child, 2009; para. 3) states:

> [Participation] has evolved and is now widely used to describe ongoing processes, which include information-sharing and dialogue between children and adults based on mutual respect, and in which children can learn how their views and those of adults are taken into account and shape the outcome of such processes.

However, Article 12 does not give children a right to govern the outcome of decisions, but rather have their views taken into account; it is legitimate to override children's wishes, if this is considered to be in their best interests, as protected under Article 3 of the UNCRC (Daly, 2018; Tisdall, 2015, 2021). The importance of child participation is multifaceted. Participation can lead to the improvement of services and decision-making with and for children (Thomas, 2007). It enhances democratic processes, as children gain opportunities to become active members of their communities in settings like schools and local authorities (Sinclair & Franklin, 2000, p. 1). There is also instrumental value to the child, in fostering a sense of belonging and empowerment (Rap, 2019; Thomas, 2007). Children learn valuable skills for decision-making, such as debate, communication and negotiation and prioritisation (Sinclair & Franklin, 2000, p. 1).

Children and Policymaking

Children can be involved in participation about matters that affect them, but can also be involved in more political forms of participation (Thomas, 2007, p. 206). For example, the Committee on the Rights of the Child (2009) has confirmed that the obligations under Article 12 apply to law and policy development and has stated:

> The views expressed by children may add relevant perspectives and experience and should be considered in decision-making, policymaking and *preparation of laws and/or measures as well as their evaluation*. (para. 12, our emphasis)

This includes children participating 'through research and consultations' (Committee on the Rights of the Child, 2005, para. 14(b)). In this regard, the Committee itself has consulted with children and young people on the development of recent General Comments on children's rights and access to justice (2024), the environment (2023) and the digital environment (2021) through child advisory teams and child-friendly consultation documents. However, it is rare to involve children in law and policy development, due to scepticism over their capacity or doubt that they will have valuable ideas (Greig et al., 2013). There are also concerns that giving children more control will undermine authority and that complying with their views will divert resources away from other priorities (Lundy, 2007, pp. 929–930). In addition, decision-making bodies often lack the practical means to include children, meaning children are included too late or have too little time to respond (Tisdall, 2017, p. 61). Bureaucratic processes are often not set up to include children's views (McMellon & Tisdall, 2020) and child-friendly consultation documents are rarely developed (Byrne & Lundy, 2019). In this respect, a child-friendly version of the Law Commissions' consultation document (2019a) on surrogacy was not produced.

Nonetheless, it is recognised that policymaking is enhanced by asking children directly about their experiences (Byrne & Lundy, 2019, p. 264). As Bessant and Broadley (2014) note:

> Children generally have clear understandings of what is happening in their lives, what is in their interest and what they want. They often see and experience events that adults and especially the professional adults in their lives know nothing of and have never experienced themselves. (p. 713)

This means that involving children in research about children's lives improves the reliability and validity of knowledge gained (Greig et al., 2013, pp. 227–228). Listening to children's views leads to more relevant decisions for them individually (Byrne & Lundy, 2019, p. 364) and can strengthen the evidence base for policy and enhance implementation (British Academy, 2022, p. 40). As Sinclair and Franklin (2000) note, better informed decisions for children are also more likely to be implemented. These reasons provide the justification for involving children with experience of surrogacy into the consultation process, which represents Phases One and Three. Many of the issues considered by the Law Commissions and in public debates about surrogacy are relevant to children, including legal parenthood, payments to surrogates and access to origin information. Arguments are made about children's interests in relation to these issues and have been used to either push for reform, maintain the status quo or abolish surrogacy entirely. There is a risk that if children are not involved in consultation, policymakers will make assumptions about children's views and experiences that may not reflect reality (British Academy, 2022, p. 40).

However, it is also important to involve children in law and policymaking even if they *do not* have experience of an issue (Byrne & Lundy, 2019), as was the case for Phase Two participants. This involved children in consultation as a democratic exercise, in the same way that the public were consulted through the Law Commissions' processes (Law Commissions, 2019a). It is instructive to draw on ideas from sociology of childhood to understand why this is important. Mayall (2002) argues that the intersections between past and present must be considered, in the sense that adulthood and childhood sit in different historical and social times. This means that:

> [s]ocial policies that impact on childhood experience are constructed, whether by design or not, by cohorts of older people drawing on their own experience, and on their ideologies of childhood and adulthood and the correct relationships between childhood and adulthood. (Mayall, 2002, p. 30)

Social policy can often reflect 'earlier cohort identities, goals and ideologies' (Mayall, 2002, p. 30). Therefore, if children's views are not considered when reforming laws, there is a possibility that it will be shaped by values or ideologies that no longer hold, when the children to whom the laws apply become adults.

In summary, children should be involved in law and policy development. First, there is value in engaging with children who have lived experience of an issue, so that their experiences can be fed into the assessment of law and law reform initiatives. Children have their own experiences of social processes, and it is important that these are also captured, because law and policy also need to include childhood experiences in the assessment of current law and law reform ideas. This is especially the case for surrogacy, since the law directly impacts children and many of the law reform recommendations from the Law Commissions are relevant to children. Second, it is also important to consult with children who are not directly impacted by an issue, as they should be included in law and policy development, whether or not they are currently impacted by a certain issue, in the same way as adults are. Third, involving children in research such as this is in line with the argument that to recognise children as social agents, we need to move beyond researching their childhood world, and include them in general social research that is not only about the child/adult boundaries, in order to fully accept them as 'agents in and of the social world' and 'potential informants of that wider world' (Uprichard, 2010, p. 11).

Involving Children in Research

There are different ways to include children in research. Christensen and Prout (2002a, 2002b), for example, speak of children as objects, subjects, social actors and co-researchers. Regarding the category 'children as objects', research is conducted on children, but children are not seen as social actors. This could involve getting adults' views on child experiences (Robinson, 2025, p. 483). 'Children as subjects' involves research in which children are viewed as having subjectivity, but researchers judge children's competencies (Christensen & Prout, 2002a, 2002b, p. 481; Robinson, 2025, p. 483). With 'children as social actors', children's independent views and experiences are sought, and with the category 'children as co-researchers' children are actively involved in data collection (Christensen & Prout, 2002a, 2002b, p. 481). Another category that has developed more recently in the latter category is 'co-produced research', which is '...an approach in which researchers, practitioners and the public work together, sharing power and responsibility from the start to the end of the project, including the generation of knowledge' (National Institute for Health and Care Research, [NIHR] 2024).[14] Co-production can be used at different stages, including identifying research questions, project design, governance, research activities, communication of findings and knowledge exchange (UK Research and Innovation, 2025). It is based on the principles of power sharing, inclusion of all perspectives and skills, respect and value for the knowledge of all contributors, reciprocity, building and maintaining relationships (NIHR, 2024). The use of co-produced research is growing 'because of its potential to improve the quality and relevance of research and its effect on policy and practice' (Redman et al., 2021).

[14]See 11 co-produced studies with children in Sevön et al. (2022). These are categorised as a 'research with children approach' and a 'participatory action research approach'. For co-produced research with children, see Lundy et al. (2011), Little et al. (2023) and Åkerström and Brunnberg (2013).

This project is not co-produced, but falls into the third category above; the children were seen as 'social actors'. The reason for not using co-production is that the project was time sensitive. As noted, the Law Commissions did not directly engage with children and had a set consultation window. Therefore, in order to include the views of children, there was a time limit on the research. Co-produced research takes more time and resources (Redman et al., 2021, p. 1). It also raises ethical complexities around the management of power imbalances and sharing responsibilities with children, which require additional time to manage (Tisdall, 2017). It should be noted, however, that before Phase Three, the team carried out a process of consultation with eight young people on the research questions, methods and outputs from Phases One and Two, which led to adjustments to the data collection method (card game) for Phase Three.[15]

The next section detailed the tools used to seek to ensure the method was participatory, grounded in the Lundy model of participation and the Mosaic approach of listening to children.

Facilitating Participation: The Lundy Model

The Lundy model originated in education and has gained widespread recognition as a way to realise children's Article 12 rights (Daly et al., 2025, p. 570). It was chosen here as it has been adopted by many organisations (Department of Children and Youth Affairs, 2015; European Commission, n.d.; World Health Organisation, 2018) and is recognised as an approach which clearly reflects the Committee on the Rights of the Child's understanding of participation under Article 12 (Bessant, 2022).[16] The model has four elements, namely, 'space', 'voice', 'audience' and 'influence' (Lundy, 2007, p. 933). With regards to space, Lundy notes that children must be afforded a safe space where they can express

[15]Space does not allow for a full exploration of adjustments made. Appendix 4 includes Phase One and Phase Three card examples. This consultation involved three focus groups with participants from Phase One and two additional participants (aged 7–19). We brainstormed what kind of questions they would ask if they were the researchers. We asked them if they had ideas for card design/redesign (supported by an artist) and asked for feedback on the artwork space and output design.

[16]For other theories on participation, see Hart's 'ladder of participation' (1992). The bottom three rungs of the ladder are manipulation, decoration and tokenism and are categorised as non-participation. These rungs are participatory: assigned but informed, consulted and informed, shared decisions with young people (adult-initiated), young people-initiated and directed and shared decisions with adults (young people-initiated). Shier's (2001) 'pathway to participation' is based around three concepts: openings, opportunities and obligations. It provides practitioners with questions under the categories: listening to children, supporting the expression of views, taking views into account, involving children in decision-making, and sharing power and responsibility. Sinclair (2004) suggests a model with four dimensions: participation level (the extent of children's engagement/control); the decision-making focus (private or public and individual or group); the participation activity (e.g., survey, one-off consultation, etc.); and the group of children included.

their views without fear of rebuke or reprisal (Lundy, 2007, p. 934). The space must also be inclusive, and include children of all abilities (Lundy, 2007, p. 934). In terms of 'voice', Lundy notes that the restriction in Article 12, i.e., that it is afforded to children who are capable of forming their own views, only applies to the second part of Article 12(1), i.e., the obligation to give views due weight. Therefore, 'children's right to express their views is not dependent upon their capacity to express a mature view; it is dependent only on their ability to form a view, mature or not' (Lundy, 2007, p. 935). She notes that this means that children may need assistance to express views, in line with Article 5 of the UNCRC (Lundy, 2007). Lundy also notes how children identified plays, puppet shows, videos and drawing as ways to engage with children (Lundy, 2007, p. 935). Regarding 'audience', Lundy (2007, p. 936) argues that the obligation to give children's views 'due weight' means that those views should be listened to in decision-making. The fourth element, 'influence', is about acting upon children's views, where appropriate. The next sections consider the 'space', 'audience' and 'influence', before moving on to a fuller discussion of the third element 'voice', to explain in detail the methods used.

Space for Children

This project provided a 'space' for children to express their views on surrogacy. Phase One and Two involved group interviews, ranging from two to six children. Phase Three involved one interview with two participants and three individual interviews. In this regard, the space was set up in a way to make participants feel at ease.[17] Participants were in a circle on the floor or at tables and each child had their own 'play-space' with a card game. Various steps were taken to create a safe space for expression of views. For example, there was a 'code of conduct' card, which asked participants to listen, to wait to speak, to be nice and respectful, to not interrupt and to ask questions if they did not understand. Participants were told that there was no right or wrong answer and that they did not have to answer any question they did not want to. There was a 'not sure' card that participants could hold up for this purpose. Two or three researchers were present to assist a child in need of help or to allow them to take a break. Participants were given time at the start to become familiar with the space (Greig et al., 2013, p. 114). A core feature of providing an inclusive space was also the 'art space'. This was set up on a table or floor with a range of art materials.[18] Participants sat in a group and individually made art at the start and during the breaks. Such an 'art space' was also held at SUK's annual conference in 2022 with one of the researchers and a member of SUK. In most groups, one researcher also did artwork alongside participants or helped them locate the art

[17]The locations for Phase One were venues in central London and a University seminar room. The location for Phase Two was school classrooms. The locations for Phase Three were participants' homes and a University seminar room.
[18]See Appendix 4, Fig. 8.

materials they wanted to use. Participants were able to speak to each other and the researcher while making art, which led to rapport-building before and during the interviews. The way in which the 'art space' facilitated the participants' 'voice' is explained below.

Audience and Influence for Children's Views

In respect of the 'audience' element of the Lundy model, preliminary findings of the research were disseminated widely to national and international policy makers, law makers, surrogacy organisations and academics. Preliminary findings of Phase One were presented to the Law Commissions in September 2022. This was invited by the Law Commissions after the publication of a blog about the project for Surrogacy Awareness Week (Wade, 2022). This presentation resulted in citations to the research in the Law Commissions' 2023 report. The Nuffield Council on Bioethics also requested a meeting and cited the project in its Briefing Paper on Surrogacy (2023). The preliminary findings of Phase One and Phase Two were written into two separate Reports (Children's Voices in Surrogacy Law, 2023a, 2023b) which were sent to the Department of Health and Social Care (DHSC), the Human Fertilisation and Embryology Authority, Cafcass, the Nuffield Council on Bioethics, the UN Committee on the Rights of the Child and the APPG on Surrogacy. The reports were published on the project website and sent out via the team's professional social media accounts. The reports were also developed into child-friendly animated versions, available on the website. The website also hosts artwork from Phase One in a video format ('Digital Wall') and artwork from Phase One and Three in an artbook format.[19] The preliminary findings and methods, as well as the 'digital wall', were presented at national and international conferences.[20] The research was the subject of an in-person art exhibition,[21] two invited podcasts[22] and featured in an Economist documentary (The Economist, 2023). The team also organised a

[19]Phase Three was not included with this artwork, as it had a different prompt, which was 'What I learned about surrogacy today'.

[20]These included the second International Surrogacy Forum, Copenhagen, June 2023 (Wade); International Social Service Workshop, Geneva, October 2024 (Wade); Child Identity Protection Conference, Sierre, Switzerland, November 2023 (Wade), Association of Lawyers for Children Annual Conference, November 2024 (Wade); 27th Annual Family Law Conference, March 2025 (Mahmoud); University of the Western Cape, South Africa; Contemporary Parent-Child Relationships and the Law Conference, University of Galway, Ireland, November 2023 (Mahmoud).

[21]CVSL Art Exhibition, Attenborough Arts Centre, Leicester, 24 June 2023–9 July 2023, funded by the University of Leicester, Knowledge Exchange, Impact and Proof of Concept Fund. The launch event showcased the card games, animations, and preliminary reports alongside the framed artwork.

[22]See podcast 'Children of Surrogacy' for SUK (https://surrogacyuk.org/podcasts/) and 'Listening to Children: Children's Perspectives on Surrogacy Law' for the Mason Institute Investigates series (https://blogs.ed.ac.uk/mason-institute/2023/08/09/season-2-episode-5-listening-to-children-childrens-perspectives-on-surrogacy-law/).

conference called 'Future Directions in Surrogacy Law' during this project,[23] which hosted a 'children's panel'. It included five children with experience of surrogacy who shared their views on the law through an interactive simulation of a group interview with cards, mini whiteboards and a 'show and tell' of objects that held meaning for participants in relation to surrogacy. The audience included representatives from the Law Commissions, family law judges, legal practitioners, social workers, counsellors, surrogacy organisations and academics.

Regarding 'influence' of children's views *on law and policy*, this depends on the actions of the government, i.e., whether reforms are implemented and whether they would engage with our findings in doing so. The interim response from the government to the Law Commissions' Report in 2023 stated that there was no parliamentary time to take forward the recommendations (Caulfield, 2023). In April 2025, the Law Commissions received a letter from Baroness Merron, the Parliamentary Under Secretary of State, DHSC, stating that the Government will consider the issue in the future (Merron, 2025). It is hoped that any law and policy reform in the future will engage with this research. Moreover, as noted in the Introduction, law and policy is not the only type of influence; it is hoped this research will enhance academic debates by including understandings of children's views on law and policy in surrogacy and present a new method to include children in future law reform agendas.

'Voice' of Children

In terms of the third element of the Lundy model, to facilitate hearing the 'voice' of children, the method drew on the Mosaic approach from early childhood studies. This is a 'multi-method, polyvocal approach' which recognises the different 'voices' or languages of children (Clark, 2017; Rogers, 2005; Rogers & Boyd, 2020). It originated in research about the evaluation of early childhood services (Clark & Moss, 2008) and the design of indoor and outdoor play spaces (Clark, 2001, 2010). The studies utilised interviews, photography, map-making, child-guided tours and voice recordings. The model has since been used in research with children on social services research (O'Kane, 2000), health education (Morrow, 2001) and mental health (Punch, 2006). The model is based on the provision of an array of resources and environments to children to capture verbal and pre-verbal communication (Clark, 2017, p. 16). It is creative and recognises that children can 'speak' to adults through their play, their actions and reactions (Clark, 2017, p. 16). Examples of methods include photo-taking, drawing, map-making, playing, etc., thereby combining the 'visual' with the 'verbal' (Clark, 2017, p. 16). The 'mosaic' concept refers to how different

[23]'Future Directions in Surrogacy Law', Institute of Advanced Legal Studies, 30 November 2022, funded by a Society of Legal Scholars Small Grant. The presentations from this conference formed the basis of an edited collection (Horsey et al., 2025).

methods can be used to 'piece together a child-directed account of their interests and priorities' (Clark, 2017, p. 16).

In line with a children's rights-based approach and sociology of childhood, children are viewed as 'experts in their own lives' (Clark, 2017, p. 14). As Clark (2017) notes,

> The aim is to identify methods that position children as holders of unique insights into the lived experience of their lives and that open up as many different ways for children to communicate this competency as possible. (p. 17)

The epistemological approach is that knowledge is created, as opposed to gathered (Clark, 2017). The tools are not used to extract 'one truth', but rather to co-construct meaning from a range of realities (Clark, 2017, p. 12). The model is also reflexive: listening is seen as an active process, with children and adults constructing meaning and responding (Clark, 2017, p. 17). Clark is clear that this is a method that can be adapted to any context working with children, as it is 'a way of conceptualising "listening" and the relationships and processes involved' (Clark, 2017, p. 17). Indeed, it is now an established approach in research with children to recognise that they communicate through verbal and non-verbal means, such as plays, songs, drawings and stories (Blaisdell et al., 2019; O'Kane, 2000, p. 139). While the age-range for the interviews was 8–18, and the Mosaic approach was originally used with younger children, using a range of tools to capture children's views was seen as accessible and engaging and was therefore used for all age groups.

In line with the Mosaic approach, our framework is built around three communicative elements, namely, 'playing', 'speaking' and 'creating', as set out in the next section.

The CVSL Method

Playing: The Use of Card Games

We used play in the interviews through the means of a specially designed card game.[24] These were designed by members of the team with two professional illustrators.[25] They included a 'code of conduct' card, explanation cards of main concepts in surrogacy and cards for the games. All efforts were made to use plain unambiguous language (Greig et al., 2013, p. 116). Simple definitions for the terms: 'surrogacy', 'traditional surrogacy', 'gestational surrogacy' and 'parental order' were placed at the top of the play space. These were visible during the interview, so that children could refer back to these definitions at any point. The

[24]Card examples are included in Appendix 4, Figs. 2–6.

[25]The card deck and activities were designed by Katherine Wade and Charlotte Mills and the illustrators were: Sara Digregorio and Claudia Dagostino, with additional illustrations by Jasmine Thompson (Phase Three).

interview opened with a brainstorming activity on the question: 'What makes someone a parent?'. Children were invited to write sentences, words or draw pictures on Post-it notes, which were gathered and placed in a shared area for discussion.[26] For three topics: parenthood, contributions and origins/contact, there was an initial card game at the start of the topic discussion. The first game asked children to vote on the question: 'Who do you think the parents of a child should be when a child is born through surrogacy?' and asked them to choose between three illustrated cards: the intended parent/s, the surrogate, and the surrogate and partner. The second game asked children to sort items such as 'car', 'food', 'gift', 'money' into piles on top of 'Yes', 'No' or 'Not Sure' cards in response to the question: 'Do you think it is OK for intended parents to give these things to the surrogate?' The third game involved circling 'Yes', 'No' or 'Not Sure' on cards with a list of questions about whether children should know about the surrogacy arrangement, the people involved and whether they should have contact with these people. For Phase Three, there was also a 'Maybe' option.[27]

The use of play in research fits with a children's rights approach. Article 12 UNCRC, interpreted in line with Article 5, means that there is an obligation to ensure that children have direction and guidance in expressing their views, in a manner consistent with their evolving capacities (Głos, 2024, pp. 806–807). There were many benefits to the use of play. First, the play element made the interviews engaging, which is important in holding the varying attention spans of children (Tinson, 2009). Since play is a 'natural language of children', it can be a medium through which their voice is exercised and meaning is made (Głos, 2024, pp. 806–807). Game-based research is motivating and engaging for young participants (Barwick et al., 2018); participants were physically interacting with materials to complete tasks which was good for engagement (O'Kane, 2000). Second, game-based research creates a controlled space/structure for the research (Barwick et al., 2018); the game broke the interview up into distinct sections, thereby providing structure. Moreover, as Barwick et al. (2018) note, 'as controlled environments, [games] offer a safe space to explore sensitive issues' (p. 246). Within the card game, participants were not asked direct questions about their own personal experiences. Instead, they were asked general questions which they could follow up with personal insights if they wished. This helped to create a relaxed discussion. Third, the game also meant that the team captured participants' initial reactions to questions. Participants revealed their answers at the same time for some questions or worked with their own card deck for others. This helped to guard against participants replicating the views of their peers, which can be a concern in research with children, particularly when some may feel marginalised, inhibited or less confident speaking in front of others (Bessant, 2022, p. 22). While there is always a risk of certain participants dominating a

---

[26]See Appendix 4, Fig. 7.

[27]This card was added as a response to feedback to the consultation with children on the card games noted above (n. 15).

discussion (Greig et al., p. 117), the card games also meant that everyone was prompted to give their views.

Speaking: The Use of Interview Questions

Each topic for discussion began with a game, as described above, which then led to a set of questions. It is important to note that in the first three topics the aim was to seek participants' views on ethical issues that the law regulates as opposed to gathering personal insights about their own experiences. For example, the questions were not framed as: 'Do you have contact with your surrogate?', but rather 'Should children have contact with their surrogate?' Similarly, participants were not asked: 'Was your surrogate paid and were you OK with this?' but rather: 'Is it OK for intended parents to give surrogates money?' This approach was important because the aim of the project was to elicit their views on how the issue of surrogacy should be regulated. Participants were asked about 'children born through surrogacy' and 'intended parents' as abstract figures to seek to explore what rules participants thought should be applied to everyone. Participants were then asked follow-up questions from the games, such as 'Why do you think the parents should be the intended parents?, 'Should the surrogate be able to change her mind?' and 'What age do you think parents should tell their children about surrogacy', for example. This part allowed for free-flowing conversation between the interviewer and participants.

It is also to be noted that with the exception of parental orders (a major element of potential reforms), we did not explain the current law. First, this meant that we did not spend time in the interviews on explanations of law, which may have bored the children or taken a lot of time. Second, if participants were told what the law was and then were asked whether it should be changed, they are already being told the status quo, which children may have interpreted as something which must be followed.[28] We sought to capture participants' unique insights without them being told the current legal position and to see if there are things that are important to children that adults have not considered. In this sense, it does not follow a 'law-first approach'; it focuses on children's perspectives rather than foregrounding the research with abstract legal concepts or specific laws (Watkins et al., 2018). We therefore presented the children with scenarios or questions that arise in surrogacy, which present ethical and legal dimensions and explored their responses and reactions to these (see Watkins et al., 2018).[29]

---

[28]One insight that supports this is from a study on legal capability, which showed that when children adopted legal or quasi-legal terminology, criminal law terms tended to be used over civil law terms (Watkins et al., 2018). This could indicate that children may not see law as having a more enabling/regulatory function.

[29]The Watkins et al. study (2018) did not focus on ethical questions, but explored familiar situations in children's everyday lives, to observe their choices and reactions, as a way to gain insights into how they make sense of the law in those scenarios. However, it is similar in the sense that it is not 'law first'.

We recognise that there are limitations to this method. First, what children say in general about normative issues might not be what they think the law should be, as an objective rule, for everyone. Nonetheless, we still believe that asking normative questions about issues in surrogacy is better than asking children to evaluate law. Law begins with a stance; a decision has been made that certain interests are weightier than others or that certain ethical principles must be respected. It is therefore better, when trying to assess children's views and to be truly participatory, not to present them with the law or proposals for reform from law reform bodies.[30] As noted, they may defer to law, seeing it as a set of rules to be followed, and it presents them with adult-centric frameworks for the regulation of human behaviour. Secondly, law is sometimes indirect about the principles that justify these frameworks (Huxtable, 2017, p. 94), and so if children side with law or law reform stances, the justification or ethical principles for their positions may not be readily apparent. Therefore, if we uncover the ethical principles that the children appear to resort to, such as fairness, autonomy or identity (even if not worded in this way), this provides us with a richer insight into what they think of the law or how the law should be.

Creating: The Production of Artwork

Children were invited to make a creative contribution on the topic: 'What surrogacy means to me' in Phases One and Three, and on the topic: 'What I learned about Surrogacy Today' in Phase Two. This was done at home, at a surrogacy event, and in the 'art space' at interviews. Children were provided with a range of materials, such as paper, cut-out card shapes of people, markers, pencils, plasticine, crayons and craft materials (e.g., pipe cleaners, googly eyes, glitter, etc.). They were told they could make any creative outputs they liked, including drawings, collage, word clouds, poems or models. This method aimed to capture the subjective and experiential 'voice' of participants. This approach allowed unique and visually powerful insights into how surrogacy was experienced or perceived by participants. In direct contrast to the card games, the activity was structured around a non-law focused open question. This aspect of the project was grounded in legal consciousness (Ewick & Silbey, 1998) and law and visuality (Mulcahy, 2017; Rose, 2022). We were able to gain insight into the way in which law impacted participants' lives. While law was not directly portrayed in the artwork, the pieces illustrate the kind of experiences and emotions that the current regulation facilitates (Wade & Mills, 2025). There are many benefits to the use of artwork. Children can express experiences, emotions and ideas they may find difficult to articulate (Farmer & Cepin, 2017; Karlidag-Dennis et al.,

[30]This is the opposite approach to 'pre-figurative approach' (Cooper, 2023), whereby ideas for law reform ideas (which are not mainstream) are posed to participants as already being on the reform agenda. We did not take this approach, as children may be more susceptible to giving answers that they think the researcher/adult thinks is 'right' (Greene & Hill, 2005), due to power imbalance, and so might consider reform ideas put forward by researchers as the 'right' answer.

2025). Visual methods also challenge power imbalance between researchers and children, by allowing children to determine what is important (Fane et al., 2018). Being able to choose what to produce meant the children exercised a high level of control over the process (Green, 2017). Children were able to express as little or as much as they liked, and they had time to reflect on experiences (Coyne et al., 2021). It also facilitated a non-confrontational basis for the initial interactions, as eye contact and direct questions were not needed (Einarsdóttir et al., 2009, p. 220). An analysis of the Phase One and Phase Three artwork was conducted (Wade & Mills, 2025). The four themes that were produced – connections, love, positivity and rationalisation – showed a positive perception of surrogacy from participants. The artwork showed that UK surrogacy law facilitates practices based on collaboration and mutual respect, surrogacy is not necessarily harmful to children, children accept non-heteronormative models of parenthood and children value altruism in surrogacy. This book does not explore the artwork themes; however, it refers to the findings from the artwork, where relevant to the findings and arguments made.

All three elements of the method complement each other, with games and artwork breaking up interviewing and allowing for rapport-building and flow of conversation. In line with the Lundy model and the Mosaic approach, different methods were used to seek to capture different ways that children express themselves. In addition, the different methods allowed us to form a rich picture of the participants' views and experiences. The games and questions gave insights into participants' views on ethical issues in surrogacy. The artwork gave insights into their experiences and perceptions of surrogacy, as it is currently practiced in the United Kingdom and the United States, which is shaped by the law and policy that regulates it.

Data Analysis

The interview recordings were transcribed verbatim, and analysis was conducted using Braun and Clarke's (2022) reflexive thematic analysis. First, all three authors conducted a 'familiarisation stage', where all transcripts were read, to become familiar with the data as a whole (Braun & Clarke, 2022, p. 6). In the second stage, all the transcripts were separately coded with manual codes. The third stage involved 'collaborative coding' (Braun & Clarke, 2022, p. 285), where all codes were shared, allowing for reflection upon individual ideas and assumptions and a set of common codes were produced. The fourth stage involved all three authors separately grouping these codes to develop themes on the topics: parenthood, contributions, origin information and surrogacy in children's social worlds. The team then met to agree on a final set of themes for each topic. Different authors took the lead for some chapters but all chapters were jointly reviewed and co-authored. The artwork was also coded under this framework. However, given the visual nature of the data, we also considered the way the image was composed and the atmosphere we interpreted from the image

(Rose, 2022). We also drew on some participants' own explanation of their artwork (Leitch, 2008; Wade & Mills, 2025).

The process was reflexive in the sense that we reflected on how our values, methods and academic discipline shape knowledge production, including personal, functional and disciplinary reflexivity (Braun & Clarke, 2022, p. 13, 2023, p. 4). The collaborative coding was undertaken to guard against bias in the development of codes and themes, since it allowed each researcher to see how the language of the participants was interpreted by the others.

Limitations

A common concern with doing research with children is that children will simply reflect the views of parents or influential adults in their lives. A child is already in a network of power relationships in terms of peer relations, family processes or institutional relationships (Fraser et al., 2014, p. 47). It is of course the case that children are influenced by their social networks and their views are likely to reflect the views and political/social positioning of their carers. For children, in particular, their moral development and socialisation are influenced by parents/carers and family members (Padilla-Walker & Memmott-Elison, 2020). This is not a reason not to do research with children, however. This challenge is one which is present for all empirical research, since all participants are embedded in social networks and influenced by the views of those around them. People craft answers to questions to match their own intentions and the intentions of others (Bucknall, 2014, p. 72).

Another limitation of research with children is to do with the power dynamic between researchers and child participants. Researchers have power over the way in which the research is conducted. As Flewitt (2014) notes:

> Whatever format is chosen for interviews, they are infused with complex relations of power: who chooses what (and what not) to discuss, who asks what questions, when, and how, who is allotted the status to answer and who is not, who determines when to end a line of questioning, and so on. (p. 143)

Even where an engaging and inclusive method for hearing children's views is used, children will often see researchers as authority figures. Children may respond to questions according to their expectations of what the researchers want to hear (Hill, 2006). Children may also feel they are expected to give an answer, whether or not they have a view (Flewitt, 2014; Hill, 2006). Environments can also play a role; children being interviewed in school are already in a power relation with teachers and may see researchers as part of this hierarchy (Greig et al., 2013, p. 116). It is therefore essential to build rapport with research participants, in order to earn their trust, so that they feel comfortable in giving their own views (Flewitt, 2014). As noted, the card games and the artwork helped to build rapport and trust with participants, since the children could easily interact with the researchers and other participants. These activities also allowed the research team to engage in joint activity with the children to establish rapport and to ease hierarchy. The interviewer also had their own play space and sat on the floor or at tables with the participants. They did the brainstorm activity and told the participants their answers. As noted, the researchers were also present at the 'art space' and, in some groups, made their own artwork.[31] The children also explained their art to the researcher, which eased the power imbalance, by giving them an instructional/authoritative role.

Other potential limitations are to do with participant recruitment. First, the participant number in this project is small. Therefore, we do not claim the results are generalisable. Nonetheless, the data are valuable, given that this is the first time children were consulted on surrogacy law reform in the United Kingdom and to our knowledge in English speaking jurisdictions.[32] Second, there is the issue of self-selection bias. This is particularly relevant for Phases One and Three. Participants were recruited through sending recruitment adverts to the main non-profit surrogacy organisations: Brilliant Beginnings, Childlessness Overcome through Surrogacy (COTS), My Surrogacy Journey and SurrogacyUK, who forwarded these to their members and shared our social media advertisements.[33] These organisations are actively involved in supporting surrogacy in the United Kingdom, meaning their members are mostly surrogates, intended parents and/or organisation staff. Such involvement (presumably) means that these individuals have a positive attitude towards surrogacy and that their views may be known to participants and may influence them. Children, as is also the case for adults, are shaped by the cultural context and the dominant discourses that surround them (Greene & Hill, 2005). However, self-selection bias is a limitation of all empirical research (Costigan & Cox, 2001) and is not possible to circumvent, since voluntary participation is required for ethical research (Costigan & Cox, 2001; Robinson, 2014). What is important is to be aware of the possibility of selection bias in the interpretation of data (Robinson, 2014). Therefore, we do not argue that the findings in this study represent *all* children's experience of surrogacy in the United Kingdom. Rather, the data give an insight into surrogacy from a group who have been involved in surrogacy conducted with the support of these organisations. However, these perspectives are valuable, since the support of the surrogacy organisations is a unique feature of UK surrogacy practice (Pott & White, 2025). It should also be noted that this was one

[31]Such instances of 'joint action' with children can be seen as reflecting the 'least-adult' approach (Mandell, 1988) whereby the researcher acts in as least an adult manner as possible; they act as an observer, neither directing or correcting children's actions and joining in where invited. For example, if participants made art which was not relevant to the topic, the researcher listened to explanations and joined in by making similar art.

[32]Internet-based and library-based searches revealed no empirical studies with children on surrogacy law.

[33]Such approaches are common, since recruitment of children is rarely direct but controlled through agencies, professionals and carers etc. (Powell & Smith, 2009).

of the reasons for conducting Phase Two, as we wanted to explore diverse views from children with and without experience of surrogacy.

Another limitation is around diversity of participants in terms of gender, ethnicity and socio-economic backgrounds. In this respect, the only participant background information collected was age and gender (all Phases) and connection to or experience of surrogacy (Phase One and Three). For Phases One and Three, we included all participants whose families contacted us. This was necessitated by the limited pool of potential participants, due to the small number of children born through surrogacy annually and the requirement for the children participating in this study to be aged eight and over. Therefore, we did not undertake sampling methods to seek to increase diversity. For Phase Two, however, efforts were made to do so. We visited four schools in Southeast England. Two of these were primary schools, each in different socio-economic catchment areas. For the two secondary schools, one was part of an Academy Trust (non-selective), and the other was a Grammar school (selective). However, we do not claim that the data across all three Phases reflect a fully representative sample of children, in terms of gender, ethnicity and socio-economic background. It is also to be noted that there was an age range of 8–18 years for the interviews, which is the basis of this book's analysis. It could be argued that age restrictions should not have been in place, since children's participation should depend on their capacity to understand and agree to take part, which for some children, could be earlier. However, the age of eight was chosen in the following way. Originally, the age of nine was chosen due to the subject matter of the research, which is human reproduction. This is covered in Year 5 in primary school, when children are 9–10 years old. The reason for the involvement of 8-year-olds was that in Phase One, a number of parents asked whether their 8-year-old child could be involved. This is likely because such children have experience of surrogacy and therefore know information about reproduction at an earlier time than it is taught in school. This new age range was ethically approved and kept in place for Phase Two, to allow young children to be involved if they wished, with agreement from their parents. Children of any age could take part in the art element of the research.[34]

Conclusion

This chapter set out the methodology of the project, which is based on the premise that children are both social agents and holders of rights. Under the new sociology of childhood, children are seen as creating meaning through their everyday experiences. A rights-based approach under the UNCRC places obligations on States Parties under international law to respect children's views in decisions that affect them. There is therefore an obligation on States Parties and those who work with children to facilitate the inclusion of their views in line with

[34]The youngest participant in the art-making part of the project was five years old. They took part at the SUK Annual Conference 2022.

their capacities, in order to secure compliance with UNCRC obligations. The Committee on the Rights of the Child (2005, 2009) has interpreted Article 12 as meaning that children should be involved in public decision-making more broadly. This has led to involving children as active participants or co-collaborators in research projects, as opposed to merely being research subjects. Respecting children's agency and their right to have their views heard means that a diverse range of methods may be needed to support participation with children. It falls to researchers to design methods and channels to hear from children with diverse ages and abilities (Sevön et al., 2022). The Lundy model, which emphasises space, voice, audience and influence, and the Mosaic approach, which advocates for verbal and non-verbal methods to capture different communication styles of children, were used to shape the methods. The interviews had 'playing', 'speaking' and 'creating' elements, with card games, interview questions and artwork, to capture children's views on ethical issues in surrogacy law that are currently under discussion in law reform debates. Through card games and interview questions, we asked direct questions about issues that the law regulates in an objective way. With artwork creation, we explored the way in which current law and policy shaped the everyday experiences of children, and their perceptions of surrogacy, removed from legal and ethical frameworks. Through the use of these varied methods and collaborative thematic analysis, we were able to construct a rich picture of the participants' views on surrogacy law and law reform.

The following chapters detail the substantive findings from the data on the topics of legal parenthood, contributions, origin information and how children navigate surrogacy in their social worlds.

Chapter 2

Children's Views About Parenthood in Surrogacy Arrangements

> '[The law] should be changed to as soon as the baby comes out of the tummy, it should, first, straight away, be the person who is intending to look after it'.[1]

Introduction

This chapter addresses the first topic under consideration in the interviews: children's views about parenthood following a surrogacy arrangement. The chapter first explores concepts used by participants to explain their understanding of the meaning(s) of parenthood, generated through a brainstorming activity where participants were asked the question 'what makes someone a parent?'. Secondly, it explores participants' views on who they thought the parents of a child *should* be following a surrogacy arrangement. Thirdly, it examines how participants view the law regarding parenthood. Participants were asked about their views on who should be recognised as the parent(s), the parental order process, whether the surrogate should be able to change her mind and the requirement that at least one intended parent must have a genetic link for them to be eligible for a parental order.

The chapter explores what concepts underpin the participants' understanding of parenthood, how they think (legal) parenthood should be assigned and their perceptions of the role of genetics, gestation/birth and intention/agreement in determining parenthood. These issues fit into ongoing domestic and global debates regarding parenthood in surrogacy, debates on the role of genetics in parenthood in assisted reproduction more widely, and proposals to reform the law on parenthood following surrogacy in the United Kingdom. The findings provide insights into the extent to which direct experience of surrogacy or lack thereof, or experiences of different types of surrogacy, may have impacted participants' views.

[1] Scarlett (11, born through gestational surrogacy).

Children's Voices in Surrogacy Law, 51–85

doi:10.1108/978-1-83549-642-820261003

We note that participants in Phase One were recruited through domestic non-profit surrogacy organisations committed to altruistic and ethical surrogacy and that their involvement and often continued connection with these organisations may have shaped their views, understandings and vocabulary. Similarly, for those in Phase Three, their knowledge of being born through an international surrogacy arrangement, and the more contractual nature of this, may impact how they understood parenthood. Our findings, therefore, likely reflect the discursive environments within which the children have grown up.[2]

This chapter begins with an overview of the current law on legal parenthood following surrogacy in the United Kingdom. There then follows a detailed discussion of the data under the themes that were identified. The interviews revealed different, varied (and sometimes conflicting) understandings of what makes someone a parent and views on the law. Sometimes this reflected participants' personal experiences, while at other times it was based on preconceptions. The participants generally recognised parents as those who care, provide and support, but also sometimes bestowed special meaning to genetic relationships (not necessarily conferring parenthood), meaning an interesting interplay between intention and genetics sometimes arose. Participants generally supported intention-based parenthood. Nonetheless, for many, genetics retains a certain level of importance, even within an intention-based model. Five main themes were identified. First, *being* a parent/parenting is about love and care, while biology is secondary. The remaining four themes relate to what children thought should determine parenthood following surrogacy: children attach importance to choice, agreement and assumed responsibility; children consider that surrogates should be held to their decisions, especially gestational surrogates; children recognise the suboptimality of the parental order system; and children believe that having a genetic link should not be a requirement for legal parenthood. The final section of the chapter explores the implications of these insights for the law on parenthood following surrogacy.

The Law on Legal Parenthood Following Surrogacy: An Overview

It is the law that determines who the legal parents of a child born through surrogacy are, notwithstanding any agreements made between the parties of a surrogacy arrangement. The provisions apply equally whether the insemination or embryo transfer took place (or the child was born) in the United Kingdom or overseas. Section 33 of the Human Fertilisation and Embryology (HFE) Act 2008 provides that the 'woman who is carrying or has carried a child as a result of the placing in her of an embryo or of sperm and eggs, and no other woman' is the legal mother.[3] Any second parent – male or female – is determined depending

[2]This idea is discussed further in Chapter 1, p. 48. The interview questions are included in Appendix 5.

[3]Following *McConnell & Anor, R (On the Application Of) v The Registrar General for England and Wales* [2020] EWCA Civ 559 this includes a trans man who gives birth.

on their relationship to the birth parent, though this depends on a determination of various issues about consent and intention. The legal framework allows only a maximum of two people to be legal parents at any one time, an ideological position that continues to reflect the dominance of the traditional hetero-normative nuclear (or sexual) family (Brown, 2018, 2019; Fineman, 1995; Horsey & Jackson, 2023; McCandless, 2025; McCandless & Sheldon, 2010a, 2010b; Sheldon, 2005; Smith, 2010). Increasingly, and not exclusively related to surrogacy, we see the problems this engenders with the binary terminology used to define legal parents (Brown, 2018; Dunne & Brown, 2024; Horsey & Jackson, 2023; Mahmoud & Romanis, 2023; *McConnell & Anor, R (On the Application Of) v The Registrar General for England and Wales* [2020] EWCA Civ 559; *FZ* v *MZ & FZ* v *Y Council* [2025] EWHC 3338 (Fam)).

The law is complicated and at times internally and terminologically contradictory (Horsey & Jackson, 2023). If the surrogate is married or in a civil partnership, her spouse or partner will be either the 'father' (s. 35 HFE Act 2008) or the second legal 'parent' (s. 42 HFE Act 2008) at birth, depending on whether they are a man or a woman. However, a statutory exception exists wherein the spouse/civil partner can show that they did not consent to their spouse/partner being treated (i.e. inseminated or having an embryo transfer). Where the surrogate is single, that is unmarried or not in a civil partnership, an intended father can be registered as the legal father if he is biologically related to the child, where desired.[4] Alternatively, if it is desired that a *non*-biological intended father become the (legal) father at birth, he can do so if the 'agreed fatherhood conditions' are met (ss. 36–37 HFE Act 2008). Otherwise, the parties may decide that an intended mother (biologically related or not) can be a second 'female parent' according to the 'agreed female parenthood conditions' (ss. 44–45 HFE Act 2008). It does not (legally) matter which intended parent is registered on the birth certificate, but an intended mother cannot be a legal 'mother' – only a 'parent' – whereas an intended father (biologically related or otherwise) will be the 'father'. As the Law Commission and Scottish Law Commission (2023, para. 2.3) recognised:

> [W]hile it is possible for one intended parent to acquire legal parental status upon the birth of the child, it is never possible for both intended parents to be the legal parents at birth. Further, the surrogate will always be the legal parent, whether she wishes to be or not.

This reflects what has been termed 'family form ideology' (McCandless, 2025, p. 138), in which the 'unitary ideological model of the nuclear family' dominates

---

[4]This is according to the common law rules that existed prior to the HFE Acts which make the genetic father of a baby born to an unmarried/civilly partnered woman the legal father (subject to the mother registering him as such). See *Leeds Teaching Hospitals NHS Trust* v *A and B* [2003] 1 FLR 1091.

the rules on legal parenthood, leaving no room for parenthood to be determined by other 'concepts such as dependency, care or vulnerability; or perhaps even safety or social justice' (McCandless, 2025, p. 137). Though the Law Commission and Scottish Law Commission' (2023) proposed a new 'pathway' (see below) that would represent a substantial change to legal parenthood following surrogacy, it still rests on an assumption that the *shape* of the traditional nuclear family (if not the *content*) should prevail. It assumes that in regulated arrangements the intended parents would be legal parents at birth '*to the exclusion* of the surrogate' (McCandless, 2025, p. 138), framing surrogacy as inevitably about substitution and exchange rather than, perhaps, the collaborative process some consider it to be. This replicates a binary understanding of parenthood: *either* the surrogate *or* the intended parent(s) will be the parents (Brown, 2018). To counter this, McCandless argues for simultaneous recognition of the legal status of *both* the surrogate and the intended parents at birth.

Birth registration processes are governed by the Births and Deaths Registration Act 1953. While the surrogate has an obligation (as the legal mother) to register the birth within 42 days, it is possible for her to register the child with the intended parents' surname. If one intended parent is to be jointly registered on the birth certificate alongside the surrogate, they must attend the registration with her. If that person is not the biological father, then anecdotally it seems that it is best practice to take copies of the Human Fertilisation and Embryology Authority (HFEA) consent forms signed at the time of treatment, which confirm that the 'agreed fatherhood' or 'agreed female parenthood' conditions were met.

Parental orders are a bespoke court order created to enable the transfer of legal parenthood from the surrogate (and her spouse/partner where relevant) to the intended parents post-birth, provided certain conditions are met (ss. 54 and 54A HFE Act 2008).[5] These conditions include that the intended parent/s be over 18 and be domiciled in the United Kingdom, Channel Islands or Isle of Man. Where they are a couple, they must be married, in a civil partnership or an 'enduring family relationship'. At least one of the applicants (where a couple applies) must have a genetic link to the child. In the case of a single applicant, they must have a genetic link. At the time of both the application and the making of the order, the child's home must be with the applicant/s. Applications cannot be made before the child is six weeks old but should be made before the child is six months old. An application cannot be granted without the surrogate's free and unconditional consent, unless she cannot be found or lacks capacity. Additionally, the court must be satisfied that no money or other benefit, other than for 'expenses reasonably incurred', has changed hands in relation to the

[5]See Introduction, p. 10. Parental orders were first introduced by the HFE Act 1990. Until that time, intended parents would have to adopt a child born through surrogacy. S. 54 HFE Act 2008 applies to couples seeking a parental order; S. 54A applies to single applicants.

arrangement, unless authorised by the court. Such authorisation can be retrospective.[6]

Parental orders are granted by the family courts[7] and have the effect of making the intended parents the legal parents and permanently extinguishing the legal status of the surrogate and any other legal parent at birth (even if this was one of the intended parents). Parental order applications are assisted by a Parental Order Reporter (POR), a Children and Family Court Advisory and Support Service (Cafcass) social worker appointed by the court (Cafcass, 2016). The POR investigates whether all the criteria for making a parental order are met and whether it would be in the child's best interest for an order to be made. This includes visiting the child with their intended parents in their home. Like adoption orders, parental orders have a 'transformative' effect, reflecting the child's lifelong identity within their family (Brown & Wade, 2024). After an order is made, a new birth certificate is issued to replace the original certificate.[8] Without a parental order, one or both intended parents will not have their relationship with the child secured in law, with implications, for example, for inheritance and succession rights and decisions about medical care and other important aspects of the child's life. Without an order, the surrogate remains the legal mother of the child, meaning that (in the absence of a court order conferring parental responsibility on the intended parents) her consent would be needed for various decisions to be taken and that (unless disinherited by will) the child would inherit from her if she died.

The very fact of parental orders has been criticised (Horsey, 2010), as have several of the individual requirements that must be met for an order to be granted (Horsey, 2016; Horsey & Sheldon, 2012; Park-Morton, 2026). One criticism is that, by the time a parental order application is heard, the court is presented with a *fait accompli* and, given that the court must treat the child's lifelong welfare as paramount[9] and the child concerned will be being cared for by

---

[6]This is how intended parents who enter international commercial surrogacy arrangements, or those who give gifts that might be deemed more than expenses connected to the surrogacy can obtain parental orders (providing the other conditions are met) (Jackson, 2016). Several of the other requirements have been purposively interpreted or 'read down' (in the context of human rights legislation) by the courts, which have an obligation to make decisions reflecting the child's lifelong welfare (HFE (Parental Orders) Regulations 2010). The need for the surrogate's consent and the six-week period within which no application can be made are immovable *(Re C (Surrogacy: Consent)* [2023] EWCA Civ 16).

[7]The family courts in England and Wales are the Family Court and the Family Division of the High Court. The Family Court sometimes delegates straightforward parental order applications to magistrates. Complex or international surrogacy cases are typically handled by the High Court.

[8]The original birth certificate is then sealed from public record. If the birth occurred overseas and the child has an overseas birth certificate (which usually recognises the intended parents as parents but has no legal effect in the United Kingdom), the new UK birth certificate is issued in addition to this.

[9]The HFE (Parental Orders) Regulations 2010.

the intended parents, it is unlikely that an order would be refused (see also *A & B* v *C & D* [2026] EWHC 972 (Fam)). The Law Commission and Scottish Law Commission (2023, para. 2.5) explained that:

> Under the current regime, the paramount consideration for the court in deciding the parental order application is the welfare of the child. If the child is living with and being cared for by the intended parents, it will almost always be in the child's best interests for a parental order to be made. The courts are consequently generally reluctant to refuse to grant parental orders, due to their legally transformative nature in making the child a member of the intended parents' family.

In their Final Report, the Law Commission and Scottish Law Commission (2023, para. 2.7) acknowledge that:

> [T]he current allocation of legal parental status to the surrogate at birth is contrary to the fundamental objective of a surrogacy agreement which is that all parties intend the intended parents, and not the surrogate, to be the legal parents. This current allocation operates against the interests of the child, who is initially raised in a family that is not legally recognised as their family. It also runs counter to the interests of the surrogate, who will be the legal parent of a child that she does not consider to be her own or part of her family.

They also note that the current position allows intended parents to 'walk away' from an agreement with no consequences, leaving the surrogate responsible for the child.[10] This position led them to recommend at the 'heart of [their] proposals for the reform of surrogacy law' a '"new pathway" to legal parental status' (2023, para. 2.1) that would allow (some) intended parents to become legal parents from birth, where there is ongoing consent from the surrogate to this.[11] To be able to proceed on the new 'pathway' (and therefore to become legal parents from birth), intended parents would have to follow a defined administrative process, overseen by a Regulated Surrogacy Organisation (RSO), building in safeguards and other aspects of good practice, some seemingly based on the practices of existing non-profit surrogacy organisations. The RSO would ensure defined steps have been followed, including medical/criminal checks, the uptake of counselling and legal advice and insurances etc. and, crucially, record the details of the arrangement in a Regulated Surrogacy Statement (RSS) before

[10]It should be noted that in practice, it is very rare in UK surrogacy arrangements for either side to renege on the agreement, though it is the case that some relationships have broken down, including at/after the point of birth (see NGA Law, n.d.).

[11]There would be no requirement for the surrogate's spouse/partner to give consent under the new proposals, and they would not be a legal parent at birth (2023, para. 4.151).

conception is attempted. There are also some eligibility criteria (for example, relating to the surrogate and intended parents' age) for entering the pathway. Intended parents who do not meet the requirements for the pathway (including those who undertake international or 'independent' domestic arrangements) would be required to apply for a parental order to transfer legal parenthood to them post-birth. One of the requirements that the Law Commissions recommend should remain for both being able to enter the pathway and for residual parental orders is that at least one applicant be genetically related to the child (Law Commission and Scottish Law Commission, 2023, p.163, para. 6.145).[12]

It is in this legal context that we sought to ascertain children's views on (legal) parenthood following surrogacy.

Parenting Is About Love and Care; Biology Is Secondary

We wanted to explore participants' initial reactions about what makes someone a parent, without having first explained the law. We therefore did not explain what legal parenthood means in practical terms, nor did we distinguish legal parenthood from the concept of parental responsibility. Participants were asked to write or draw on Post-it notes their thoughts in response to the question 'What makes someone a parent?'[13] The Post-its were placed in a shared space, and the ideas on them were discussed. The first theme (which also features in later themes in differing ways) was constructed from this activity.

In Phase One, where the 25 participants had either been born through surrogacy, had a cousin born through surrogacy or had a mother who was a surrogate, the most common single words used on their Post-it notes were 'care' (n = 15), 'support' (n = 12), 'responsibility' (n = 11) and 'love' (n = 10),[14] suggesting they understood parents as being (their) primary caregivers. Other words and phrases used by these participants included 'looks after', 'kindness' and 'birth'. Similarly, in Phase Two, where the 24 participants had no prior connection with surrogacy, the most prevalent terms used included 'care' (n = 17) and 'love' (n = 8). Some mentioned 'birth' or 'having' a child/baby (n = 4). Being 'biologically related' (3) was mentioned, as was 'adoption' (n = 4).[15] While again this indicated an understanding of parents as caregivers, there were more references to biological terms and to adoption. In Phase Three, where the five children were born through surrogacy in the United States, 'care' (n = 2) and the concept of 'looking after'

---

[12]This proposal has been criticised, for example because it precludes a parental order in couples where both parties are infertile, or where a solo female applicant can neither provide ova nor carry a pregnancy (Park-Morton, 2024b).

[13]See Appendix 4: Fig. 7.

[14]A word cloud depicting the most prevalent terms provided can be seen in the Phase One preliminary report, Fig. 3, page 7 (Children's Voices in Surrogacy Law, 2023a).

[15]A word cloud depicting the most prevalent terms provided can be seen in the Phase Two preliminary report, Fig. 2, page 8 (Children's Voices in Surrogacy Law, 2023b).

($n = 3$) were highlighted, with two of the five participants also mentioning that a parent was about responsibility for the child's 'safety' or 'keep[ing] them safe'. Two also included a timeframe in relation to that care, i.e., 'for life'/'whole life'. One said that the responsibility to care for a child came with parenting, whether that was biological or not.

In follow-up discussions following the brainstorming activity in Phase One, some participants focused on parenthood being about 'having babies', which they explained in different ways. Some reflected biological understandings of conception, as seen in the following quotes:

> If you are a parent, the way you do it is by having a baby. The way a baby is made – if you don't use surrogates – is by having sex. (Raven, 9, child of surrogate)

> To become a parent, you need a sperm and an egg. A parent is someone who has a child or has had a child for someone else via IVF. (Oliver, 11, child of surrogate)

Others considered alternative social or legal means of becoming parents as an alternative to biological parenthood, as follows:

> You become a parent by having kids, either adopting, surrogacy, foster, having your own – all that makes you a parent. (Ava, 10, child of surrogate)

> A parent would be a person who is your guardian, and it doesn't have to be your biological parent. (Valeria, 10, child of surrogate)

In Phase Three, the sentiments were similar. For example, Camille (13, born through US gestational surrogacy) told us that:

> A parent can be biological or not. You can have adopted parents or obviously surrogate parents.

The level of biological, social and even legal understanding may reflect the participants' backgrounds and their exposure to surrogacy throughout their lives. As indicated above, longstanding connections with surrogacy organisations may shape views and understandings. All the Phase One and Three participants knew they (or a close relative) had been born through surrogacy or had a mother who acted as a surrogate and had an understanding of the processes (and sometimes the law) involved. For example, Scarlett (11, born through surrogacy) said:

> It is not just the person who gave birth. It is the person who looks after the child or baby. When I was first born, obviously, the surrogate was by law my proper mother, but obviously she is not, and it's my parents that are my parents.

In Phase Two, participants tended to focus on parents as caregivers and being those who raise, protect, support, look after and love a child; there was less discussion of the biological processes by which birth might be brought about. Rose (13) said 'a parent is someone who loves and takes care of their children and raises them', while Ella (14) said 'loving, caring, when I think of the word parent it makes me think about caring'. James (11) said 'a person who is caring for that person... kind, always there to help, doesn't need to be biological', and Annabelle (10) said 'a parent is someone who raises a child, someone who looks after you until you are old enough to live by yourself'. Other examples of how Phase Two participants articulated this include:

> What I think a parent is, is caring of a child, protective, can provide for the child, loving, supportive network, understanding, known since birth/a long time. (Ivy, 15)

> People who care for and look after a child, person, people the child sees as their parental figures and the people who give birth to or adopted child. (Harry, 16)

Very few answers were wedded to biological connections and generally included a broader understanding of other parenting relationships. Natalie (15) explained that 'you have different types of parents', adding:

> So, I was thinking about godparents and how those people who – even though the child might not be genetically related to them, or who haven't raised a child since birth – still promise to love and protect this child, and how parenting is about being accepting of this child, because it's someone you love deeply.

Similarly, Harry (16) said he thought parents are 'whoever the child sees as their parents', adding: 'like a step-parent, or something like that, would play an important role'. Tim (11) said that: 'either you have the baby or you adopt them and you have to care and love them, either way'. Generally, it seemed that the Phase Two participants were aware of and accepting of different family forms and different ways of *doing* parenthood. This may reflect general societal changes, in that it is common for children to be exposed to a multitude of family types due to the prevalence of divorce, remarriage and various kinds of 'blended families'. It may be that participants in Phase Two were aware of, but less exposed to, families created via third-party-assisted reproduction, in that their understandings of non-genetic parental relationships generally referred to adoption and step-parenting.

However, in Phase Two there was sometimes a notable linkage of genetics and parenthood in the context of discussions about telling children they were born through surrogacy.[16] Ella (14) appears to refer to parenthood being based on genetics, since she refers to physical similarities:

---

[16]Knowledge of origin information is explored fully in Chapter 4.

> Say when they grow up and they ask questions, like if you don't look alike or something, then I think you should tell them because they do deserve to know and to know who their *real parents* are.[17]

Alan (8) said that children should know they were born through surrogacy 'because if they don't know, if you tell them that they were born through surrogacy, they should – they'll want to know who their *actual parent* is'.[18] It is unclear whether Alan is referring to gestational or traditional surrogacy and whether 'real parenthood' is being attributed to gestation, genetics or both. However, it is clear that surrogacy, in some way, makes the surrogate a 'real parent' for some. For example, Natalie (15) noted the idea that a non-genetically related parent may not be seen as a real parent. In relation to the question of whether a child should know who their surrogate is, she said:

> I said "yes", so that the child could make an informed decision about whether or not perhaps they want to meet the surrogate, whether or not they care about it. It could be different for them if they feel that maybe that the intended parents aren't their real parents because one of them is not genetically related to them. It's just so that they know everything about the surrogacy.

Among some of the younger children, the idea of sadness came up in relation to a lack of genetic or gestational link with parents. Jax (8) mentioned children may be sad 'because their parents didn't actually create them'. Thomas (8) said 'it might feel a bit sad for them' to be told they were born through surrogacy, later explaining this may be because they 'don't know who their real like mother is or something'. Katie (10) also mentioned sadness:

> I mean, it is kind of true, or fair, to know who your actual person that's like gave birth to you and that, because say if you didn't know they you ask and then like, maybe say I was like born through surrogacy but like, then I would be sad because I wouldn't really know who my real parents are and stuff like that.

It might be expected that there would be more acceptance of intention-based parenthood among Phase One and Three participants. However, in Phase One Ava (10, child of surrogate) referred to a 'real mum', and Emily (8, child of surrogate) referred to 'actual mum' when speaking about traditional surrogates. Annabelle (10, child of surrogate) also mentioned sadness regarding a lack of genetic connection with parents. She said:

[17]Emphasis added.
[18]Emphasis added.

> They might be sad because they might be like, they might feel like they are different to everyone else. And they might feel like "well they're not my real parents"...because only...maybe only their mum donated her egg, or her dad donated the sperm, and it might only one of them donated it, so they might feel like "well, only my dad's my parent", or "only my mum is my parent".

In Phase Three, Alison (12, born through US gestational surrogacy) said that children born through traditional surrogacy might want to know who their 'parent' was. Similarly, Camille (13, born through US gestational surrogacy) said that if you do not disclose gamete donation to children, 'they might want to find out who their actual parent is', and her sibling, Bill (11, born through US gestational surrogacy), referred to children's donors as their 'biological parent'.

There is a great deal of sociological and anthropological literature on kinship, which space does not allow in-depth consideration of here.[19] However, briefly, these insights support the idea that 'there is every reason to suppose that children are likely to be creative in their approach to kinship' (Mason & Tipper, 2008) and that while kinship is not a 'given', sometimes genetic relationships are understood as creating kinship ties that are fixed and cannot be chosen (Finch & Mason, 1993). Participants referencing 'sadness' about not knowing genetic parents seems close to arguments that it is essential to know one's genetic lineage to establish meaning and structure in our lives (Nelson, 1992) or, further, that children also need to have *relationships* with genetic relations to flourish (Velleman, 2005). Such comments mirror studies that revealed sadness of parents who use donor conception about 'lost genetic lineage' (Nordqvist & Smart, 2014, p. 142). They also suggest that while first-hand experience of surrogacy in childhood normalises intention-based parenthood and/or the day-to-day *doing* of parenting (care), genetics still play an important (though sometimes inconsistent) role in children's conceptualisations of parenthood.[20] For example, while both Camille (13, born through US gestational surrogacy) and Bill (11, born through US gestational surrogacy) referred to those with a genetic link as 'parents', they

---

[19]Kinship has varying meanings in different disciplines and across cultures. In the context of anthropology, Strathern defines kin as 'relatives connected to one another without any supposition of what kind of social group or family they make up' (Strathern, 2005, p. 167). From a sociological perspective, Mason conceptualises kinship around four dimensions of affinities: fixed, negotiated and creative, ethereal and sensory affinities. For meanings of kinship in assisted reproduction, see Carsten (2004), Mason (2008) and Nordqvist and Smart (2014).

[20]Some research with adults in the context of donor conception also shows inconsistency in how genetics is visualised. In a study with 119 adults with experience of donor conception in their families (22 heterosexual parents, 22 lesbian parents and 30 grandparents of donor conceived children), Nordqvist and Smart (2014) found '...a paradox in that at times real kinship seemed to be imagined entirely in terms of genetic connection, while at other times genes were insignificant and subordinate to what really mattered in the doing of kinship' (p. 162).

also accepted and defined parenthood as being based on love and care. Alison (12, born through US gestational surrogacy) said a parent was defined as '[s]omeone who loves and cares for a child and keeps them safe'. Camille said: 'a parent is a guardian, biological or not, who is responsible for a child's safety and wellbeing' and Bill said that a parent is 'the person who looks after you'. It therefore appears clear that both genetics and intentional/social parenting can hold significance for kinship for children at the same time.

Following the discussions about what makes someone a parent, we explained how surrogacy works in practice, describing the difference between traditional and gestational surrogacy, and including the fact that sperm or egg donors may also be involved. A more detailed explanation was needed for the Phase Two participants; those in Phases One and Three already had some familiarity with the concepts. Once we had explained the different forms of surrogacy and the various permutations of people who might be intended parents (or donors), we moved on to ask them normative questions ('should' questions[21]) relating to specific aspects of parenthood following surrogacy.

What Do Children Think Should Determine Parenthood in Surrogacy?

We asked the participants: 'When a child is born through surrogacy, who do you think the parents should be?' We were seeking views on who *should* be recognised as parents following a surrogacy arrangement. This question thus drew upon participants' ethical understandings of surrogacy, parenthood and motherhood. The participants were asked to choose between one of three choices depicted on illustration cards: 'intended parent/s', 'surrogate' or 'surrogate and partner'. For the 'intended parents' option, various permutations of a heterosexual couple, same sex couples or solo parents were depicted. It should be noted that children were presented with a dichotomous choice – should either the surrogate, the surrogate and her spouse *or* the intended parents be the legal parent/s? This choice reflects both the current law and the Law Commissions' proposals, but forecloses the possibility of exploring views on whether a child could potentially have more than two legal parents. For the purposes of our research questions, which aimed to gain insight into participants' views on the law and law reform, this activity gave us insights into this, but if the aim was to explore understandings of parenthood more broadly, an alternative approach would be to allow participants to pick multiple cards or devise their own frameworks.

Children Attach Importance to Choice, Agreement and Assumed Responsibility

When asked to choose between the intended parents, the surrogate or the surrogate and her partner, the most common response in all phases was that the

[21] In line with one strand of understanding of empirical bioethics, seeking to find where 'an empirical 'is' can inform a normative 'ought' claim' (Ives et al., 2018).

intended parents should be the parents. In Phase One, 22 participants (88%) said this,[22] in Phase Two, 18 said this (75%)[23] and in Phase Three, all five stated this (100%).[24] A common idea was that giving birth or providing sperm or eggs was not necessarily enough to equate to parenthood, but this also depended on other (overlapping) themes discussed below. The participants gave various reasons for favouring the intended parents, including sympathy for those who may have struggled to have children, recognition of the intentions of the parties and fairness in relation to keeping promises.[25]

In Phase One, Jane (14, born through gestational surrogacy) focused on choice/intention with regards to her view that intended parents should be the parents 'cause the intended parents chose to be the parents, and the surrogate chose to be a surrogate – not a parent'. Christina (14, born through gestational surrogacy) focused on the idea of the intended parents having assumed responsibility for the child from the outset as the reason for recognising them as legal parents at birth. She said:

> At the start of the surrogacy process, the intended parents, like, took full responsibility for the child that would be born.

Interestingly, participants in two interviews mentioned the possibility of the child having three parents (the intended parents and the surrogate), as proposed by McCandless (2025). Scarlett (11, born through surrogacy) based this on a circumstance in which all adults agreed/wanted this and said:

> They could all make a group decision, if they want to do it. And if they agree they all want to be the parents, then they could go to court and get it changed. I don't know if that is possible, that three people can be the parents.[26]

In Phase Two, some participants who chose the intended parents viewed this as a matter of common sense. Lydia (16) explained that intended parents should be recognised as the parents 'because [they] would be the ones who would end up with the child'. Similarly, Ivy (15) said:

---

[22]Two said the surrogate should be the parent.

[23]The other six initially said this should be the surrogate and her partner.

[24]Intended parents were therefore chosen by 83% of the total 54 participants.

[25]There was some reflection of legal consciousness in Phase One and Three answers – due to their knowledge of surrogacy some knew who the parents 'are' in law and answered this instead of 'who should?' (e.g. Ava, 10, child of surrogate and Scarlett, 11, born through gestational surrogacy).

[26]See Introduction, p. 4 and Bella and Sienna, below.

> Because they, like, intended to be the parent of the child. I don't know how to describe it. It just kind of makes sense, if it is, like, the parents of the child that has been made.

Some reflected on the emotional significance of becoming parents for the intended parents, as shown by Henry (10), who said:

> It should be the intended parents, because if they're the people that want to be the parents, then they're obviously going to be emotionally hurt if they don't have the child that they want to look after. (Henry, 10)

Additionally, some focused on the social act of parenting, as can be seen in the following quotes:

> They're going to be the parent of the child no matter what, even if it's traditional or gestational, because they're the ones that are going to actually raise and [shape] the child and how they're going to be in later life. So, I think just the intended parents. (Jasmine, 11)

> Because if someone's wanted you to carry their baby, why would they get to keep it for themselves? It doesn't matter if you give birth to someone or not. As long as you raise them, then you count as being the parent. (Annabelle, 10)[27]

> I think it actually is the intended parents, because it's like when a child is adopted, the parents aren't...the child would feel more attached to the parents who adopted him, rather than the biological parents. (Leonard, 12)

In Phase Two, participants' answers were often based on the presence of an agreement (presumed to reflect the parties' intentions):

> [T]hey were the people who wanted it to happen and, like, they were the ones the baby was supposed to go to, because it was agreed. (Tim, 11)

> Because if they're going through the process, I guess that's kind of been the agreement to it. And because they're the ones that originally want the children. (Liam, 18)

---

[27]Despite the phrasing here, which could be read as asking why intended parents would 'get to keep it for themselves?', Annabelle said intended parents should be recognised as the parents; therefore this appears to ask why the *surrogate* would get to keep the baby.

> I think it's because the intended parents were the ones that wanted a surrogate, and they decided they wanted to do it and then the surrogate was just someone that could help that happen and they know that was the part of the thing – they had to give up the baby after it was born. (Rose, 13)

> [T]he surrogate is aware that the child won't be theirs after they've had the baby. So, they know that the intended parents are going to look after them. So, the intended parents should be the ones to help the baby. (Carrie, 17)

In Phase Three, the overwhelming response favouring the recognition of intended parents as parents was supported by similar sentiments:

> Because the child was supposed to be for them in the first place and part of it is their DNA sometimes. (Alison, 12)

> The intended parents were originally the people who wanted the child and they talked to other people to help them do that so the whole ordeal was meant to help them. (Bill, 11)

> [T]he intended parents are the real parents. They are the ones that requested the baby. They are the ones that sought help and if the surrogate and her partner wanted their own child then they could have had their own child. They were clearly capable. (Camille, 13)

These participants recognised that the child was 'supposed to be' the child of the intended parents and that was because they were the ones who initiated the arrangement and intended to care for the child (with the surrogate wanting and intending the opposite). One recognised that the child would likely be biologically related to at least one of the intended parents. This perhaps reflects some understanding of the law, which requires one intended parent to be genetically related to the child to obtain a parental order (ss. 54(1) (b) and 54A(1) (b) HFE Act 2008). However, most participants supported the idea that parenthood should follow the choices and agreements made by intended parents and surrogates.

Surrogates Should Be Held to Their Decisions, Especially Gestational Surrogates

We explained that the way the current law is formulated allows the surrogate to change her mind. This was at the forefront of the Warnock Committee's recommendations (Department of Health & Social Security, 1984) and clearly lies behind both the provision that the surrogate is always the legal mother (s. 33 HFE Act 2008) and the fact that her consent to a parental order is required (s. 54 (6) and s. 54A(5) HFE Act 2008). It also explains the provision in the SAA 1985

(s. 1A, inserted by the HFE Act 1990) that all surrogacy arrangements are unenforceable. However, the idea that the surrogate should always be the legal mother has been challenged (Callus, 2012; Douglas, 1994; Horsey, 2010; Lima, 2024; Mahmoud, 2023), including by surrogates themselves (Horsey, 2015, 2018a, 2018b, 2025a, 2025c; Horsey et al., 2022; Mahmoud, 2023). Further, case law indicates, and the Law Commission and Scottish Law Commission (2023, para. 10.140) recognised, that the unenforceability of surrogacy arrangements combined with the fact that the consent of the surrogate to the making of a parental order cannot be overridden (except if the surrogate cannot be found or lacks capacity) means she has an ultimate veto that can be used against intended parents (*Re AB (Surrogacy: Consent)* [2016] EWHC 2643). It is vanishingly rare that a surrogate changes her mind about the agreement. Even fewer cases are because she wants to keep the baby; such cases more usually reflect the surrogate's concern in some way about the intended parents (NGA Law, n.d.).

We asked participants what they thought about the law being framed in such a way as to allow the surrogate to change her mind. In Phase One,[28] 18 (90%) participants said that the surrogate should not be able to change her mind; one said 'maybe', and one said 'yes', but added she should have to go to court if she wanted to do so. In Phase Two, there was more variation, with 11 (46%) participants saying that the surrogate should not be able to change her mind and seven (29%) saying that she should. Interestingly, six (25%) said that 'it depends' on the *type* of surrogacy arrangement, suggesting that weight was attached to whether the surrogate was genetically related to the child. In Phase Three, four of the five participants had a strong sense that it would be unfair for a surrogate to change her mind,[29] for various reasons, including sympathy for the intended parents and the value of agreement, as can be seen in these quotes:

> I think that sometimes it can be unfair for the people who can't have a child themselves because they might just never end up with a child even though they tried to get one. (Alison, 12, born through US gestational surrogacy)

> I don't think that you can just change your mind that late... Because she's already agreed to do it for the intended parents. (Bart, 12, born through US gestational surrogacy)

> I don't think that's right either because if you offer to carry a child for someone then it's their child from the start. You have no right to decide what happens to that baby. If you wanted your own and

[28]The five participants in the first interview did not answer this question; therefore, the percentage calculation here refers to the 20 other children in this phase.

[29]One Phase Three participant initially said the surrogate might be able to change her mind if she would be 'lonely' otherwise but changed his mind when asked if that would still be the case if the surrogate already had her own children (Steve, 9, born through US gestational surrogacy).

> you were clearly capable of carrying then you should have made it your mission to have your own rather than taking someone else's child. (Camille, 13, born through US gestational surrogacy)

As seen from the quotes, these participants were not open to changes of mind, because they saw agreements as something you should stick to. Camille even introduced the language of rights to justify this, suggesting a strong moral conviction behind her statement. Evalynn (11, born through gestational surrogacy) was similarly dogmatic:

> I don't think the surrogate could change their mind, because it is not the surrogate's baby. It is the intended parents' [baby]. And so, I think that shouldn't really happen.

However, younger participants tended to be more concerned about the happiness of the entire group and an overall concept of 'fairness' as Lilly (9, child of surrogate) explained:

> My mum said that you have to trust. . .the intended parents have to trust the surrogate and the surrogate has to trust the intended parents, because, they need to trust them, because if the surrogate wants to keep the baby, then that's not going to be fair, because they waited for a long time.

Some noted it was important for surrogates to understand what they were agreeing to from the outset; for example, Lucy (15, child of surrogate) stated:

> I think they should give consent, but right at the start of the pregnancy. So that you know they understand, and they give consent that it's not their child and they are doing it for someone else.

Jack (17, child of surrogate) agreed with her, adding:

> I think if the surrogate is in the state of mind where she isn't certain whether she wants to keep the baby or not, then she shouldn't be a surrogate because it is kind of the agreement of, you know, you're having this baby to help these other people. It's not yours.

Anna (16, cousin of a child born through surrogacy) raised the issue of a power imbalance between the intended parents and the surrogate, explaining that she did not 'know how to [say] this right' but that there was:

> A power dynamic between the surrogate and the [intended parent], in that the surrogate has more of a choice afterwards,

> and it can frighten [intended parents] off getting a surrogate at all if they're worried that at the end of it their baby can be taken from them.

For those without experience of surrogacy, the reasons given for participants' answers tended to focus on understandings of what was 'fair', often based on the value attached to the agreement entered into. Carrie (17) said that surrogates should not be able to change their minds 'because they've agreed that it's not going to be their baby', adding:

> It's the intended parents'. So, for [surrogates] to change their minds, it's not very fair on the intended parents, because the intended parents could have picked someone else to be the surrogate knowing that they'd be the intended parents by the end of it. It's not fair.

Similar points were expressed by others:

> I don't think that's fair for the intended parents because the surrogate obviously agreed before the process began, that she would give the baby to the intended parents. So, I'm not sure it's right, they're willing to change their mind when they're born. So, like, there should be, um, like, an agreement sort of thing before just to say like, "Yes, I am going to give the baby to you". (Jasmine, 11)

> It's just not very fair because it's kind of their child yet someone's sort of taking it and I feel like maybe they should – like, the surrogate should, like, they should have, like, not a contract, well, you know, like, sort of, write up like a statement saying that they give it to the intended parents or something. (Alice, 13)

> It's not really fair on the intended parents because they're having to wait, they're waiting nine months to get a child, I mean, it's the same, like, normal but, like, they're waiting nine months and then it's just to be told, "Actually, no, I want to keep the baby. You're not going to get it". (Leonard, 12)

Other aspects of 'fairness' were associated with practicalities, such as the costs incurred and preparation undertaken by intended parents. For example, two participants talked about the impact a change of mind by the surrogate would have on the intended parents in terms of time, emotions (care), effort and expenditure, as follows:

> The intended parents have gone through all this and they've bought everything for this child, they really cared all through it

> and then the actual surrogate is just saying "Scrap that, I'm keeping the baby". (Diego, 10)

> They'll probably be sad because that's wasted their time and basically, they could have got all the stuff ready, like the nappies and that, and the clothes, and they could have like wasted all their money and that. (Katie, 10)

As indicated above, some Phase Two participants thought that the surrogate should be able to change her mind and, in contrast to Diego and Katie, imagined being in the position of the surrogate. Honey (16) said that this could be 'because they might have a connection to the child', later adding 'like carrying'. This prompted Liam (18) to contemplate whether surrogates should be able to change their minds up to 'a cut-off point within the pregnancy'. He said:

> Maybe after, because obviously once they actually feel more pregnant and can see a bump, that's when they could potentially have more of an attachment to it. So, maybe after 20, 25 weeks or something, that could be the real end cut-off point where they go, "I now decide that I don't want to parent the child".

Other participants' responses reflected the tension between protecting the surrogate's ability to change her mind and the value of upholding agreements. Natalie (15) recognised that a surrogate might want to change her mind due to her changed feelings during pregnancy and birth but also recognised that she should honour her agreement. She stated:

> I can understand wanting to protect someone to change their mind, because how you feel about something that hasn't happened to you yet can be different to how you feel after nine months of carrying a baby and then giving birth. But also, if you make an agreement to do something and you decided that that's what you're going to do, you should still be honouring that, in a way. But it's a very difficult kind of issue because how you feel is something you can't really police. You can't tell yourself not to feel that way.

As with previous discussions on this topic, in both Phase One and Two, for some participants, the distinction between gestational and traditional surrogacy prompted further discussion. For example, some Phase One participants were open to a traditional surrogate being able to change her mind, as Oliver (11, child of surrogate) explained:

> 'Cause she used part of her body to make it so, if you just, like, gave birth to a baby that was also sort of made of her, then I don't think it'll be that fair.

Eliza (11, child of surrogate) said that even if a traditional surrogate changed her mind and kept the child, the intended parents should remain involved with the child in some way. She said:

> Because the baby is genetically related to [the intended parents] and if they wanted to have something to do with that baby then both sides should have something to do with that baby because they are both related.

This is reflective of what can happen in practice in the case of disputes, where child arrangements orders may allow for whichever parties do not have legal parenthood to have contact with the child. However, others stated that traditional surrogates should not be allowed to change their mind. For example, Valeria (9, child of surrogate) said:

> The traditional surrogacy that we said, um, even though she's offered and used her own egg, they still asked her to be the surrogate and so that doesn't make it...Even though she's used her egg, they've asked her to be a surrogate. So, it doesn't matter what egg it comes from, it should still be theirs, because they've asked to have a baby, or, for help.

Similarly, in Phase Two, Rose (13) thought that even if the surrogate used 'her egg for someone else' then:

> Surely she knew that, and the fact that it – I get it's genetically her baby – but she didn't really want her baby, she wanted to give up the, like, her egg so another family could have it.

Later, she said:

> It's like she decided she wanted to give up an egg so someone else could have a family. I get you might change your mind because, like, once you have seen the baby and, like, you knew that anyway, you knew the fact that you were going to give, it was from the first place, so you can't really change your mind at the end, after you have promised this family that it would be their child.

In the same interview, following this discussion, Sienna (13) said 'I think there should be two different laws because they are two different kinds of surrogacy. So, it's a different, like, situation'. When asked about what the difference should be, she said that 'with gestational you can't change your mind, and traditional you can', adding:

> Because gestational you [the surrogate] are not, like, the genetic parents, so it would just make it more difficult for the other parents, because then if she keeps the baby, then she's got someone else's kid.

Additionally, in traditional surrogacy, because the surrogate is genetically related to the child, she said 'it should be, like, co-parents'. This was another example of a participant entertaining the idea of parenthood shared by both the intended parents and the surrogate.

The idea that the surrogate should not be able to change her mind was supported by most participants. In Phase One, opinions on this sometimes depended on participants' ages. Younger participants were keen to ensure that no-one was 'sad', or that everything was 'fair'. In Phase Two, there was more dogmatism: 11 participants did not think that a surrogate should be able to change her mind, with a further six saying 'it depends'. There was a strong sense of it being 'unfair' for her to do so. Phase Three participants did not support the surrogate changing her mind in similar terms, perhaps reflecting those participants' understanding of the contractual nature of the arrangements that led to their conception. It could be said that these responses illustrate a lack of awareness or empathy for the reproductive labour undertaken by the surrogate (see Armstrong, 2021, 2022; Isard, 2025; Vertommen & Barbagallo, 2021). This is perhaps not surprising among children, given the value they placed on the surrogate's choice to enter the agreement and on the importance of upholding agreements. Additionally, it reflects the empathy demonstrated towards intended parents who cannot have children. Interestingly, despite the 'common sense' approach many Phase Two participants had towards recognising the intended parents as legal parents, it was this group of participants who more clearly acknowledged the reproductive labour of the surrogate when discussing the financial contributions she should be able to receive.[30]

Children Recognise the Suboptimality of the Parental Order System

After the discussion about surrogates changing their mind, we outlined who the law currently regards as the parent(s) following surrogacy. We explained how legal parenthood can be transferred from the parties who have it at birth to the intended parents via a parental order.[31] We explained the basic principle of what

---

[30]See Chapter 3, pp. 99–100. In addition, when participants discussed ongoing contact between the surrogate and the family she helped to create, 'the significant role of the surrogate' was recognised by participants (see Chapter 5, p. 160).

[31]Legal parenthood can also be transferred via adoption and in some cases (and all cases before 1990), this remains the only option available to intended parents. However, it is widely accepted that adoption is not the preferred method for intended parents to achieve legal parenthood (Park-Morton, 2024a).

a parental order is and how it works, illustrating this with the explanation card, before asking the participants their views about this.[32]

Twenty participants in Phase One said that they did not agree with the parental order process; for example, Scarlett (11, born through surrogacy) said:

> [The law] should be changed to as soon as the baby comes out of the tummy. It should, first, straight away, be the person who is intending to look after it.

Similarly, Ellie (13, born through surrogacy) stated that she did not understand the necessity for the parental order process and said:

> It's a bit unnecessary. I don't think going through a middleman is really. . .I don't see why it should be the surrogate at all in the first place.

Some participants referred to intended parents' expectations and the effort expended by them, reflecting sympathy towards intended parents and their (possible) situations and the idea that it would be 'unfair' not to recognise them as parents. Indicating some knowledge of the law and process, Eliza (11, child of surrogate) said:

> I think it's wrong that you should have to apply for that. You've done all this work, put all this time to find a surrogate, like you could be on a waiting list for two years, and then to have to go to court like six weeks after the baby's born – that's when they have to apply for the parental order – and that can take quite a while to change even then. So, I don't think it's right, "cause I think that the intended parents from the start should be the parents".

Again, several participants focused on the idea of 'fairness'. For example, Valeria (9, child of surrogate) connected the 'work' undertaken by the intended parents to the fairness of them being recognised as parents, saying:

> The parents aren't the surrogate. They've worked hard, and they have given their sperm, and then if somebody else takes their baby, and they've been wanting to have a baby, and they've worked really hard, that's not fair.

In Phase Two, 'fairness' was regularly connected to biology and/or the fact that an agreement was in place. For example, Liam (18) said:

---

[32]See Appendix 4: Fig. 2.

> It kind of makes sense why, but at the same time – especially if they've had no sperm or egg involved, if it was the intended parents' sperm and egg – then surely they should be the ones who are legal parents. And I suppose if you are becoming a surrogate mother, you kind of agree to the terms and conditions of the fact that you won't be their mother, like you won't be the caregiver of that child.

Similarly, Ella (14) thought that:

> If they wanted – the parents – if they wanted the child, and the surrogate knew and was fine with it, but then they have to go to court just to have a baby that they wanted, that they both wanted to do, then I just think it's wrong. It's not really a point if you have to go to court for a child.

In Phase Two, some participants' opinions were clearly influenced by the potential genetic relationships (or lack of) involved. For example, Sienna (13) said:

> I think it should be changed, because if it's gestational surrogacy then she's just carrying the baby, she's not like related to it in any way, so if the intended parents didn't win the court case, then she would have someone else's baby.[33]

Following a group discussion about the difference between gestational and traditional surrogacy, Rose (13) said:

> I get like, you don't have to be genetically [related] to a baby for it to be your child, but you agree to the fact that you wanted to do it to help someone else out. But I get more towards the court case for traditional.

Rose seems to be suggesting that the parental order process may be suitable for traditional surrogacy more than gestational surrogacy. This might reflect that in traditional surrogacy the child would be genetically related to the surrogate. Some participants (particularly from the older groups) gave very nuanced responses. Again, these often reflected sympathy towards intended parents and a sense of unfairness if they could not become parents, especially if this was because the surrogate changed her mind. This can be seen in the following quotes:

---

[33]This also reflects a (relatively common, especially in Phase Two) misunderstanding of the parental order court process, viewing it as adversarial rather than the administrative process that it is.

> I mean, I understand why it's in place, because the law wants to protect the person who is carrying the baby. But it's also making it harder for people who cannot have a baby the traditional way to go through surrogacy. Because if you want to be a parent, for people who are in a heterosexual relationship who just get pregnant and then give birth, you go home with your birth certificate and you are the parents. Whereas some people can't do that. It's a lot harder. I'm not sure I would want to go to court to prove that I was the parent after nine months of waiting and hoping. And then there's still potential that they say "No, actually, you're not". (Natalie, 15)

> I don't really understand, I mean, I kind of understand an element of why the law is like that. But then again, if they've gone through surrogacy, so the surrogate has agreed once, or what I know about it, is that the surrogate has agreed to then give the baby to the intended parents. I don't really understand why they have to go to court. (Ivy, 15)

> I can understand why the law is there but it doesn't seem like it's particularly good. Because I think that if they've already made an agreement to give the child over to the intended parents, and they did it, they should continue with that. And it feels like if something were to go wrong halfway through, and the surrogate decided that they wanted to keep the child specifically to negatively impact the intended parents, then it feels like there's nothing protecting the intended parents as well. (Harry, 16)

It is interesting that these participants seemed to believe that involving the law in the determination of parenthood was unnecessary, where an agreement was already in place. In Phase Three, the idea that intended parents should need to complete a court process to become legal parents was also questioned. Some participants thought that there was just no point in a court process, particularly when everyone was already in agreement. For example, Camille (13, born through US gestational surrogacy) said:

> I think it is a bit unnecessary because the whole point of the surrogate is someone who carries the baby for a couple or maybe a person who can't have their own child biologically, or along those lines and then keeping it just goes against that entirely. The fact that we need a court order to discuss who the real parents are in that situation I don't think it's right.

Similar ideas were expressed by other participants born through surrogacy in the United States, as seen from the following quotes:

> [I]f they don't want the baby they could just give the baby over without going to court. That would be a better idea I would say. (Steve, 9, born through US gestational surrogacy)

> Personally, I think that is wrong because the child was intended for the intended parents. So if the surrogate parents can keep the child the other parents would have to go through that all again and try that again and that can take time and money. (Bill, 11, born through US gestational surrogacy)

> I mean it could be good but also the child is supposed to be from the people already so why would they have to go and get it in court? (Alison, 12, born through US gestational surrogacy)

> I think if the surrogate mother just agrees that it's the intended parents' child then it's okay... They don't have to go through the whole process of going to court. They can just sign a couple of papers and then it's the intended parents' child. (Bart, 12, born through US gestational surrogacy)

As can be seen from these responses, there is a strong idea that going to court is perceived as contrary to the intentions behind the agreement; a court process is not required where parties agree about parenthood.

It is important to note the context here: participants in Phase Three were born through surrogacy in the United States, which has a commercial, contractual model of surrogacy. While a parental order is still required when intended parents who enter international surrogacy arrangements return to the United Kingdom in order to obtain legal parenthood, these children may have knowledge of the use of contracts and payment in the United States.[34] Bart, however, does reference the idea of signing papers. This may show some indication that he thinks some legal or procedural process is appropriate, with his reference to 'a couple of papers' perhaps referring to a contract.

Children Consider That Having a Genetic Link Should Not Be a Requirement for Legal Parenthood

We explained to the participants that for intended parents to be eligible for a parental order, at least one of them must be genetically related to the child, and asked what they thought about this requirement. In Phase One, genetic relatedness generated much discussion, both here and in other parts of the interviews where it was sometimes spontaneously raised.[35] Sometimes participants both

[34] See chapter 3, p. 89.

[35] The participants in Interview 6 did not really engage with this issue: one said they thought the genetic link requirement was a good idea after it was further explained. In Interview 1, participants nodded, but it is not clear that there was full understanding.

attributed importance to a genetic link and said that it should not matter, as illustrated by Freya (12, child of surrogate):

> It's right that you [need to have the genetic connection], because then you at least have something to do with the child. But if you don't, then I don't think it matters as much because, like, even if you don't, then you're wanting to take a child, because you've agreed to. You've gone through a whole process of wanting to for so long. Because then it's, "cause even if it's a sperm donor and [the surrogate's] egg, then it's going to be their child". It should be their child.

Lucy (15, child of surrogate) recognised that families could be created without genetic or biological relationships, supporting the idea that even where there was no genetic connection between the intended parents and the child, nor a biological link through gestation, their commitment and intention should make them parents. She said:

> Family nowadays is made-up of so much more than genetics and biological relations, and I just think if the intended parents have made that commitment already before, you know, the child is even conceived, then – and they're not related – I don't think it matters. I think they should still [be] able to apply for a parental order. And I think they should still be able to be the parents no matter what, because they have made that commitment. They have taken that responsibility of that child.

Some participants initially thought the genetic link requirement may be justified by creating a distinction between surrogacy and adoption but nonetheless acknowledged problems with mandating it. For example, Jane (14, born through gestational surrogacy) stated:

> Although it makes sense to separate the idea of surrogacy and adoption, I can also see why someone might choose to go down the route of surrogacy, rather than adoption, even if they cannot provide the egg or sperm, because they may feel more connected with the child, because they were there from the start of the process.

This reflects recognition of intention-based parenthood and captures some of the criticism of the current genetic link requirement and the Law Commissions' recommendation that it be retained (Park-Morton, 2024b, 2025). Christina (14, born through gestational surrogacy) also mentioned adoption but was clear that surrogacy should be an option for parents even in the absence of a genetic link:

> I think that, if the parents... even if they are not genetically related to the child, decide to go down the route of surrogacy, I think that they should be able to get a parental order, because... it is not the same as adoption. But I think that if they – like, the parents – might feel more connected to their child or they might want to be a part of that part of the child's life.

For couples where both parties are infertile or, for example, where a solo female applicant can neither provide ova nor carry a pregnancy or a single man is unable to provide sperm, achieving legal parenthood through a parental order is impossible. Eliza (11, child of a surrogate) identified problems the genetic link requirement could cause for single applicants for parental orders:

> If there was an intended parent who was, like, a woman by themselves... And they, say, have something wrong with their eggs, they wouldn't have a sperm and they wouldn't have any eggs so, therefore, it would be the surrogate's egg or a donor egg and a donor sperm, which means they have no relation to that baby. But, at the same time, they could still be a mother, because they will look after that baby and care for that baby just as well as someone genetically related to that baby could.

In Phase Two, some younger participants struggled with the idea that there should be a genetic link requirement and could see arguments on both sides:

> Sometimes it will be right because it is genetically connected to them. But sometimes people can't have babies and two people may not be able to have babies, so it's kind of fair, but not, at the same time. (Tim, 11)

> I think that it's fair, because it means they're actually related. But I think it's also not fair because maybe they're not able to give an egg or a sperm to the surrogate. (Annabelle, 10)

Others thought that requiring a genetic link was not 'fair' or did not make sense:

> I don't think that's really fair, because say you, like, they both wanted to, but they both couldn't donate, you know? I think they should like still be able to have it. (Leonard, 12)

> I don't think anyone should have to have a genetic involvement in it, because you could have instances where both partners are sterile or infertile. And they could still want to have a child, it doesn't really make a huge amount of sense why it has to be genetic. (Harry, 16)

> It's hard because if they can't then it's unfair to almost take that away from them again. (Liam, 18)

In Phase Three, there was broad agreement that a genetic link should not be necessary, with some recognition that it might be nice to have one; there was further insight that it might be divisive for intended parents, as indicated in the following quotes:

> A biological link is great but if you don't have a biological link that's fine too. It is still going to be your child. (Camille, 13, born through US gestational surrogacy)

> I don't think there should be a genetic link between them or biological link between them because if, let's say, one of the parents has difficulty with one of those things they might not be able to do it and then the other parent might not be comfortable doing it. (Bill, 11, born through US gestational surrogacy)

Bart (12, born through US gestational surrogacy) started from the position that the requirement should remain:

> I think it's good. It should stay the same because if it's not one of the parents' genetical child then it's not their child at all because they have nothing to do with it.

However, he later changed his mind when given a hypothetical situation where a single woman could not provide an egg and could not be pregnant (as identified by Eliza, earlier). When asked why he changed his mind, he said 'because then everyone can have a child'. Alison (12, born through US gestational surrogacy) also summed up this dilemma, also introducing the idea of 'unfairness':

> It makes sense because otherwise they wouldn't really be related to them. It could also be hard as well if they didn't give their DNA then they wouldn't be able to have the child. I don't think that's fair.

When presented with the single woman example, she added:

> She can't do it herself but she still wants to take care of a child and have her own child. She's gone to do surrogacy. I think she should just be able to do it as well if other people are able to do it because she can't do it herself.

Steve (9, born through US gestational surrogacy), however, was adamant that the genetic link requirement is wrong. He said:

> I would say that is kind of mean as if it is a male that wants a child, if the sperm doesn't work then that would be very sad for the male if they are not allowed to have the child. If it is a female and the egg doesn't work that would also be very annoying so I would say they should have the child whatever the case.

Despite having no connection to surrogacy, several participants in Phase Two reflected some of the ideas of those in Phases One and Three. Natalie (15) said 'I don't think parenting is about genetics. You don't need to be related to someone to love them and to care for them'. Rose (13) explained that she thought 'it's okay even if they are not genetically related to them', adding:

> Because I guess that if you didn't want to do, like, an adoption or something, and you wanted something more like a closer relationship and, like, see the baby growing and, like, kind of, I guess that is different.

Like others in Phases One and Three, Jasmine (11) identified the potentially disproportionate effect on solo intended parents. She said:

> I'm not sure actually they had to write that part of the parental order, because what if it was like just a single person and they couldn't donate because for some medical issue?

These ideas are interesting as they demonstrate that many of the participants across the three phases were accepting of 'pure' intention-based parenthood. Conversely, some Phase Two participants regarded a genetic link as a legitimate requirement because of similarities they saw to adoption, as seen in these quotes:

> If they are not genetically related then it's like an adoption because, like, it is a bit, because if you get adoption, like, the kid probably won't look like you. So, it's pretty much the same, if you are not the parent who donates an egg or sperm, because it's not going to look like you and you just, you are not really part of it, you are just waiting for the baby. (Sienna, 13)

> The law should say how it is, because if they are related, it brings the parent and the child closer and then sort of like not being related, because then, even if they don't know, you are always going to know, you are not going to be as close as you want to be, and not look like each other or anything. (Ella, 14)

Carrie (17) saw this more starkly and said that 'if there's no genetic link, then they may as well just adopt'. Bella (13) also saw this as an alternative for intended parents. She said:

> I think it's fair for the parents to get a parental order if – to not be able to get one – if the child isn't related to them, because it's not theirs and technically, they could resort to adoption.

She justified this by saying that as the child was in the early stages of life, they would not remember. She was also concerned by 'proof', saying 'I think they can't prove that the child is theirs unless they are related to it. So, if they can't prove it, then technically the court can't do much about it'. However, this idea was refuted by Leonard (12) in the same interview, who saw the agreement between the parties as potentially more important:

> But then, like, as it's surely [intent] if you only have an agreement. Like, say, it could be a contract, like, just even a simple one that says 'I, the undersigned, we are willing to hand over the child to you', and then they both sign it. Then they would have an actual way to prove the point that actually it is what we have agreed on that being right, so that they can actually show that it is theirs, that they can, like, maybe bypass the system of needing a genetic requirement.

During discussions about parenthood in Phase One, two participants mentioned that the presence of a genetic link might affect who should be legally recognised as the parents. The six participants in Phase Two who did not say the intended parents should be legal parents said that the surrogate and her partner should be recognised as such. They clearly based this on genetics (though this was sometimes misunderstood). For example, Jax (8) said the surrogate and her partner should be recognised as the parents because 'they are the original ones who would...which actually had the eggs and stuff'. Other discussion illustrated that not all participants fully understood the concept and purpose of surrogacy, more so in the younger groups. For example, Diego (10) said the surrogate and her partner should be recognised as the parents because:

> It's only fair that they go through all that pain. What's the point of going through all that pain and then give it to another person?

Two Phase Two participants who initially said that the surrogate and her partner should be recognised as the parents (Bella, 13; Alice, 13) later said that this might depend on whether the surrogacy was traditional or gestational. If it was gestational, they changed their answers to say that the intended parents should be the legal parents. Interestingly, Bella (13) also entertained the idea of 'all' parties being recognised as parents:

> Well, I think it depends because if it's the gestational one, then I think the intended parents would be the actual parents. But then if it's the traditional one, I think it should be both, because the child is still genetically connected to the surrogate.

This suggests that there is some sense that where a surrogate also provides the egg, she has a stronger claim to parenthood than one who does not. This is not reflected in law, where gestation and birth are the determinant of motherhood, but does reflect earlier empirical studies with gestational surrogates, where the only deviation from a strong sense that intended parents should be legal parents at birth arose in discussions of traditional surrogacy (Horsey, 2025a, 2025b, 2025c; Horsey et al., 2022). This idea is also seen in the earlier discussion of whether surrogates should be able to change their mind. There was also some suggestion that a court should only be involved in the determination of parenthood where traditional surrogacy is used and a dispute arises between the parties and that disputes might be more likely in the case of traditional surrogacy.

However, as also seen from participants' responses to questions about origin information, genetics had varying and sometimes contradictory importance to the participants. While this might be more expected from the children with connections to surrogacy, due to their understanding of their and others' family circumstances and different means of family creation, it was also seen among the children in Phase Two. At the same time, some participants highlighted that, to them, birth does not equal parenthood. For example, Thomas (8) indicated that the 'baby is related to both' the surrogate and the intended parent, one by birth and one by genetics:

> The baby is like basically related to both now thinking of it, because like the baby was in the other person's womb, but the original mother and the father gave their egg and sperm to, like, to the surrogate.

Some who had initially agreed with the genetic link requirement later changed their mind, suggesting sympathy with those who cannot provide gametes and a broader, inclusive understanding of parenthood. As Leonard (12) pointed out, even where there is no genetic connection, intended parents' (pre-conception) intention could be proved with an agreement.

Conclusion: Insights for Law, Policy and Practice

The first insight is that participants support intention-based parenthood and would therefore likely support the Law Commissions' proposed new 'pathway' to parenthood, which would confer legal parenthood on the intended parents at birth. Their insights may even support a rebuttable presumption in law that intended parents in all domestic surrogacy arrangements would be legal parents at birth, with the potential for the surrogate or other interested parties to challenge that presumption (in a court process) within a certain amount of time (Horsey, 2010). Across all phases, children thought that care, love support and/or responsibility for/the act of raising a child is what makes someone a parent.

Most participants recognised that people can become parents in different ways, with adoption, fostering, step-parenting and being a godparent or guardian all being mentioned. Though there was some (sometimes contradictory) weddedness to biology in the sense of both gestation/birth and genetics, actually *being* a parent was not defined this way by most of the participants. In addition, across Phases One and Three, most participants thought parental orders unnecessary and/or that the process should be changed. In Phase Three, participants viewed the post-birth input of a court as wholly unnecessary.

The second insight is that participants were concerned that the parties should stick to their agreements. Many of them thought that it was not fair for people who had entered an agreement to change their mind. Therefore, the Law Commissions' proposal to create RSOs that have a role in facilitating, overseeing and supporting agreements, which would be detailed in RSSs from before conception until beyond the birth of a child through surrogacy would appear to align with the participants' views. Notwithstanding strong support for the importance of abiding by agreements, the views of some participants also seem to be in line with the mechanisms in the new pathway that accommodate a change of mind by the surrogate. A minority of participants thought that the surrogate should be able to change her mind, and some thought she should be able to have parental rights or contact, if she had used her own egg. The Law Commissions' recommendations would differ depending on the point in time that a surrogate changes her mind (referred to as 'withdrawing her consent to the agreement') (Law Commission and Scottish Law Commission, 2023; para. 2.14). They propose that if she withdrew consent *before* the birth of the child, the agreement would 'exit the pathway': parenthood would rest initially with the surrogate and fall to be decided by an application for a parental order, as now (with some modified criteria).[36] If consent were withdrawn *after* the birth (within a statutorily defined six-week period), the intended parents would remain legal parents, but the surrogate could apply for a parental order. Since this protects surrogates' ability to change their mind while also giving the intended parents more protection than they currently have, it would seem that this would be supported by those participants who were simultaneously concerned about the value of upholding agreements, empathised with what the intended parents had gone through, and wanted to protect the surrogate. However, some participants talked about recognition of more than two parents (particularly in the case of traditional surrogacy). This could be considered in law reform in various ways, including, for example, (a) allowing three (or more) parents to enter the new pathway by agreement; and/or (b) in case of a dispute or the withdrawal of the

[36]Internationally agreed (albeit non-binding) principles of good practice support the idea that surrogates should be able to change their mind, certainly up to the birth and probably afterwards (ISS, 2023).

surrogate's consent, there could be a way for courts to assign parenthood to more than *either* the intended parent/s *or* the surrogate.[37]

A third insight from the participants regarding parental orders is to do with international surrogacy. The Law Commissions have stated that they hope that the new pathway, if introduced, would incentivise prospective intended parents to undertake surrogacy in the United Kingdom.[38] Another reason for the Law Commissions wanting to incentivise surrogacy in the United Kingdom is over concerns about potentially unethical practices in some other jurisdictions (Law Commissions and Scottish Law Commission, 2023; paras. 16.9–16.33). The Law Commissions ruled out (between their earlier consultation and final Report) establishing a Home Office 'recognised list' of 'suitable' jurisdictions where the issuance of a foreign birth certificate naming the intended parents as the legal parents at birth would enable recognition of that on return to the United Kingdom. As well as deeming post-birth court involvement as unnecessary, as will be evident from the analysis in Chapters 4 and 5, the five participants born through US surrogacy had positive experiences; they were proud and open about their birth through surrogacy and all five had contact with their surrogate and had visited their place of birth. Therefore, perhaps the development of a 'recognised list' of suitable overseas surrogacy jurisdictions should also be reconsidered, or there could be a lighter touch process for granting parental orders in overseas surrogacy cases where the destination (or even agency/provider[39])

[37]The Law Commissions' proposals, and indeed the current law, do not distinguish between gestational and traditional surrogacy. We recommend that this should continue to be the case. However, given participants' concerns for (especially traditional) surrogates, as well as acknowledgement in case law that traditional surrogacy may require higher safeguards (*Re C (Surrogacy: Consent)* [2023] EWCA Civ 16) and recognition in some empirical work with surrogates that traditional surrogacy may be 'different', should the 'pathway' be implemented, we recommend that RSOs have a duty to ensure there is specific advice and support tailored to traditional surrogacy arrangements. This could be included in any Code of Practice for RSOs developed by the regulator. It should also be noted that traditional surrogacy may be more likely in the context of 'independent' surrogacy arrangements (those not supported by a non-profit organisation). While the Law Commissions propose that such arrangements would continue to require post-birth applications for parental orders, there would be no formalised opportunities for independent advice. Consideration could be given as to how to reach parties involved in independent surrogacy, such as the inclusion of advice from RSOs for traditional surrogacy in the DHSC guidance (Department of Health & and Social Care, 2018a).

[38]Many international surrogacy destinations are chosen by intended parents precisely *because* the surrogate is not recognised as the legal parent at birth in that destination, and the intended parents are. However, this reflects a misunderstanding of the recognition of legal parenthood, which would still require an application for a parental order from intended parents who had a child through international surrogacy upon their return to the United Kingdom (Hirst, 2026).

[39]The organisation Growing Families is campaigning for and working on accreditation of individual surrogacy agencies/clinics etc., which would enable intended parents seeking surrogacy overseas to make more informed choices. Though based in Australia, the information is available globally.

is recognised as providing 'ethical' surrogacy that would align with the UK regulator's expectations.[40] In this respect, it would be important to ensure that any country placed on the list makes origin information (about surrogates and donors) available, to enable contact to be made.[41] This would reflect what our participants said about the value of openness and ongoing contact, including among those who were born through international surrogacy. The conceptual difficulty with this is that it would mean recognising some commercial arrangements undertaken overseas, while at the same time trying to incentivise domestic altruistic (or at least non-commercial) arrangements within a model of good practice (Law Commissions and Scottish Law Commission, 2023; paras. 12.94–12.95). There would also be practical difficulties and cost implications of creating such a list and keeping it under review and up to date. Whether this is contradictory in terms of underlying policy or a pragmatic response to international surrogacy in the absence of international treaties or agreement is a matter for debate.

The fourth insight is that participants did not seem very supportive of the genetic link requirement. Phase One and Two participants said that they did not view having a genetic link as being a particularly important requirement for becoming a child's parent. It was also thought unnecessary by participants in Phase Three, with the two who initially viewed the requirement as sensible later changing their mind when hypotheticals about single women unable to produce eggs or sustain pregnancy were raised. The argument for allowing 'double donation' has been outlined by the Law Commissions and academically (Law Commission and Scottish Law Commission, 2019a, 2019b; paras. 12.39–12.43; Park-Morton, 2024b, 2025). In the Law Commission and Scottish Law Commission' (2019a, 2019b) original consultation paper, it was proposed that the genetic link requirement could be removed where it was not possible for either of the intended parents (or a single intended parent) to provide gametes, for 'medical reasons' (para. 12.59). This was proposed only for the new 'pathway' and not for residual parental order cases. The findings suggest that the recommendation that the genetic link requirement should be retained could potentially be revisited, at least in the context of surrogacy arrangements undertaken on the 'pathway' overseen by a RSO. Potentially, this should also occur for residual parental order cases, especially where there is medical need.

Lastly, it is clear that these participants accepted intention as the basis of parenthood and also accepted different family forms. Nonetheless, genetics has a strong hold on their understanding of kinship. This was seen around some

---

[40]See also the recent Australian Law Reform Commission (2025) proposal seeking to 'limit access to overseas surrogacy to jurisdictions with regulatory systems which provide for non-exploitative surrogacy arrangements' by creating 'registered overseas surrogacy arrangements' in 'permitted destinations' (Proposal 37).

[41]The Law Commission and Scottish Law Commission (2023. Para. 10.164) recommend that information about the surrogate, gamete donors and intended parents should be provided to the court as a prerequisite for parental orders (which would be used for international surrogacy in all cases). The recommendation suggests that the requirement can be dispensed with, if information is not available. For a critique, see Wade (2025).

participants' use of language such as 'proper', 'real', 'actual' and 'original' parent. Mostly this was used in the context of genetic 'parents' rather than referring to those who gave birth. It is difficult to draw meaning from the use of these descriptors as there was sometimes contradiction in their use. For example, Camille used 'real' in the context of intended parents providing genetic material, but later used it to suggest that 'real' parents are the 'legal' parents. Though different family forms are accepted, we found that the language available to participants to define different genetic or gestational links is limited. Some of this framing regarding 'real' parents when referring to surrogates or donors, for example, could be hurtful to those born through assisted reproduction. For these reasons and more, including increasing problems with the terminology used to define legal parents (Dunne & Brown, 2024; Horsey & Jackson, 2023; Mahmoud & Romanis, 2023), it may be that a full reconsideration of legal parenthood in the context of assisted conception and the increasing variety of modern family forms should be undertaken. This should include consideration of whether and in what circumstances it might be possible to legally recognise more than two parents (McCandless, 2025), as was indicated by some of our participants. In addition, we think it is important to introduce education on alternative family forms in schools to expand children's understandings of parenthood, as discussed in Chapter 5.

Chapter 3

Children's Views About Contributions to Surrogates

'Even though you pay for [a pet], it doesn't affect how much you'll like it or not'.[1]

Introduction

This chapter focuses on children's views on the acceptability of various contributions (e.g., reimbursement of expenses incurred, material contributions) made by intended parents during surrogacy arrangements. Payments made during surrogacy arrangements are 'situated in an ambiguous regulatory position' (Brown, 2021, p. 125), with various 'concerns as to transparency as to what payments are being made for' (Law Commissions, 2023; para. 12.41). In part, this is due to a central tension in domestic surrogacy regulation, namely the formal commitment to altruism alongside a practice in which payments are routinely made and retrospectively authorised. By analysing how participants distinguished between reimbursement, gratitude and payment, the chapter offers an empirically grounded perspective on whether the current expenses-based model and the Law Commissions' proposals regarding payments align with children's views and lived experiences.

Terminological clarification is necessary, given the significant legal and conceptual work that distinctions between categories of financial provision carry in this area (Lee, 2023; Mahmoud, 2023). The term 'payments' is used throughout this chapter as the primary descriptor for money provided by intended parents to surrogates, in alignment with the terminology of the Law Commissions' Final Report (2023), which structures its proposed regulatory framework around 'permissible payments' and 'prohibited payments'.

[1] Alison, 12, born through US gestational surrogacy.

Children's Voices in Surrogacy Law, 87–118

doi:10.1108/978-1-83549-642-820261004

Within the proposed framework, the most significant categorical distinction is between financial provision to reimburse or compensate the surrogate for costs, losses or burdens arising from the surrogacy arrangement and financial provision made for the act of gestation itself. The Law Commissions designate the latter as 'payment for gestational services'. This term is used in this chapter to refer to payments that are not connected to any identifiable cost, loss or inconvenience incurred by the surrogate (more commonly referred to as 'expenses'), but which are made for the gestational role itself. This category is among the Law Commissions' proposed 'prohibited payments', on the ground that permitting it would be incompatible with the altruistic model of domestic surrogacy (2023, para. 12.22, paras. 12.81–12.110).[2] The broader term 'contributions' is used in this chapter to encompass a range of financial and non-financial provisions – including gifts and material support – evaluated by participants, some of which fall outside the Law Commissions' formal payment categories. No implication of legal permissibility is intended by the use of this term.

Unlike other areas of its consultation, instead of making concrete proposals about what payments might or might not be permissible, the Law Commissions' Consultation Paper (2019a, Chapter 15) merely set out eight categories of potentially permissible payments and invited consultees' opinions on these. These included essential pregnancy-related costs (such as for fertility treatment and routine obstetric and postnatal care), additional pregnancy-related costs (for example, childcare and domestic support) and surrogacy-specific costs (including legal advice, recuperation and postnatal counselling). Their categorisation also included lost earnings arising from time off work, compensation for pain, inconvenience and medical complications, and payments designed to preserve eligibility for means-tested benefits. The Law Commissions' framework also allowed for modest or reasonable gifts, conceptualised as symbolic rather than remunerative. The most contested category was payment for gestational services, understood as direct compensation for carrying a pregnancy. It was these categories we discussed in the interviews in this project. To elicit participants' views, participants aged 8–14 were first asked to consider a set of 'contribution cards', each depicting a contribution selected to map onto the eight

---

[2]It should be noted that 'compensation' is not used as a general synonym for financial provision to surrogates. Within the Law Commissions' proposed framework, 'compensatory payments' (understood as payments for pain, inconvenience or distress arising from the pregnancy) are expressly prohibited. The terms 'remuneration' and 'fee' are similarly avoided, as they carry connotations of employment or contractual service that neither accurately characterise the legal structure of domestic surrogacy arrangements nor reflect the Law Commissions' principle that the surrogate should be neither better nor worse off financially as a result of the arrangement. The line between these categories is legally significant and contested. The Law Commissions' taxonomy seeks to articulate it with greater precision than the current framework permits, but the distinction between a payment that reimburses a real cost and one that compensates for the burdens of gestation remains inherently a matter of evaluative judgement.

categories as outlined in the Law Commissions' (2019b, p. 18) infographic.[3] These were maternity clothes, doctors' fees (medical expenses), vitamins, lost wages (loss of earnings connected to unpaid leave from work), spa vouchers and holidays. Participants were asked to classify whether each contribution should be allowed, using response cards labelled 'yes', 'no' or 'not sure' (Phases One and Two), and 'yes', 'no', 'not sure' or 'maybe' (Phase Three).[4] Participants aged 15–18 were shown the Law Commissions' original infographic and were asked to evaluate the acceptability of each category directly.[5]

To explore broader normative concerns regarding commodification, participants were asked: 'Should intended parents be able to pay a surrogate?' This question related to 'payment for gestational services', defined as money given to the surrogate for her role in carrying the child, and this was explained to participants. The question engages longstanding ethical and legal debates about whether paid surrogacy risks transforming reproduction, pregnancy and children into market commodities (Anderson, 2000; Radin, 1987, 1996; Warnock, 1985). To further probe perceptions of commodification, participants were also asked: 'Some people think that surrogates should not be paid because children born through surrogacy would not want to know that their surrogate had been paid. What do you think of that?'

As discussed in Chapter 1, participants in Phases One and Three were recruited through domestic non-profit surrogacy organisations committed to altruistic surrogacy.[6] Phase One participants' responses may reflect internalised discourses in which surrogacy is explicitly characterised by ideas of kindness, altruism and non-commercialisation. Previous empirical research demonstrates that surrogates reproduce the language of any organisation with which they are affiliated (Mahmoud, 2023); it is plausible that children with lived experience of domestic surrogacy will similarly internalise that framing. For Phase Three participants, their knowledge of having been born through international commercial surrogacy in the United States may similarly have shaped both their vocabulary and how they relate to payments. Phase Two participants did not have direct experience of surrogacy, and their familiarity with and understanding of surrogacy were likely shaped by mediated representations, including celebrity narratives and television portrayals, through which surrogacy is frequently encountered.[7] The findings presented here reflect both participants' reasoning and the discursive environments within which they have been raised and offer several important insights for the regulation of payments in surrogacy arrangements.

---

[3]See Table 8, Appendix 2.
[4]The 'maybe' card was added after consultation following Phase Two, see Chapter 1, p. 43.
[5]See Appendix 3.
[6]See Chapter 1, p. 48.
[7]As we see in analysis of how children navigate surrogacy in their social worlds: Chapter 5, p. 171.

This chapter starts with an overview of the current regulatory approach to contributions, highlighting the challenges arising from the opaque framework. Following this, the chapter presents a detailed discussion of the data under the three themes that were identified. The first theme, 'Fairness is important to children', explores how participants grounded their reasoning in three frames – non-disadvantage, parental responsibility and distributive justice – when deciding on the acceptability of various contributions. The second, 'Gratitude expressed through gifts is acceptable', explores how participants implicitly developed a nuanced typology of gifts (symbolic, recuperative, potentially coercive) by considering the function of these gifts and the potential impact on the relationship between surrogates and intended parents. The third theme, 'Altruism acts as a normative anchor', explores how children used altruism as a moral anchor and viewed it as fundamentally important in ensuring surrogates exercised autonomy in these arrangements. Importantly, the findings suggest that no single model adequately captures the range of participants' expressed reasoning. The final section of this chapter discusses what these insights mean for the legal regulation of payments in surrogacy.

The Law on Financial Contributions: An Overview

As discussed in the Introduction, the Warnock Committee objected to payments to surrogates, as these were seen as exploitative of women and degrading to children.[8] However, when Parliament passed the Surrogacy Arrangements Act (SAA) 1985, it did not explicitly address the acceptability of payments to surrogates made by intended parents (Mahmoud, 2023; 2026a). Instead, it focused on the criminalisation of commercial surrogacy (Freeman, 1989; Montgomery, 1986). Section 2(3) of the SAA 1985 differentiated commercial payments made to third parties 'in respect of making, or negotiating or facilitating the making of, any surrogacy arrangement' from 'payments to or for the benefit of' surrogates made by intended parents. Notwithstanding the distinction between these payments, they are commonly conflated, with this remaining at the heart of debates on the legitimacy of surrogacy and contributing to policymaking (Horsey, 2018b, pp. 16–19; Mahmoud, 2023).

The introduction of parental orders by s.30 of the Human Fertilisation and Embryology (HFE) Act 1990 stated that only 'expenses reasonably incurred' during the pregnancy were prima facie permissible payments, without providing a definition of what these payments encompassed. However, through retrospective authorisation, the courts were able to approve payments other than for 'reasonable expenses' (*Re: Adoption Application (Payment for Adoption)* [1987] 2 FLR 291; *Re MW (Adoption: Surrogacy)* [1995] 2 FLR 759; *Re Q (A Minor) (Parental Order)* [1996] 1 FLR 369). This was an attempt 'to restrain the "deviant" form of surrogacy by implying that legal parenthood could be jeopardised if payments (other than for expenses reasonably incurred) were made'

[8]Introduction, p. 7.

(Mahmoud, 2023; 2026a). As the courts have been influenced by their assessments of whether surrogates were 'acting altruistically' (Brown, 2021, p. 107) when determining whether payments were 'reasonable expenses', this requirement was an early attempt to enshrine altruism into the legal framework. The 1998 Brazier Review was also concerned with payments in surrogacy, as it was required to consider 'whether payments, including expenses, to surrogate mothers should continue to be allowed, and if so on what basis' (Brazier et al., 1998, para. 1.2).[9] The Brazier Review recommended that payments should solely cover the reimbursement of bona fide expenses incurred during the pregnancy, with no payment provided for loss of potential earnings. The Review outlined a list of 'genuine' expenses, including maternity clothing, healthy food, vitamins, all medical expenses, any loss of earnings connected to unpaid leave from work in connection with the pregnancy and/or birth, travel to/from appointments, necessary accommodation and childcare (Brazier et al., 1998, para. 5.24). This approach reflects a broader normative position that any additional payment risks undermining the altruistic framing of surrogacy,[10] though the government did not act on Brazier's recommendations.

There is a widespread and persistent misconception that surrogates cannot be paid beyond reasonable expenses (Gamble, 2017, 2018; Mahmoud, 2023, 2026a), notwithstanding the fact that this prohibition does not appear anywhere in the legislation. In addition, ss. 54(8) and 54A(7) of the HFE Act 2008 permit courts to retrospectively authorise payments other than 'expenses reasonably incurred', including those made in international commercial arrangements. At the same time, the court is bound to uphold the paramountcy of the child's lifelong welfare, and it is unlikely that this would be achieved by refusing a parental order where payments beyond reasonable expenses have been made. The courts' approach to payments in domestic arrangements reflects the view that the surrogate neither gains financially from the pregnancy in any real sense nor is left to incur the costs related to it (*Re A, B, C (UK surrogacy expenses)* [2016] EWFC 33). The framework for retrospective authorisation was clarified significantly by Williams J in *A & B v C & D* [2026] EWHC 972. He held that the authorisation of payments under s. 54(8) of the HFE Act 2008 is governed by a paramount welfare test such that pure public policy considerations have no independent traction in the authorisation decision: the questions previously identified in *Re X and Y (Foreign Surrogacy)* [2008] EWHC 3030 (Fam) concerning the proportionality of payments, the good faith of intended parents and the absence of fraud remain relevant only insofar as they bear upon the welfare of the particular child, for instance, by illuminating the suitability of the intended parents or any risk of harm to the child. However, the belief that parental orders may be refused

---

[9]See Introduction, p. 15.

[10]This restrictive understanding sits alongside judicial acknowledgment that payment itself is not inherently unlawful; in 2001, Hale LJ, as she then was, acknowledged that 'surrogacy arrangements are not unlawful, nor is the payment of money to a surrogate mother in return for her agreeing to carry and hand over the child' (*Briody v St Helen's and Knowsley Area Health Authority* [2001] 2 FLR 1094).

where intended parents make payments beyond 'expenses reasonably incurred' remains pervasive, despite no evidence that this happens in practice (Brazier et al., 1998, para. 5.3; Horsey et al., 2022; Horsey & Sheldon, 2012).

Surrogates in the United Kingdom are typically reimbursed for expenses they incurred by being a surrogate, with most receiving between £15–20,000 (Horsey, 2025a; 2025c) and parental orders being routinely granted. Sometimes this includes 'payment for expenses incurred as a result from the need for physical and emotional recuperation from pregnancy and birth' acknowledging the fact that surrogates prioritise the intended parents during the arrangement (Horsey 2018b; Mahmoud, 2023; *Re A, B and C (UK surrogacy expenses)* [2016] EWFC 33). Additionally, it is common practice for surrogates to receive sentimental gifts from intended parents, such as charm bracelets, spa breaks, flowers, jewellery, alcohol and 'pamper packs' (Mahmoud, 2023; van den Akker, 2003).

As discussed above, the Law Commissions' original consultation invited responses on the acceptability of potential contributions on 'a spectrum from essential costs related to the pregnancy, to unrestricted payments' (para. 15.4). However, in their Final Report, the Law Commissions shifted from this categorisation and proposed a new regime for regulating payments within surrogacy arrangements, aiming to ensure surrogates 'are neither left financially worse off nor do they financially benefit' (2023, para. 12.15). The Final Report specifies 10 categories of 'permissible payments' and four categories of 'prohibited payments' (para. 12.22, paras. 12.81–12.110). 'Payments for gestational services' fall within the prohibited category, albeit without sustained normative engagement on whether surrogates should be paid for being surrogates (Brown, 2025). Research reveals academic support for the idea that surrogates should be reimbursed for expenses incurred and receive a modest payment on top acknowledging their reproductive labour (Alghrani & Griffiths, 2017; Horsey & Sheldon, 2012; Sifris, 2024; Walker & van Zyl, 2017a, 2017b). However, the proposed framework is supported by surrogates in the United Kingdom who have a limited appetite for a model allowing payment for gestational services (Horsey, 2025a; Horsey et al., 2022; Mahmoud, 2023).

The current landscape reflects some level of pragmatic accommodation between principle and practice: while domestic surrogacy remains framed around altruism, various financial aspects reveal a more complex global economy of compensation (Iliadou, 2025b; Luo, 2026; Mahmoud, 2026a). The Law Commissions' proposals consolidate this position by seeking greater clarity and transparency rather than fundamentally reconfiguring the underlying model. In doing so, they leave intact the central tension identified across the literature, namely, that domestic surrogacy in the United Kingdom operates within an 'expenses-plus' framework that resists explicit characterisation as payment for gestational labour, yet nonetheless acknowledges the material and relational demands placed on surrogates.

This unresolved tension goes to the heart of what the following empirical analysis illuminates: the legal framework never conclusively determined whether payment is problematic in principle or merely in excess of permissible expenses. The categories of 'reasonable expenses' and 'retrospective authorisation' are not so much a coherent regulatory scheme as a pragmatic deferral of a question the legislature has consistently declined to answer. This conceptual gap – between formal legal prohibition and routine practical accommodation – is elucidated through participants' reasoning and subsequently used to assess the Law Commissions' proposals regarding payments in surrogacy.

Fairness Is Important to Children

As explained in the previous section, while the legal framework allows intended parents to reimburse surrogates for costs incurred during the surrogacy, there is neither a defined list of acceptable 'reasonable expenses' nor a 'universally acceptable figure to pay for surrogacy expenses' (*Re A, B and C (UK surrogacy expenses)* [2016] EWFC 33; *Re C (Surrogacy: Payments)* [2002] EWHC 157). When participants decided on the acceptability of various contributions, fairness was their primary organising principle. However, it would be imprecise to treat 'fairness' as a single criterion, as participants' reasoning operated across three related but distinct normative frames. The first is non-disadvantage: surrogacy should not leave the surrogate financially worse off than she would otherwise have been. The second is parental responsibility: because intended parents are responsible for the resulting child, they should bear the costs that pregnancy creates. The third, expressed by a smaller group of Phase Two participants, is distributive justice: certain costs arising from surrogacy ought to be met by public provision rather than private ordering. These three norms are analytically distinct – the first is corrective, the second is relational, the third is structural – and participants moved between them in ways that did not always map onto the existing legal framework.

In relation to 'non-disadvantage', participants identified 'essential expenses' in terms of whether a cost was linked to the pregnancy and whether the surrogate would otherwise have incurred it herself. Underpinning this was a broader concern that surrogacy should not leave the surrogate financially worse off as a result of the arrangement. For example, Camille (13, born through US gestational surrogacy) suggested that acceptable payments were 'anything that the intended parents would have to pay if they were having the child themselves and nothing else'. Participants recognised that pregnancy-related costs are ordinarily borne by those choosing to have children and reasoned that surrogacy should not alter this allocation of financial responsibility. Rather than viewing such payments as exceptional or commercially problematic, participants framed them as analogous to the ordinary expenses associated with pregnancy and parenthood. Some contribution cards were implicitly deemed 'essential expenses', like 'maternity clothes', because they obviously related directly to the surrogacy. For example, Jack (17, child of surrogate) said:

> Yes to maternity clothes, but not like designer maternity clothes that you get hand-tailored and everything like that. It just needs to be a reasonable level.

This reasoning was reflected consistently across participants' accounts. Anna (16, cousin of a child born through surrogacy), for example, argued that intended parents should cover essential costs because, had they been carrying the pregnancy themselves, 'it's something they would be paying for'. Similarly, Harry (16) reasoned that intended parents 'should have to – or should be able to – pay for the pregnancy' because they would otherwise incur those costs 'through a kind of more traditional way'. Carrie (17) likewise emphasised that intended parents 'would be paying for it anyway', and therefore the surrogate should not personally absorb essential pregnancy-related expenses. Participants discussed the provision of these essential expenses as a matter of fairness: it would be unfair for surrogates to be left financially disadvantaged due to their involvement in surrogacy arrangements. For example, Oliver (11, child of a surrogate) said: 'the intended parents shouldn't make the surrogate pay for the surrogacy'. Similarly, Natalie (15) explained:

> If you're a surrogate and you weren't considering getting pregnant before they [the intended parents] approached you, then it's unlikely you would have to pay for those costs without the intended parents.

Camille (13, born through US gestational surrogacy) also noted that:

> Intended parents should take responsibility for just anything on the responsibilities of taking care of [the surrogate] while she is pregnant, if anything is the result of the pregnancy.

As participants considered essential expenses to be any cost that would not have existed if the surrogate was not pregnant, they distinguished between reimbursing surrogates for income lost due to pregnancy and paying them for the role of being a surrogate; this latter category is akin to the Law Commissions' prohibited payment for 'gestational services'. Across participants' accounts, this distinction was consistently grounded in fairness and the need to avoid financial detriment to the surrogate. Valeria (9, child of surrogate), for example, emphasised that:

> It's not fair that she has to pay for it all because she didn't have to do the surrogacy in the first place, but she offered to, so she didn't have to do it, but she did it.

Within this framework, 'lost wages' was commonly identified as an acceptable category of contribution, particularly where pregnancy disrupted paid employment, as the following quotes reveal:

> Because they [surrogates] could lose wages because of the pregnancy. Because they wouldn't be in work, and they might have to work less hours when they do work. So really, that isn't their fault. (Eliza, 11, child of surrogate)

> If [the surrogate] had, like, maybe not a very good job and she wasn't earning that much money, and then she had to stop work, it would be quite nice to pay her lost wages. (Evalynn, 11, born through gestational surrogacy)

> I think if the intended parents were in a position where they can pay for [loss of earnings], then that's something they should consider. (Natalie, 15)

Participants' divergent views towards payment mirrored academic debate on whether surrogacy should be conceptualised as labour (and therefore compensable) or as a form of altruistic care (and therefore not). Within this context, some participants rejected the idea that intended parents should be responsible for compensating lost wages, reasoning that surrogates had autonomy in deciding to undertake the arrangement and therefore should have anticipated its financial consequences. For these participants, fairness required balancing intended parents' financial position against surrogates' responsibility for their own choices, as the following quotes reflect:

> [The surrogate] chose to do it and she didn't have to miss work. (Alison, 12, born through US gestational surrogacy)

> I feel like everything shouldn't be put on the intended parents, because surrogates are putting themselves forward to doing this, and they should accept the responsibility of that as well. (Anna, 16, cousin of a child born through surrogacy)

> Because they [the intended parents] don't know what job they [surrogates] have, and if it's, like, a job that pays a lot, then they might not be able to cover it. (Bella, 13)

Participants usually excluded contributions deemed inessential or 'luxuries' from what they considered appropriate for intended parents to cover. This was particularly evident in responses to the 'car' card, which allowed exploration of how far intended parents' financial responsibility might extend beyond clearly pregnancy-related needs. Younger participants used this contribution card to distinguish between necessary and unnecessary costs, often expressing uncertainty where the link to pregnancy was unclear, as shown here:

> I chose "not sure", just because I don't know how the car would be related to the surrogacy. (...) I don't know how a car would help the surrogate. (Scarlett, 11, born through gestational surrogacy)

> I just think the car is random! It doesn't really have anything to do with a child or having a child. You don't need a car. (Alison, 12, born through US gestational surrogacy)

By contrast, participants who viewed a car as acceptable justified it through functional necessity rather than as a luxury. These participants framed acceptability in terms of need and affordability, as these quotes demonstrate:

> I put the car in "yes", because [surrogates] can give it back to [intended parents] just after they had the baby, and it would help [surrogates] get around and then they can give it back to the [intended parents]. (Emily, 8, child of surrogate)

> If [the surrogate] needs a car to get to work or do her shopping, and she can't afford to get a car, then I feel, like, if the intended parents want to give them a car to help out, I don't see why not. (Ellie, 13, born through gestational surrogacy)

> If [the surrogate] needs to get transported around to more places, I would say they should have a car and that would be very useful for them. (Bart, 12, born through US gestational surrogacy)

Bill (11, born through US gestational surrogacy) expressed a more conditional view, indicating that a car could be justified if a surrogate's existing vehicle was too small during pregnancy ('then maybe'), but that otherwise it would not be appropriate ('no'). In this sense, the permissibility of the contribution again depended on its relationship to facilitating the surrogacy arrangement and preventing practical disadvantage to the surrogate.

Taken together, participants did not apply a strict essential/luxury dichotomy. Instead, they evaluated the acceptability of contributions through a contextual fairness lens grounded in perceived pregnancy-related need and the avoidance of financial disadvantage. Judgements about acceptability, therefore, depended on whether a cost could be plausibly connected to the practical demands of surrogacy, rather than on fixed categorical exclusions of non-essential goods.

This concern over intended parents' potential financial vulnerability is a significant finding, and it reorients the focus of surrogacy regulation. Legal frameworks have historically been driven by concerns about surrogates' presumed financial vulnerability (Busby & Vun, 2010; Horsey, 2010; Horsey et al., 2022; Jackson, 2001; Mahmoud, 2024; Ragoné, 1994), alongside associated fears that financial need may distort consent and increase the risk of exploitation (Belliotti, 1988; Oliver, 1989; Purdy, 2018; Rothman, 1992). However, participants' reasoning under the theme of fairness complicates this framing by attending to the potential financial vulnerability of intended parents. In this sense, fairness was not conceptualised solely as protection of surrogates, but as a balancing exercise between potentially competing vulnerabilities. This is reflected in empirical research on surrogacy arrangements, which shows that surrogates themselves may take into account intended parents' financial constraints when considering expenses and contributions (Mahmoud, 2023). While intended parents are often assumed to be affluent, data indicate considerable variation in household income, ranging from below £29,000 to over £200,000, with multiple social and structural factors shaping this distribution (Horsey et al., 2025). Recent estimates further suggest that domestic surrogacy arrangements typically cost between £40,000 and £60,000, with a substantial proportion allocated to surrogates' expenses and medical costs (Horsey, 2025a, 2025c). Read through the lens of fairness, these findings underscore participants' implicit concern that surrogacy involves financial interdependence between parties whose resources may both be constrained in different ways, rather than a simple model of affluent intended parents and vulnerable surrogates.

The second normative frame participants employed in reasoning about fairness was 'parental responsibility' Participants reasoned that intended parents should bear the financial costs associated with the pregnancy because they were responsible for the resulting child. Participants linked ideas of fairness to parental responsibility, reasoning that intended parents should bear the financial costs associated with the pregnancy because they were responsible for the resulting child. As Alison (12, born through US gestational surrogacy) explained, 'it is your child. It's not really her child. I feel like you should pay for it yourself rather than let her pay for it'. This was particularly evident in discussions concerning healthcare and medical expenses, where participants viewed payments for medical needs as part of the intended parents' obligations towards their future child. Participants were specifically asked whether intended parents should contribute financially to surrogates' 'doctors' fees'. We explained that these 'doctors' fees' related primarily to privately funded fertility treatment – particularly given that at least 70% of treatment cycles are privately funded (Human Fertilisation and Embryology Authority, 2025).[11]

Following this clarification, participants consistently framed responsibility for medical costs as flowing from intended parenthood and from the desire to ensure the child's wellbeing. Ava (10, child of surrogate), for example, explained that 'if the actual [intended] parents want to keep the baby healthy, they should pay for the medication and things'. Bella (13) similarly described doctors' fees as 'necessities for pregnancy' and reasoned that intended parents should cover them, 'as it is their child'. Camille (13, born through US gestational surrogacy) likewise emphasised that, because it was 'technically the intended parents' child', they should 'take responsibility' for paying the fees.

Participants were concerned with fairness in relation to surrogates' health and wellbeing, particularly when discussing whether 'vitamins' constituted an acceptable pregnancy-related expense for intended parents to cover.[12] Participants reasoned that, where vitamins were necessary to support the pregnancy or the surrogate's health, it was fair that intended parents bear the associated costs.

[11]Recent research similarly indicates that intended parents incur approximately £16,000 in medical costs when undertaking domestic surrogacy arrangements (Horsey, 2025a, 2025c).

[12]As explained above, 'vitamins' were included within the Brazier Review's list of genuine expenses (Brazier et al., 1998, para. 5.24) and have also featured in case law and reform discussions (*A Y* v *ZX* [2023] EWFC 39; Law Commission and Scottish Law Commission, 2019a, 2019b, para. 3.65; *Re A, B and C (expenses)* [2016] EWFC 33). Similarly, SUK includes vitamins within its overview of surrogacy-related costs.

At the same time, many participants expressed concern about surrogates' wellbeing and autonomy, worrying that intended parents might purchase inappropriate vitamins or pressure surrogates into taking supplements with which they were uncomfortable. Participants therefore distinguished between financial responsibility and decision-making authority: while intended parents should fund pregnancy-related needs, surrogates were viewed as better placed to determine what was medically appropriate for their health. This was an understandable concern, as participants may not have been aware that certain prenatal vitamins are routinely recommended during pregnancy (National Health Service, n.d.). Similar concerns for surrogates' wellbeing were seen in discussions surrounding the acceptability of gifts in Theme Two.

Older participants developed this idea of fairness further and emphasised the importance of discussing financial matters in advance, particularly to ensure affordability, avoid misunderstandings and clarify expectations regarding responsibility for costs. Participants reasoned that intended parents and surrogates should reach a shared understanding beforehand about which expenses would be covered and in what circumstances. Participants consistently emphasised the need for clear, upfront discussions to avoid uncertainty and potential conflict. As Lucy (15, child of surrogate) explained, '[c]osts should be discussed by the surrogate and intended parents, and they should come to kind of an agreement on what they feel is right and necessary'. Jack (17, child of surrogate) similarly stressed the importance of anticipating all possibilities 'so then no party ends up... at a loss or being like all this isn't what I thought was gonna happen'. Harry (16) extended this reasoning, suggesting that intended parents' should have to – or should be able to – 'pay for the pregnancy'. This emphasis on prior discussion and mutual understanding aligns with current practice. Though surrogacy contracts are not legally enforceable under the SAA 1985 s 1A, written agreements are commonly used by surrogates and intended parents to structure their relationships and are widely recommended as good practice (Law Commission and Scottish Law Commission, 2023; Mahmoud, 2023). SurrogacyUK (SUK) and Brilliant Beginnings both provide draft agreements for intended parents and surrogates, while the Department of Health and Social Care (2018a) similarly advises that written agreements promote 'effective communication and mutual understanding'. Their importance is further reflected in the proposal for Regulated Surrogacy Statements (RSS) within the Law Commission's proposed New Pathway (2023, Chapter 9).

Some participants' concerns about fairness were influenced by how they understood the respective financial positions of intended parents and surrogates. In particular, participants without direct experience of surrogacy often described it as something only accessible to very wealthy individuals, reflecting a broader perception of surrogacy as a 'luxury' form of family creation. These understandings of surrogacy fed into their reasoning about fairness, as it shaped assumptions about who should bear financial responsibility, with participants tending to view intended parents as better placed to absorb the associated costs. Their perceptions were shaped by mediated representations, including celebrity narratives and television portrayals, through which surrogacy is frequently encountered. As discussed in Chapter 5, several Phase Two participants described learning about surrogacy through television and media, which tend to foreground high-profile, affluent intended parents. This framing is also reinforced within certain strands of anti-surrogacy advocacy, where surrogacy is characterised as a practice driven by wealthy individuals exploiting the reproductive labour of poorer women. For example, campaign materials produced by Stop Surrogacy Now UK (2025a, 2025b) frequently emphasise the role of affluent intended parents in shaping the global surrogacy market. While such representations are influential, they risk oversimplifying a more socio-economically diverse set of experiences and may reinforce unfounded assumptions that surrogacy is exclusively a 'luxury' form of family creation (Horsey et al., 2022; Mahmoud, 2023).

The third, distinct dimension of fairness – distributive justice – was identified among a small but significant group of Phase Two participants, who reframed surrogacy as a practice with public implications, arguing that certain costs should be met through government support rather than individual responsibility. This represented a meaningful departure from the dominant framing of payments as a private matter between intended parents and surrogates, and it implicitly located surrogacy within broader welfare structures. It should be noted that this position was articulated by a minority of Phase Two participants; they may have been responding to their own relative unfamiliarity with surrogacy's costs by reaching for public provision as a solution, without full appreciation of how domestic surrogacy arrangements operate in practice. Harry (16), for example, suggested that:

> If it's a loss of earnings, that's something the government should probably pay back instead of the intended parents...doctors' fees... should be something that the government can take care of as well.

Ivy (15) further developed this position by emphasising the need for state protection, arguing that intended parents 'shouldn't be forced to pay for [essential expenses], just in case the intended parents don't have the money to pay for it, or if they just don't want to pay for it'.

When participants suggested that the government should cover costs associated with 'lost wages', they framed surrogacy-related absence from paid work as something that could, in principle, warrant public financial support. For example, when discussing 'lost wages', Sienna (13) argued that 'lost wages' and related costs should be 'something that the government takes care of'. This echoes broader scholarly accounts that conceptualise surrogacy as a form of labour, sometimes described as 'gestational labour' or 'work' (Alghrani & Griffiths, 2017; Armstrong, 2021, 2022; Berk, 2020; Isard, 2025; Jacobson, 2016; Lewis, 2017, 2019; Parry, 2018; Stoeckle, 2018; Vertommen & Barbagallo, 2021; Walker & van Zyl, 2017a, 2017b). However, participants did not explicitly engage with this terminology. Rather, their suggestions can be understood as reflecting a view that some financial losses arising from surrogacy could be met through public mechanisms, analogous in structure (though not explicitly framed as such) to statutory forms of earnings replacement such as maternity-related payments.

As described in the Introduction, surrogacy regulation has historically been structured around a binary of altruism versus commercialisation (Lee, 2023). These Phase Two participants moved beyond this binary by suggesting that certain costs associated with surrogacy should be met through public provision, particularly where financial vulnerability might otherwise arise for intended parents. Their reasoning departs from dominant private-ordering assumptions that underpin current regulatory approaches in ways that the legal framework does not accommodate. This is a significant finding, and it is returned to in the final section of this chapter.

Additionally, some participants' support for payments in surrogacy was grounded in fairness reasoning linked to the time, effort and physical demands of pregnancy. They justified payment in terms of the burden of pregnancy and the sacrifices involved. As Bella (13) explained, 'I think they should be paid because pregnancy is long and it's hard'. Similarly, Harry (16) reasoned that intended parents should be able to pay the surrogate because 'you are asking for them to give up nine months of their life to go through this for your benefit'.

Rather than focusing on abstract notions of commodification, these participants emphasised the embodied burden of gestation when justifying financial recognition. This connects with wider debates about whether surrogacy can be conceptualised as 'work'. While surrogates in the United Kingdom are generally reluctant to describe their participation in these arrangements as employment-like and tend to remain in paid work during pregnancy due to the non-substitutable nature of gestational labour (Mahmoud, 2023), judicial approaches have similarly rejected a straightforward work-based framing. In *PQ v SSWP* [2026] UKUT 1, Wikeley J held that 'to describe surrogacy as a form of employment or work (or indeed as a vocation) is to stretch the natural and ordinary meaning of the word beyond breaking point', noting that it is a '24/7 responsibility… it cannot be re-arranged' [para. 57].[13] However, the court also acknowledged that payments may function as 'reassurance that both parties are committed to the successful completion of the agreement' [para. 73].

The data revealed that fairness was the key organising principle through which participants evaluated contributions in surrogacy; however, this 'fairness' encompassed three analytically distinct normative frames that the current legal approach does not clearly distinguish. The first, non-disadvantage, maps most closely onto the legal concept of 'expenses reasonably incurred': surrogates should not be left worse off, and the costs of pregnancy fall to those who initiated the arrangement. This reflects the view adopted by the courts, wherein the surrogate should neither gain financially from the pregnancy nor be left to incur the costs related to it. The second, parental responsibility, operates as a relational

[13]This case was concerned with whether payments received as expenses incurred during a surrogacy arrangement amounted to income (or capital) for the purposes of benefit entitlement.

allocation norm that justifies intended parents' bearing of pregnancy-related costs based on their relationship to the resulting child. This reasoning precedes, and is not reducible to, legal parenthood. The third, distributive justice, is the most significant: it moves beyond private ordering altogether and suggests that certain surrogacy-related costs belong within public welfare provision. While this third frame was expressed by a minority of Phase Two participants, it represents a meaningful challenge to the dominant assumption that surrogacy is, and should remain, a private arrangement. The law's silence on the distribution of surrogacy-related financial burdens across welfare structures – and the Law Commissions' failure to engage with this question – reflects an unexamined assumption that this chapter's empirical findings make visible.

Gratitude Expressed Through Gifts Is Acceptable

As mentioned above, it is common practice for surrogates to receive sentimental gifts from intended parents, as well as a recuperative break.[14] Participants implicitly distinguished between three types of gifts: (a) sentimental/symbolic gifts, which functioned as relational affirmations, (b) recuperative gifts, which acknowledged the toll of pregnancy and (c) incentivising gifts, where high-value contributions risked undermining altruism or creating subtle coercion. Their distinction was not necessarily monetary – instead, participants considered the function of various gifts and the potential impact on the relationship between surrogates and intended parents.

This tripartite typology reflects what Zelizer (2011) identifies more broadly in her account of how people manage the intersection of economic and intimate life: individuals actively earmark different types of payment or gift to preserve the moral character of relationships. By distinguishing between gestures of appreciation, expressions of care and contributions that could function as inducements, participants were doing precisely this work: using social distinctions to insulate the relational meaning of surrogacy from the corrosive potential associated with purely transactional exchanges. On this account, the function of a gift matters more than its monetary value: a modest bunch of flowers and a luxury holiday are not merely different in quantity but different in kind because they occupy different positions within the relational economy of the arrangement.

Participants recognised the importance of gifts as a means of expressing appreciation and making surrogates feel valued within the arrangement. They understood these gifts as enhancing wellbeing by signalling gratitude and acknowledging the significance of pregnancy for the intended parents and surrogates, as seen in these quotes:

[14]The Brazier Review held that surrogacy should be grounded in the 'gift relationship', arguing that this constituted 'the core value, on which many social arrangements in the United Kingdom are based, including blood and live organ donation' (1998, para. 4.36). Otherwise put, the Brazier Review adopted what Zelizer (2011, p. 174) terms the 'hostile worlds' doctrine: the belief that intimacy and market logic occupy morally distinct spheres, discussed later in this chapter.

> Presents, because it'll make [surrogates] happy, and cards to show appreciation. (Ava, 10, child of surrogate)
>
> Flowers because it's, like, something that's not expensive, but it's just nice. (Oliver, 11, born through gestational surrogacy)
>
> It shows that [the intended parents are] grateful for what the surrogate's doing, because pregnancy is such a big part of someone's life for nine months. I think it's just nice for [intended parents] to show their appreciation. (Carrie, 17).

These participants highlighted the symbolic but low-cost nature of such gestures, framing gifts in relational terms. In this sense, the primary function of these gifts can be understood as relational affirmation, signalling appreciation, reinforcing interpersonal connection and maintaining a moral framing of surrogacy as grounded in gratitude rather than transaction (Mahmoud, 2023).

As explained above, spa vouchers are a relatively common, modest gift sometimes given to surrogates, aimed at expressing appreciation and acknowledging the demands of pregnancy. This contribution was generally viewed positively and was framed in terms of recovery and rest. Some participants, however, qualified their support by expressing hesitation grounded in a fairness-based evaluation of cost, as shown by these quotes:

> A spa voucher is like a vacation, because, like, pregnancy can be hard, so, like, to have a relaxing something. (Rose, 13)
>
> With the spa voucher, I wasn't sure. Because sometimes spas can be quite expensive. But then also if the surrogate is going through a lot of stress carrying the baby, she might need to relax. (Scarlett, 11, born through gestational surrogacy)
>
> [Spa] vouchers in 'maybe', because it could be nice to go to the spa before giving birth or while pregnant. It's also probably quite expensive. (Alison, 12, born through US gestational surrogacy)

The inclusion of this contribution card allowed for exploration of participants' views on gifts that sit between symbolic appreciation and more practical forms of support. Participants' responses were structured by a fairness-based concern for intended parents' financial vulnerability, alongside recognition that such gifts might support surrogates' wellbeing. Rather than drawing a sharp distinction between different categories of gifts, participants tended to assess acceptability in functional terms, focusing on whether the gift was appropriate, proportionate and beneficial to the surrogate. In these cases, spa vouchers were evaluated through a proportionality lens, balancing intended parents' financial capacity with the perceived legitimacy of supporting surrogates' wellbeing. However, acceptability remained conditional: where participants expressed hesitation, it was again grounded in a fairness-based evaluation of cost.

While many participants accepted spa vouchers and holidays as forms of recuperative gifting, some expressed concerns about perceived discomfort experienced by surrogates or potential risk to the foetus. For these participants, acceptability was not primarily about balancing intended parents' financial vulnerability with surrogate wellbeing, but about avoiding any potential harm to the surrogate or foetus, leading them to restrict acceptable use of such gifts to the post-birth period; this is seen in the following quotes:

> Like, you can have it after, cause then you have time to relax. But you don't really need a spa if you're pregnant... it's normally really hot and stuffy and steamy. (Valeria, 9, child of surrogate)

> That would be uncomfortable. You know how they have to lay down when they [go to] a spa? Well, how are you meant to lay down when you're pregnant with quite a big belly? (Diego, 10)

> A spa voucher, I believe, can sometimes be harmful to babies – to unborn babies – so, if the voucher has an expiry date after the pregnancy, so that it could be used after so it wouldn't interfere with the pregnancy, I think it would be fine. (Leonard, 11)

In this way, some participants reoriented the assessment of 'appropriate' gifts towards safeguarding pregnancy itself, reinforcing that even recuperative forms of support remain conditional on perceived safety and timing.

A modest 'holiday' (recuperation break) is a common contribution that functions as a recuperative gift, acknowledging surrogates' labour and their decisions to put their lives on hold and prioritise intended parents during the arrangement. Across all phases, participants were divided on the acceptability of providing a holiday, and the discussion of this contribution card illustrated the boundary between recuperative and incentivising gifts most sharply. Holidays were understood by some as appropriate expressions of gratitude for the physical and emotional demands of pregnancy. Aoife (10, child of surrogate) described a holiday as a reward after birth when 'all the stress should just go away', while Lilly (9, child of surrogate) similarly focused on the opportunity for the surrogate to 'just relax' after pregnancy. Participants also evaluated holidays through the lens of timing and pregnancy safety, as seen in the following quotes:

> Like, if say you're on the plane and she was. like, about to give birth, it might be a bit risky. But also, it might be nice. (Scarlett, 11, born through gestational surrogacy)

> Maybe it would be quite nice to go on holiday, but I think, like, she should go...the surrogate should go on holiday not too late – at the start of the pregnancy – 'cause you don't want anything to happen whilst on the holiday. (Evalynn, 11, born through gestational surrogacy)

> If the holiday was like an intense holiday, it should be like after the pregnancy. I think that would be fine because it's not going to interfere with the pregnancy. (Leonard, 11)

As discussed earlier in the Introduction, older participants engaged directly with the Law Commissions' proposed 'gifts' as one of the categories of permitted contributions (Appendix 3). This involved one group interview, with three older participants aged 15-17. These participants similarly distinguished between sentimental or symbolic gifts, recuperative gifts and incentivising gifts. Some rejected the provision of gifts altogether, where they perceived them as extending beyond necessary expenses into forms of undue inducement or exploitation. Jack (17, child of surrogate) explicitly rejected holidays as inappropriate, arguing that 'it should be what needs to be covered for the surrogate pregnancy', and warning that non-essential gifts such as holidays could attract individuals 'not in the right mental space for that', potentially leading to situations where people become 'really, really desperate turning to surrogacy'. In his view, limiting gifts was a safeguard against potential vulnerability and exploitation.

Practical affordability also shaped participants' views. For example, Lucy (15, child of surrogate) accepted that a holiday could 'show their gratitude' but cautioned that 'some families can't cover that extra cost on top of the surrogacy itself'. Within this framework, the holiday contribution remained contested: for some participants, it was within the bounds of acceptable gratitude, particularly as post-birth recuperation; for others, its higher cost placed it closer to inducement than appreciation.

Some participants drew a sharper boundary around high-value or costly gifts, which they associated with potential pressure, discomfort or inappropriate inducement. Jane (14, born through gestational surrogacy) articulated this concern, noting that 'surrogacy is already a really expensive process', suggesting that expensive gifts 'might make the surrogate feel uncomfortable, the amount spent on the gifts'. Anna (16, cousin of a child born through surrogacy) similarly emphasised relational effects, arguing that 'there should definitely be a limit', because high-value gifts can 'put pressure on intended parents' and make it seem 'like [the surrogate's] lives [are] being controlled through gifts'. Camille (13, born through US gestational surrogacy) went further, arguing that excessive gifting risks functioning as a 'bribe... to keep their baby', thereby distorting the meaning of gratitude into transactional exchange. These accounts indicate that participants actively regulated the meaning of gratitude, distinguishing between acceptable expressions of appreciation and forms of gifting that might introduce expectation or obligation.

Alongside this restrictive position, other participants emphasised that the acceptability of contributions ultimately depended on intended parents' autonomy and, crucially, the surrogate's desire to receive them. For example, Leonard placed all contribution cards in the 'not sure' category and explained:

> I think you should be allowed to, but I think you shouldn't be allowed to if the person [the surrogate] says, "No, I would not like anything from you", or "I would not like that from you". Because, I don't think you should, like, forcefully give somebody something that they don't want.

In this way, gift-giving was understood as conditional upon relational agreement rather than unilateral provision.

Participants did not treat gift-giving as a simple question of acceptability, and conceptualised autonomy within surrogacy arrangements, particularly in relation to intended parents' freedom to make financial decisions. Phase Two participants especially emphasised that intended parents should retain discretion over their decisions to provide various contributions to surrogates, framing this as a matter of protected choice, as these quotes reveal:

> It's their [the intended parents'] choice. The government can't stop them [the intended parents] from using their money, so it's their choice to do what they want to do. So, why would you block them, when it's their choice? (Jax, 8)

> If the intended parents want to give the surrogate more money willingly, then I think they should be allowed to give them however much they want. (Carrie, 17)

> I don't think it should be expected because the cost of surrogacy could already be quite an extortionate amount, especially for some couples and whatever their circumstances are. So, it shouldn't be a necessity to give a gift. But if they wanted to, I guess they could. (Liam, 18)

For some participants, intended parents' provision of money beyond incurred expenses was understood as an acceptable form of gratitude, particularly where it functioned as a simple 'thank you' rather than as 'payment for gestational services'. Participants described this contribution as an optional gesture of appreciation that could sit alongside other gifts, as long as the sum remained modest and did not undermine the surrogate's altruistic motivations. For example, Scarlett (11, born through gestational surrogacy) suggested:

> I think you can give her a bit, like paying for things for the baby, or like just for herself to say, "thank you." But, like she shouldn't get offered loads, because she is doing it out of kindness.

Participants born through surrogacy in Phase One and those born through international surrogacy in Phase Three were generally more permissive regarding gift-giving and were less likely to view financial or material contributions as undermining surrogates' altruistic motivations, as these quotes demonstrate:

> If [intended parents] want to give money, they can, and if they don't, they don't have to. (Ashley, 12, born through traditional surrogacy)

> She's doing a really big thing for the family, making their child or carrying their child. I think that she deserves some kind of gift as well. (Alison, 12, born through US gestational surrogacy)

Participants emphasised the relational basis of gifting. Indeed, across the data, participants developed a differentiated framework structured around the function and relational impact of gifts rather than their presence or monetary value – and this framework maps directly onto Zelizer's (2011, p. 67) account of money as a 'material expression of gratitude' that acquires meaning from its social context. Gratitude was treated as an expected and legitimate feature of surrogacy arrangements. Symbolic expressions of gratitude – such as flowers, cards or small presents – were consistently framed as appropriate because they signalled appreciation without generating financial pressure or altering the underlying character of surrogacy arrangements. Recuperative gifts, such as spa vouchers or holidays, occupied a more contested middle position: they were accepted where they acknowledged the embodied demands of pregnancy but rejected where they appeared disproportionate or potentially coercive, as these participants discuss:

> I would say definitely a thank you card with money inside. (Steve, 9, born through US gestational surrogacy)

> I think it's all up to the intended parents. I think [surrogates] shouldn't get paid, but they could give them money as a gift after. (Bart, 12, born through US gestational surrogacy)

Their accounts indicate that modest financial gifting could be understood as *post hoc* gratitude rather than remuneration.

Potentially more expensive gifts provided as contributions were more likely to be interpreted as shifting the meaning of gratitude into something closer to inducement or obligation. In these instances, participants drew on concerns about pressure and relational imbalance, suggesting that excessive gifting risked compromising voluntariness and reframing the arrangement as transactional exchange. Therefore, participants assessed various contributions as gifts through their perceived relational effects, asking not merely whether a gift was affordable, but whether it preserved the surrogacy arrangement as a non-coercive, voluntary and ultimately altruistic one. This is consistent with Zelizer's (2011) broader argument: it is not the presence of money or material exchange that renders a relationship commercial or intimate, but the social meanings attached to how, when and why it is given.

Altruism Acts as a Normative Anchor

To ascertain participants' views on whether payment is acceptable, participants across all phases were asked: 'Should intended parents be able to pay a surrogate?'[15] The findings are presented in Table 2. Just over half of all participants said that intended parents should be able to pay a surrogate. One-fifth of all participants did not think that intended parents should be able to pay a surrogate. The remaining participants were unsure whether intended parents should be able to pay a surrogate.

Phase Two participants (who did not have direct experience of surrogacy) were more likely to assume that surrogates were necessarily primarily motivated financially, reflecting dominant societal understandings of surrogacy (Mahmoud, 2023, 2026a; Shaw et al., 2024). This was evident in participants' own accounts:

> I think with being a surrogate, it is like, a deal, like, the intended parents are paying for you to carry a child. (Natalie, 15)

> They're also getting paid quite a lot of money to be a surrogate. (Carrie, 17)

These accounts suggest that for Phase Two participants, payment was treated as a key feature of surrogacy. This transactional framing sits in tension with how

Table 2. Breakdown of Participants' Views on the Acceptability of Payment[a].

	Yes	No	Not Sure	Maybe
Phase One	9	10	6	
Phase Two	18	1	5	
Phase Three	1		2	2
TOTAL	28	11	13	2

[a]The 'Maybe' response card was introduced in Phase Three only and was not available to participants in Phases One and Two. This methodological difference should be borne in mind when comparing response distributions across phases, as the availability of an additional response option may have drawn responses that would otherwise have been recorded as 'Not Sure'.

[15]The Brazier Review unquestioningly held that surrogacy undertaken in exchange for financial benefit contravened societal norms (1998, p. i); financially motivated surrogates were deemed less likely to be capable of making an informed choice about becoming a surrogate and more susceptible to exploitation. This concern persists in contemporary policy discourse and remains central to critiques of unregulated international surrogacy, where fears of coercion and exploitation continue to be invoked to justify restrictive approaches (Iliadou, 2025b; Mahmoud, 2026a).

surrogacy is structured and understood within practice in the United Kingdom, where altruistic motivation is central.

In the United Kingdom, non-profit surrogacy organisations play a significant role in the practice of surrogacy and supporting surrogates by raising awareness about surrogacy, providing information and support, and hosting social events and conferences (Baslington, 2002; Horsey, 2025b; Mahmoud, 2023; Pott & White, 2025; Prosser & Gamble, 2016). Participants in Phases One and Three were primarily recruited through two non-profit organisations formally recognised by the Department of Health and Social Care (DHSC): SUK and Brilliant Beginnings. SUK (2025) defines itself as 'based on trust, mutual respect and, above all, friendship', and clearly states its interest in altruistic domestic surrogacy only. Brilliant Beginnings (2020) is 'dedicated to ethical surrogacy based on strong relationships, honesty and transparency', and supports UK-based intended parents engaged in domestic or international surrogacy arrangements primarily in the United States.

For participants with lived experience of domestic surrogacy, altruism functioned as a moral anchor to assess the acceptability of contributions. However, as stated in this chapter's introduction, it is important to recognise that for Phase One participants in particular, altruism may function as an institutionally reproduced discourse rather than simply as a spontaneous personal value. SUK's explicit commitment to altruistic domestic surrogacy, combined with its role in organising the social communities within which many of these families participate, means that the vocabulary of altruism and kindness has been available and valorised within the environment in which many Phase One participants have grown up.

Altruism operated as a constraint on the meaning of payment in that payment became problematic where it was perceived to displace altruism as the primary motivation for participation in surrogacy arrangements, reflecting what Zelizer (2011, p. 174) terms the 'hostile worlds' doctrine. Importantly, altruism was not merely an ideology that participants (or policymakers) hold, but instead it was a structuring logic shaping how participants categorised contributions and evaluated their legitimacy. The 'hostile worlds' framing does not simply reflect a prior moral commitment; it actively organises the space within which contributions appear as acceptable or problematic. Within this logic, the mere presence of money is sufficient to raise the spectre of commodification, not because money is inherently harmful, but because the 'hostile worlds' framework does not easily accommodate money as compatible with genuine care. This may explain why participants consistently anchored their acceptance of payment in its perceived subordination to altruistic motivation rather than treating the two as simply co-existing.

This framing was most strongly reproduced among Phase One participants socialised within domestic altruistic surrogacy contexts. Research on the influence of metaphorical framing on people's beliefs demonstrates the extent to which they reinforce certain stereotypes (Mohnke et al., 2022). This may explain why these participants were more likely to express concerns about payment that were consistently centred on its perceived capacity to distort motivations, as seen in the following quotes:

> I don't think it's fair that they [surrogates] get paid to do it, because they're probably going to do it just for the money, and it's not about the money, it's about helping other people out. (Ava, 10, child of surrogate)

> I think that the surrogate shouldn't be paid for doing that, because it is an act of kindness, and you shouldn't have to be paid to do something out of kindness. (Scarlett, 11, born through gestational surrogacy)

> Women would just end up doing it for all the wrong reasons. (Lucy, 15, child of surrogate)

> I feel like it's a really big thing having a baby for somebody, but I think it could be not great if the surrogate is asking for a lot of money and they don't really want to do it. They're not doing it to help; they're doing it to get lots of money. (Ellie, 13, born through gestational surrogacy)

> The surrogate shouldn't expect to have bought [for them] these different things, like a holiday or something, if they're going into this wanting to help someone and not to get a holiday from it. (Eliza, 11, child of surrogate)

These participants framed payment as incompatible with the practice, at times demonstrating concerns over the motivations of surrogates themselves, suggesting that financial incentives risked displacing altruistic motivations. They distinguished between helping and receiving significant payment for gestational services, rejecting high-value contributions on the basis that they were inconsistent with a helping-oriented entry into surrogacy.

Participants did not reject payment outright; instead, they constructed a boundary condition in which payment was only acceptable insofar as it remained secondary to, and, crucially, did not displace altruistic motivation. The underlying logic is therefore not anti-payment per se but protective of motivation: what matters is whether financial elements are perceived to reframe surrogacy from a relational act of helping or 'kindness' (to use Scarlett's words) into a transactional exchange.

As explained above, under the current framework established by the SAA 1985, payments to surrogates beyond reimbursement of expenses incurred are not explicitly prohibited. However, ss. 54 and 54A of the HFE Act 2008 state that for a parental order to be granted, only 'reasonable expenses' are permitted unless retrospectively authorised by the courts. This approach contributes to public misunderstanding and reinforces the perception that surrogacy operates within a legal grey area. Empirical evidence further complicates this perception.

Contrary to dominant anti-surrogacy rhetoric, surrogates based in the United Kingdom and surrogates based in the United States generally do not receive payments that could plausibly be characterised as a major financial gain. In the United Kingdom, the mean amount received for expenses is approximately £13,535–£15,535 (Horsey, 2025a; Law Commissions, 2023; para. 12.30). In the United States, average compensation (including both expenses and a compensatory element) is around $23,000 (Berthonnet & Clos, 2024), although higher payments are observed in certain jurisdictions, such as California, where figures of up to $85,000 have been reported (Mahmoud, 2023; West Coast Surrogacy, n.d.). The Law Commissions (2023) similarly note that surrogacy agreements occurring in the United States had a mean total payment of £39,875.69 (para. 12.34).

These concerns resonate with what is described as the 'hostile worlds' framing. As outlined earlier, this approach underpinned the Brazier Report's position that surrogacy undertaken in exchange for financial benefit conflicts with prevailing social norms (Brazier et al., 1998, p. i). It also reflects the broader claim that 'market logic creates a hierarchy of worth for certain attributes and characteristics of people' and can therefore contribute to the objectification of children (Bandelj et al., 2015, p. 116). In this vein, the Warnock Report similarly characterised compensated surrogacy as 'degrading to the child who is to be the outcome of it, since for all practical purposes, the child will have been bought for money' (1984, para. 8.11).

This empirical context is relevant to understanding participants' reasoning because their concerns about payment, fairness and commodification often implicitly assume scenarios involving substantially higher payments than those typically observed in practice. In other words, some of the moral weight attached to 'payment' in participants' accounts reflects the presence of money and its perceived potential to become excessive or distorting.

To examine whether this concern is reflected in children's own perspectives, participants were asked: 'Some people think that surrogates should not be paid because children born through surrogacy would not want to know that their surrogate had been paid. What do you think of that?' Participants' accounts suggest a more varied set of responses among surrogate-born participants, with little evidence that payment is uniformly interpreted through an objectification lens. Half of the surrogate-born participants expressed personal feelings of indifference regarding payment while recognising that others may feel differently depending on their experiences, as can be seen from the following quotes:

> It doesn't affect me too much. I don't think I'd mind too much if I found out she was paid. (Tom, 11, born through gestational surrogacy)

> I don't think I really care. Honestly, it's like, surrogacy isn't that big a part of my life and I think that I wouldn't really mind. We still see our surrogate quite a lot, and if I knew that she had been paid to carry us, I wouldn't really mind because I know she was

> doing it to help our parents. But I don't know if there were different situations, but that's my experience. (Ellie, 13, born through gestational surrogacy)
>
> I don't think it would affect me that much because I wasn't really alive and, personally, I wasn't part of the, like, decision. I wouldn't have been part of the decision to pay the surrogate. I don't think it would affect me that much. (Christina, 14, born through gestational surrogacy)

While these participants described their lack of involvement in decision-making as the basis for their apathy, there was no singular position on this issue. Instead, participants' responses revealed a variety of interpretations shaped by personal experience, as seen by the following quotes:

> One person just might not care but another person might feel quite strongly about that and feel like a surrogate didn't want to bring them into the world. It depends on the child, if they were just doing it to get paid. In another sense, it's not, but it's hard to tell if they got paid 'cause you'll never actually know if they do get paid. (Eliza, 11, child of surrogate)
>
> I don't think it would bother me, like I am not [born through surrogacy], and I don't know if I would feel different if I was in that situation. But I don't think it would bother me. (Rose, 13)

These participants suggested that reactions would differ between individuals and highlighted the inherent uncertainty in how payment would be perceived.

By contrast, Scarlett (11, born through gestational surrogacy) articulated a more critical concern. She said:

> The child might feel like the only reason that the surrogate wanted to give birth to them was for the money...You don't want to feel you've just been bought like a piece, like a toy or something, because you are not: you are a human being.

Participants' accounts indicate that while concerns about commodification may be present, they are not uniformly held or experienced as determinative. Instead, participants situated the meaning of payment within relational and contextual understandings of their own experiences, rather than treating payment as inherently objectifying. Their accounts sit alongside a persistent theme in policy discourse: that surrogacy's legitimacy hinges not merely on the presence of payment but on underlying assumptions about surrogates' motivations to participate, particularly where these are framed in terms of financial necessity. As discussed previously, surrogacy regulation has been based on assumptions about surrogates' motivations, rather than attaching weight to their narrated experiences, with participation in surrogacy arrangements ultimately deemed to arise out of their vulnerability, rather than a choice that was made in a self-initiated and self-regulated manner (Mahmoud, 2023).

As will be discussed in Chapter 5, participants who were the children of surrogates expressed concerns about whether their mother's involvement in surrogacy might have been due to financial necessity rather than altruistic motivation. These participants expressed views that echoed often-repeated worries that surrogates would participate in arrangements due to financial distress (Department of Health & Social Security, 1984; Einwohner, 1989; Mahmoud, 2023, 2026a; UN Special Rapporteur, 2025). These concerns were often linked to perceived health risks associated with surrogacy, particularly where payment introduced ambiguity about whether participation was motivated by need or choice. In such cases, payment was not understood as neutral but as something that could retrospectively reframe the surrogate's actions in ways that destabilised children's understanding of altruism and care. These tensions were reflected in participants' accounts:

> If I found out that my mom had been paid to be a surrogate, I would be extremely worried. I'd be thinking, why is my mom needing to be paid to have a baby for someone else? What's going on with our situation financially? Like, do I need to get a job trying to support her? And I think it would really take away from it, because I know she really, really enjoyed being a surrogate and I'd be like, "Is that real?" Did she actually enjoy it, or was it all just to try and support us? (Jack, 17, child of surrogate)

> It would kind of worry me. Like my mom absolutely loves being pregnant and having babies and helping people. She is obsessed with it. But if I knew that, you know, she was having all of these babies and she was possibly putting herself at risk every time just to get more money for us, I think I would be extremely worried. And it would definitely really, really negatively affect me mentally. (...) I genuinely think it would break my heart. (Lucy, 15, child of surrogate)

For these participants, payment altered the perceived meaning of surrogacy itself, generating anxiety about both surrogates' wellbeing and the authenticity of altruistic motivation. This extended into concerns about children's own status within such arrangements, with participants anticipating feelings of guilt, reduced self-worth, or being 'bought':

> If my parents had to pay an extreme amount of money to have me. I think I'd feel bad, because they lost out on so much money, and then they have to continue paying for me basically for a lot of my life. (Lucy, 15, child of surrogate)

> I think it could have a really bad impact on children, like, self-esteem issues, because, like, my parents paid thousands and thousands of pounds for me. Like, is it worth it? Did they regret it, you know? (Jack, 17, child of surrogate)

> It would make the child feel less wanted and a bit sad that he's been bought. (Valeria, 9, child of surrogate)

> They might feel less loved and like they were bought. (Lilly, 9, child of surrogate)

Interestingly, participants without experience of surrogacy also linked payment to children's sense of self-worth but did so through distinct interpretive logics. For some, payment was viewed through a commodification lens, where payment risked positioning the child as something 'bought'. For others, payment functioned as evidence of intense desire for parenthood and therefore of the child's value. Both interpretations drew on a shared assumption that payment communicates meaning about relational worth, but they diverged in how that meaning was evaluated. These participants echoed the often-held public misperception that surrogacy is a form of baby-selling, where if it 'isn't literally selling a child, it is selling the child out' (Anderson, 2000, p. 21). This tension is reflected in participants' accounts:

> I wouldn't want to know that I've been bought off someone, because I would think "I never knew that I was worth that much amount of money." I wouldn't mind if it was like, some sort of different stuff, but money... I wouldn't want to be, like, bought. (Tim, 11)

> If I found out I was bought, at least I know I'm worth something, to be fair. (James, 10)

Phase Three participants born through gestational surrogacy arrangements in the United States expressed a more positive stance on payments in surrogacy, often discussing payment as a proxy for the desire to be a parent. Alison's (12, born through US gestational surrogacy) account captures this interpretive move with particular clarity: drawing an analogy with paying for a pet, she framed payment as evidence of how much intended parents 'wanted' a child, rather than as a marker of commodification:

> Even though you pay for [a pet], it doesn't affect how much you'll like it or not. I feel it's the same with a child. I think maybe the fact that they did pay [the surrogate] would, maybe, show they wanted them.

This framing, characteristic of Phase Three participants more broadly, represents a different but internally coherent application of the relational logic that underpins participants' reasoning throughout the chapter: payment communicates meaning about the relationship, and for these participants, it communicates intentionality and desire rather than transaction. Unlike Phase Two participants without lived experience, whose accounts alternated between commodification and valuation, Phase Three participants generally framed payment as affirming parental desire, rather than as undermining surrogates' motivations. In this sense, the presence of payment did not render them commodities or objectify them; rather, it functioned as a signal of intentionality. Payment was understood as symbolic, akin to 'a material expression of gratitude' (Zelizer, 2011, p. 67), demonstrating the lengths and sacrifices their parents were willing to make to have them. This was reflected in participants' accounts. For example, Bill (11, born through US gestational surrogacy) said:

> It just shows that your parents really wanted you, or the intended parents really wanted you, so they were willing to give money to get you.

This interpretive difference is unlikely to be reducible simply to the fact of having been born through commercial surrogacy. It may also reflect the legal and practical context of international surrogacy in which these participants' arrangements were embedded.[16] Intended parents based in the UK frequently pursue arrangements in the United States, where a permissive, state-based regulatory framework allows enforceable contracts and legal parenthood at birth (Fischer et al., 2024; Gamble, 2025; Horsey, 2024; Horsey & Mahmoud, 2023; Jadva et al., 2021). Within this context – in which 'payment for gestational services' is not exceptional and in which contracts are enforceable rather than merely expressive of intention – it is plausible that children developed frameworks for understanding payment that do not map onto the 'hostile worlds' logic that structures domestic surrogacy discourse. Phase Three participants' positive framing of payment may reflect not merely personal experience but the legal-cultural environment in which that experience was shaped: one in which payment and care are not structurally opposed.

The data revealed altruism was a powerful normative reference point for how children understand surrogacy. For many participants with lived experience of domestic surrogacy, altruism functioned as a moral anchor, structuring expectations about surrogates' motivations and shaping the perceived legitimacy of the arrangement. This was evident in the way participants repeatedly distinguished between helping others and acting for financial gain, with acceptance of surrogacy closely tied to the belief that surrogates were primarily motivated by kindness and voluntary care. Within this framing, payment was problematic not because money was inherently objectionable, but because of what it could signal:

---

[16]The SAA 1985 does not apply extraterritorially, with the courts noting that criminalising 'the lawful resort to commercial surrogacy abroad' would be 'overkill' (*XX v Whittington Hospital NHS Trust* [2020] EWCA Civ 2832 [55], [73]).

a shift from helping others to financial self-interest. In other words, participants were less concerned with the presence of payment per se than with whether it appeared to displace altruistic motivations. These views mirrored long-standing anxieties expressed in the Warnock Report (1984) and later reinforced by the Brazier Review (1998), where compensation is viewed as undermining altruism in surrogacy. However, unlike the aforementioned, participants' accounts suggest that this concern is contingent rather than categorical, in that payment is objectionable only where it displaces – rather than coexists with – altruism. Moreover, as noted in this chapter's introduction, the strength of this altruism-anchored framing among Phase One participants may partly reflect their socialisation within organisational contexts that valorise altruism as the defining feature of surrogacy.

Phase Two participants without experience of surrogacy and Phase Three participants born through surrogacy arrangements in the United States did not treat altruism as the primary lens through which surrogacy is evaluated. This difference in framing meant that payment was less likely to be understood as undermining altruism and more often interpreted as recognition of work, sacrifice or commitment. In this context, payment did not necessarily commodify or objectify either the surrogate or the child. Instead, payment could be reframed as evidence of intentionality, desire and commitment on the part of intended parents, without displacing the underlying relational meaning of the arrangement.

These findings complicate the assumption that payment is inherently harmful to children born through surrogacy. The Warnock Report (1984) argued that compensated surrogacy would be degrading to children, on the ground that 'the child will have been bought for money'. While some participants expressed concerns about feeling 'bought' or objectified, others described indifference or interpreted payment positively. Their perspectives were diverse and context-sensitive. Rather than adopting the rigid binary between altruistic and commercial surrogacy embedded in the legal framework in the United Kingdom, participants articulated a nuanced position, evaluating payment through a relational and ethical lens, asking whether financial exchanges support, acknowledge or distort the meaning of surrogacy.

Conclusion: Insights for Law, Policy and Practice

The first insight for law and policy is that participants assessed contributions to surrogacy arrangements through a relational and contextual framework rather than through the formal altruism/payment binary that underpins current law and the reforms proposed by the Law Commissions in their 2023 Final Report. Across all phases, participants were not primarily concerned with whether a payment was made but with whether it preserved rather than displaced altruistic motivation, whether it prevented financial disadvantage to the surrogate and intended parents, and whether it reflected genuine agreement between the parties. Their reasoning was grounded in fairness, proportionality and sensitivity to coercion, rather than fixed categories. This relational mode of reasoning is not accurately captured by categorical rules.

A second insight is that participants' reasoning challenges arguments that payment is inherently commodifying for the surrogate and the child born through the arrangement. Participants did not treat payment as *inherently* problematic. Instead, concern arose where payment potentially displaced altruism or introduced coercion. Participants saw a distinction between payment that commodifies and payment that recognises effort and reflects genuine agreement. This idea was seen consistently across the phases, and was most clearly articulated by Phase Three participants, which may reflect knowledge of commercial practice in the UK. For the latter participants, payment was understood as recognition of commitment and effort rather than as the purchase of gestational services. At the same time, payments that might be seen as inducements to surrogates or putting pressure on intended parents were seen as inappropriate, and concerns were raised that both children of surrogates and children born through surrogacy might feel negatively if large sums of money were exchanged.

These insights mean the following for law and policy development. In practical terms, such a framework could be implemented within the architecture of the Law Commissions' proposals. The Law Commissions' Final Report moves towards greater clarity by specifying 10 categories of permissible payments and four categories of prohibited payments, and by introducing Regulated Surrogacy Organisations (RSOs) to facilitate and oversee arrangements (Law Commissions, 2023; para. 12.22, paras. 12.81–12.110). Permitted payments already include the costs of a modest recuperative holiday for the surrogate and her family (para. 12.19) and modest gifts to the surrogate (para. 12.20). This enhanced clarity regarding payments is significant progress. However, the categorical prohibition of payments for 'gestational services', without any mechanism for assessing the relational context or function of a payment, may fail to capture precisely the distinction that participants were drawing. The findings do not support the categorical prohibition of payments for 'gestational services'. Therefore, a framework in which the reimbursement of expenses remains central, while modest additional payments may be permissible, would seem to be more in line with participants' views. Such payments should be clearly understood, agreed upon by all parties to the arrangement and clearly outlined in the RSS, similarly to the system envisaged by the Law Commissions in their Final Report (para. 12.297). Payments should not be such that they act as an inducement to the surrogate or put pressure on intended parents. This position is consistent with participants' own reasoning across all phases: they were not opposed to financial recognition of the surrogate's effort (reproductive labour) and commitment but were consistently concerned that any financial element in the arrangement should be transparent, proportionate and free from inducement.

Such a framework would place an obligation on RSOs to seek to ensure that all payments outlined in the RSS are consistent with the non-commercial principles of the new pathway. It is already the case that the draft Surrogacy Bill would require RSOs to carry out 'pre-approval checks' of the agreement and give 'approval' having taken 'into account all the circumstances of the case' including the welfare of any child that would be born (clause 5(3) (a)-(c)). Clause 6 of the draft Bill outlines that such pre-approval checks should contain medical and criminal checks, implications counselling, separate legal advice for intended parents and surrogates, and ensuring life and critical illness insurances are in place for the surrogate. This could easily be extended to include a requirement that RSOs must check the financial terms of the agreement, what payments are proposed, and whether they contravene the non-commercial underpinnings of the pathway. Clause 3 of the Surrogacy Bill outlines that all agreements, including promises of payments that are designed to persuade anyone to enter a regulated surrogacy arrangement or sign an RSS are to be unenforceable. This seems designed to prevent any party from being coerced into entering an agreement for money (or payment in kind) and would seem to align with some of the concerns of the participants. We suggest that this oversight function of RSOs should be introduced into draft legislation and that, through a Code of Practice developed by the regulator,[17] RSOs should be empowered to develop their own guidance for assessing payments within the framework outside of the binary of 'permitted' or 'prohibited' payments, reflecting the greater flexibility our participants would appear to support. For example, the RSOs could interview surrogates and intended parents separately to seek to ensure there is no undue influence placed on the surrogate or pressure being put on the intended parents. For surrogacy arrangements that fall outside of the new pathway, such as 'independent' domestic and international surrogacy arrangements, intended parents would still need, under the existing recommendations, to apply for a parental order, though the draft Bill envisages that payments could be authorised by the court in such situations (clauses 18(11) (b), 19(8) (b), 20(1)). In domestic agreements, the Law Commissions proposed an additional level of oversight regarding payments as an option, i.e., that while courts must grant a parental order if the child's lifelong welfare demands it, they could also have the power to 'refer the intended parents to the enforcing authority for the imposition of a civil (financial) penalty' if they contravene the proposals regarding payments.[18] Therefore, such a system of oversight should be considered, given participants' concern with ensuring that payments are not coercive to surrogates or do not place pressure on intended parents.[19]

There has already been some judicial guidance that reflects the approach of the participants and should continue to be used in current cases and for parental order cases under the new proposed framework. In *A & B v C & D* [2026] EWHC 972

---

[17]The Law Commissions propose that this would be an extension of the HFEA. See Introduction, p. 15.

[18]This is not a concrete proposal but one option the Law Commissions proposed alongside the 'regulatory control only' option (where RSOs oversee payments) which they contend is likely to sit better with the altruistic character of domestic surrogacy in the United Kingdom (2023, paras. 12.285 and 12.295).

[19]A civil penalty could also be imposed on intended parents if there are 'overpayments' made on the new pathway, though, given the oversight by RSOs proposed, this would seem less likely to occur.

(Fam), Williams J acknowledged that the existing test used by judges for the authorisation of expenses remains based on the principles set out by Hedley J in *Re X & Y (Foreign Surrogacy)* [2008] EWHC 3030 (Fam), as follows: 'Was the sum paid disproportionate to reasonable expenses?', 'Were the applicants acting in good faith and without moral taint in their dealings with the surrogate?' and 'Were the applicants party to any attempt to defraud the authorities?' (at [39], [47]). Williams J is also clear that these questions must be understood in the context that the child's welfare must be the court's paramount consideration. Additional guidance could be formally developed for judges who authorise payments that go beyond reasonable expenses, which could assist them in assessing whether the payment was an inducement or coercive. A final note on this from our findings is that it would also be important that children born through surrogacy and children of surrogates understand the nature of such payments. They could be told why the payments were made and what they were for, to allay any concerns that children of surrogates may have that their mother was induced by payment or address any negative feelings for children born through surrogacy.

A final insight that should be noted is that a minority of Phase Two participants moved beyond the private-ordering model entirely, suggesting that certain surrogacy-related costs should in principle be met through public provision by the state rather than allocated between the parties alone. Although this was not a majority position, this finding marks a meaningful departure from the private-ordering assumptions that dominate current regulatory approaches, including the Law Commissions' Final Report, which does not meaningfully engage with the question of whether a purely private financial framework adequately distributes the burdens associated with surrogacy. We suggest that this question deserves explicit attention in future law and policy reform.

Chapter 4

Children's Views About Origin Information in Surrogacy

'...they helped you be born, so I think it would be good if you knew the people. They basically made you alive'.[1]

Introduction

This chapter focuses on children's views on knowledge about origin information, which includes gestational or genetic origins.[2] This issue arises because, in surrogacy, the person who gestates the child does not usually remain the child's legal parent. Surrogacy can also involve the use of sperm or egg donors.[3] Children born through surrogacy will always have a gestational link with the surrogate. They could also have genetic links with her, if traditional surrogacy were used, or have genetic links with an egg or sperm donor. Surrogacy also creates relationships between children. Children born through traditional surrogacy will be genetic half-siblings to any other genetic children of the surrogate, including her own children and/or other children she has had through traditional surrogacy. For children born via egg or sperm donation, any other children born from the same donor's gametes are also genetically related to them.

Issues which have concerned law and policymakers are (a) whether children should be told that they are born through surrogacy and/or gamete donation and

[1]Oliver (11, child of surrogate).

[2]While it can be argued that links between children (from having the same surrogate or donor) are not accurately captured by the term 'origin information'. However, for ease of reading, the term will be used to refer to information about surrogates, donors and children linked through these means.

[3]There must be a genetic link with one intended parent for a parental order to be granted under s. 54(1)(b) and s. 54A(1)(b) Human Fertilisation and Embryology (HFE) Act 2008; therefore, the use of two donors will not result in a parental order.

Children's Voices in Surrogacy Law, 119–145

doi:10.1108/978-1-83549-642-820261005

(b) the extent of the knowledge that they should have about the people involved. We asked children a range of questions about these issues, including: 'Should children know they are born through surrogacy?' 'Should children know the identity of their surrogate?' and 'Should children know whether the arrangement was traditional or gestational?' We asked most groups about whether children should know if they are born through gamete donation and whether they should know the identity of their donor. We asked some groups about whether they thought contact with surrogates and donors was important.[4] We asked these questions using polling activities and then asked participants to explain the reasons for their answers.[5] As was set out in Chapter 1, in order to explore participants' views on the issues without prior reference to the regulatory position, the law was not explained beforehand.

The chapter first provides an overview of current UK law on access to origin information in the context of surrogacy. Following this, the data are analysed under three themes. Theme One, 'openness about origins', explores participants' views about how much children should know about surrogacy arrangements, the framing of this issue and the reasons given for the appropriateness of openness. Theme Two, 'respect for children's autonomy', explores the importance participants attach to children's autonomy in relation to knowing origin information and what this means for how information is shared. Theme Three 'deference to parents', explores how participants balance the autonomy of children against that of parents in this context. The final section sets out what these insights mean for the legal regulation of origin information in surrogacy.

The Law on Origin Information in Surrogacy: An Overview

The Surrogacy Arrangements Act (SAA) 1985 and the Human Fertilisation and Embryology (HFE) Acts 1990; 2008 do not address access to origin information in relation to surrogacy. When a child is born through surrogacy, the name of the surrogate is placed on the birth certificate, and when a parental order is granted, the original birth certificate is replaced. Children might be able to decipher from their birth certificate that they were born through surrogacy. This is because the replacement birth certificate will state: 'Certified to be a true copy of an entry in the Parental Order Register'. However, a child would need knowledge of the law to be able to decipher from such wording that they were born through surrogacy, and it is perhaps unlikely children will see their birth certificate until adulthood (Wade, 2025). Such children would not be able to find out information about the identity of their surrogate, since they would not be able to access their original birth certificate (Law Commission and Scottish Law Commission, 2023; para.

[4]The issue of contact and relationships between families is explored in Chapter 5, since contact is not an issue which is regulated by law.

[5]These questions were asked with the use of cards, which set out the questions. Participants were invited to circle the options: 'yes', 'no' and 'not sure' (Phase One and Two) or 'yes', 'no', 'not sure' and 'maybe' (Phase Three).

13.19). If the surrogate used her own egg, it is unclear whether this is clearly recorded.[6] In order to know whether they have a genetic link with the surrogate, children would need to be told this or find out from DNA testing. The same is true if donor conception is used in the surrogacy arrangement,[7] since this is also not recorded on the birth certificate. However, there is legal regulation of access to information about donors who donate in clinics licensed by the Human Fertilisation and Embryology Authority (HFEA).[8] Donor anonymity was abolished in the United Kingdom in 2005. Donor-conceived people can apply for non-identifying information about their donor at age 16 and identifying information at the age 18, through an application to the Register held by the HFEA.[9]

Therefore, access to donor information is more regulated than access to information about surrogacy. As noted, birth certificates do not contain information about surrogacy, nor is there regulation of the issue of collecting and releasing identifying information about surrogates. However, these issues may not affect children born through surrogacy to a great extent. With same-sex cisgender male couples, the need for a surrogate will be clear, since neither can carry the pregnancy and, therefore, it is unlikely that the surrogacy can be hidden from children. In heterosexual families or single parent families, studies have shown general support for openness, because parents want to share with their families, or because it is impossible to avoid telling, since the family know that pregnancy is not possible (MacCallum et al., 2003). For example, a study involving children born through surrogacy in 33 families found that, at age 10, all children born through traditional surrogacy had been told about the surrogacy arrangement (Jadva et al., 2012). If surrogacy is supported by the UK non-profit support organisations,[10] children will likely know the nature of their birth and their surrogate, since these organisations advocate friendship and ongoing relations between families.[11] Under such models, as

---

[6]There is some evidence that the HFEA's position is that where a surrogate's egg is used in traditional surrogacy, she would be registered as a donor under the provisions of the HFE Act. However, this is not clear. Where a surrogate's egg is fertilised through IVF, it is also not clear if she is treated as a donor. See Wade (2025).

[7]Gamete donation can be used in conjunction with surrogacy. However, the use of both sperm and egg donation ('double donation') will not meet the requirements for a parental order for a couple under s. 54(1)(b), meaning they can use either egg or sperm donation. A solo applicant could not acquire a parental order under s. 54A(1)(b) if they use double donation.

[8]The law does not apply to donors that do 'at-home' insemination or donors used in clinics abroad.

[9]Art 2, Human Fertilisation and Embryology Authority (Disclosure of Donor Information) Regulations 2004.

[10]See Introduction, pp. 11–12.

[11]For example, SurrogacyUK (SUK) advocates a 'friendship-first' model, whereby intending parents and surrogates develop friendships before starting a surrogacy journey. See, further, Pott and White (2025). See the SUK website: https://surrogacyuk.org/. Brilliant Beginnings is built on a 'relationship-based ethos' modelled on strong relationships, honesty and transparency. See Brilliant Beginnings website: https://brilliantbeginnings.co.uk/who-we-are/.

will be seen in Chapter 5, ongoing relationships develop between the family with surrogate-born children and the surrogate and her family.[12]

In terms of children's access to information about *children* that are linked to them because of surrogacy, there is no regulation of this. First, there is no legal mechanism for children to access information about whether their surrogate had other children through surrogacy or has her own children. Where gestational surrogacy is used, these children would have a 'gestational link',[13] since they were born to the same surrogate. Where traditional surrogacy is used, such children will have a gestational link *and* a genetic link with other children born to the surrogate via traditional surrogacy and with any of her own genetic children. Second, there is no way for children of surrogates to access identifying information about children that their mother had through surrogacy or to find out whether they are genetically related to them or not. Again, this may have limited impact on children if contact between families is established, although this depends on children being told whether the relevant links are gestational alone or also genetic. In this regard, in the study above (Jadva et al., 2012) only 58% of offspring had been told that the surrogacy was traditional, meaning they would be unaware of genetic links to the surrogate, to her own children or to other children the surrogate gave birth to following traditional surrogacy. If donors are used in surrogacy at a HFEA-licensed clinic, donor-conceived people can apply for identifying information about other donor-conceived individuals born from the gametes of the same donor (donor siblings), where both individuals consent to this via the Donor Sibling Link.[14]

The Law Commissions have proposed the development of a Surrogacy Register, maintained by the HFEA, which would record information about intended parents, gamete donors and the surrogate for all surrogacy arrangements (Law Commission and Scottish Law Commission, 2023, Chapter 13).[15] This includes information about 'intention-based origins' (Brown & Wade, 2024; Wade, 2025), which can be used to refer to information about intended parents without a genetic link but who 'played a role in the formation of the agreement which led to the surrogacy agreement' (Law Commission and Scottish Law Commission, 2023; para. 13.104). The Register would also record whether or not the surrogate had a genetic link with the child. The Law Commission and Scottish Law Commission (2023, para. 13.156) recommend that children born

[12]This is not the case in all jurisdictions. For example, there have been recent cases involving anonymous surrogates in Nigerian clinics. See *Re H (anonymous surrogacy)* [2025] EWHC 220 and *B and C* v *D and H* [2025] EWFC 366.

[13]This is wording used by the Law Commission and Scottish Law Commission (2023, para. 13.187) to denote the idea of a link formed through being born to the same gestational surrogate.

[14]See HFEA Website, Donor Sibling Link: https://www.hfea.gov.uk/donation/finding-out-about-your-donor/donor-sibling-link-dsl/.

[15]HFEA donors' information would continue to be stored in the HFEA Register. Such donors are likely to refer to gamete donors used in a fertility clinic abroad. See, further, Wade (2025).

through surrogacy in England and Wales should be able to access non-identifying information from the Surrogacy Register at age 16 and identifying information at age 18, as a matter of course. This is in line with the law on access to donor information. What is different from the current law on access to donor information is that they also recommend that children should be allowed to access *identifying* information from the Register at age 16 and 17, unless they lack capacity under the Mental Capacity Act 2005.[16] In addition, the Law Commissions suggest that access to identifying and non-identifying information should be permitted under the age of 16, without parental consent, if children are Gillick competent.[17]

The Law Commissions' Final Report also considers the broader networks formed through surrogacy and recommends that people who have the same surrogate should be able to identify each other with mutual consent (para. 13.189). It also recommends that surrogate-born children and the surrogate's own child(ren) should be able to identify each other in the same way (para. 13.209). These recommendations apply regardless of whether there is a genetic link between the individuals. In this regard, the Report states:

> Throughout the project, we have tried not to overemphasise the significance of genetics, and we think that surrogate-born people should be able to decide for themselves how important it is that they are gestationally and perhaps genetically related to someone else. (para. 13.187)

The Law Commission and Scottish Law Commission (2023, para. 13.228) took a strong stance on the question of whether children born through surrogacy should know they were born this way, stating:

> ...we are not persuaded by the concerns of those who consider that the intended parents should be left to decide whether to tell their child of the surrogacy; this is a matter that the child has a right to know.

The Law Commission and Scottish Law Commission (2023, para. 13.216) propose that birth certificates should be clear that a person's birth is a result of surrogacy. These recommendations show a strong commitment to respecting the

---

[16]The capacity test operates as a presumption of capacity; therefore, there would be no assessment of capacity, but there would be implications counselling offered. See Law Commission and Scottish Law Commission (2023), paras. 13.144 and 13.147–12.150.

[17]i.e., if they have 'achieve[d] a sufficient understanding and intelligence to enable [them] to understand fully what is proposed'. See *Gillick v West Norfolk and Wisbech Area Health Authority* [1986] AC 112. Due to different capacity law in Scotland, the Law Commissions propose access to both identifying and non-identifying information at age 16, as a matter of course, and access to information under 16, where the young person meets the test for legal capacity.

autonomy of surrogate-born individuals both to know about their birth through surrogacy and to have access to information about their surrogate and other individuals with whom they share genetic and/or gestational links (Wade, 2025). However, as noted, the Commissions argue that their stance is not that special significance should be given to information about genetics, but that it is up to individuals to decide its significance (para. 13.187).

The Law Commissions' stance in relation to access to information about surrogacy is in line with trends in law, policy and practice which encourage openness in assisted reproduction, most notably in the field of donor conception. As noted above, donor anonymity was abolished in 2005. The value of openness has been recognised in public debates (HFEA, 2023b; Nuffield Council on Bioethics, 2013), in donor conception support groups,[18] and in academic literature (Allan, 2017; Blyth et al., 2009; Cowden, 2012; Guichon et al., 2012). While the first regulatory approaches to donor conception were based on secrecy (Haimes, 1988, 1992), in the 1980s and 1990s a move towards openness was influenced by donor-conceived people themselves and recipient parents (Blyth et al., 2001; Frith, 2001; Turkmendag, 2012), as well as by research supporting openness in adoption, where it has been argued that children having knowledge of their background and genetic relatives was important for positive identity development (Haimes, 1998; McWhinnie, 2001; Triseliotis, 1973). This echoed the growing recognition at that time of the need to prioritise child welfare, with the introduction of the introduction of the Children Act 1989 (Gilman & Nordqvist, 2018) and the establishment of the United Nations Convention on the Rights of the Child (UNCRC) 1989, which was ratified by the United Kingdom in 1991. Relevant provisions of the UNCRC in this area include, for example, Article 7, which protects the child's right to birth registration, name, nationality and 'as far as possible, the right to know and be cared for his or her parents' and Article 8, which provides that a child has a right to have their identity preserved, including nationality, name and family relations. The European Court of Human Rights (ECtHR) has recognised that personal identity is a 'vital interest' that is protected under Article 8 of the European Convention on Human Rights (ECHR) (*AM v Norway,* App no 30254/18; *S-H v Poland,* App Nos 56,846/15 and 56,849/15).[19] There is also strong recognition in the domestic courts of a right to know one's origins, with a focus on genetic links (*Re H (A Minor) (Blood Tests: Parental Rights)* [1996] 3 FCR 201;

[18]The Donor Conception Network publishes books in the *Telling and talking series* (https://dcnetwork.org/product-category/telling-and-talking-series/). It also publishes *Our story series* (https://dcnetwork.org/product-category/our-story-series/). The Network publishes books about donor conception (https://dcnetwork.org/telling-and-talking/books/). The Network runs 'Telling and Talking' workshops (https://dcnetwork.org/telling-and-talking/). It also runs 'What Makes Me, Me?', creative sessions for children: https://dcnetwork.org/events/activities-for-children/. See also Paths to Parenthub (n.d.). *Why telling matters – talking to your child about donor conception* [Webinar]. https://pathstoparenthub.com/webinars/; see also Kluger-Bell (2012).

[19]See also *Jäggi v. Switzerland*, App. No. 58757/00 (ECHR 13 July 2006) and *Mikulić v. Croatia*, App. No. 53176/99 (ECHR 7 February 2002).

Re T (Paternity: Ordering Blood Tests) [2001] 2 FLR 1190; *Re R (Parental Responsibility)* [2011] EWHC 1535 (Fam); *MS v RS (Paternity)* [2020] EWFC 30; *Re F (Paternity: Jurisdiction)* [2007] EWCA Civ 873 and *AB v CD* [2019] EWHC 1695 (Fam)). In 2001, in a judicial review case regarding the then-anonymous system of gamete donation, it was held that 'everyone should be able to establish details of [their] identity as a human being' and that this included the 'right to obtain information about a biological parent who will inevitably have contributed to the identity of the child' *R (on the application of Rose) v Secretary of State for Health & the HFEA* [2002] EWHC 1593 (Admin). In surrogacy, a right to 'identity' has been used as a justification for making parental orders in cases where there are questions about compliance with the requirements under s. 54 or s. 54A of the HFE Act 2008 (Brown & Wade, 2022; *X v Z (Parental Order: Adult)* [2022] EUFC 26; *A v P (Surrogacy: Parental Order: Death of Applicant)* [2011] EWHC 1738 (Fam); *Re X (A Child) (Parental Order: Time Limit)* [2014] EWHC 3135 (Fam); *Re A (A Child)* [2015] EWHC 911 (Fam)).[20]

These trends towards openness are also reflected in sociological research. It is argued that the support for openness 'draws upon a broader valorization of "transparency" in the political sphere', where increased availability of information is seen as efficient and just (Klotz, 2014, as cited in Gilman & Nordqvist, 2018, p. 317) While in the past secret-keeping (about genetic ties or lack thereof) was seen as being in the best interests of children or families, it has been argued that this came to be seen as immoral and harmful to intimate relationships (Nordqvist & Gilman, 2022; Smart, 2009, 2010).

The next sections explore participants' views on access to origin information about surrogacy.

Openness About Origins

This section begins with a breakdown of participants' answers to questions about knowledge of information in surrogacy (Table 3), before exploring their reasons for their responses. It follows with a breakdown of participants' answers regarding knowledge of gamete donors (Table 4) and a discussion of their views on this issue.

As can be seen from Table 3, the majority of participants were in favour of being open with children about surrogacy arrangements. In contrast to law and policy and trends in literature, participants did not justify openness in surrogacy by using the terminology of 'identity'. Neither did they talk about origin information in a legalistic way. They did not talk about children bearing rights which others have a responsibility to fulfil, which is the framing under a human rights based approach. For example, only nine participants (three in Phase One and six in Phase Two), mentioned the idea of a 'right to know'.[21] Three of these were

[20] On the requirements for a parental order, see Chapter 2, pp. 54–57.

[21] The breakdown is as follows. Phase One: Valeria, 9 (child of surrogate), Eliza (11, child of surrogate) and Lucy (15, child of surrogate). Phase Two: Bella (13), Jasmine (13), Cassie (17), Harry (16), Natalie (15) and Ella (14).

Table 3. Knowledge About Surrogacy Origins.

	Phase	n = 'Yes'	n = 'No'	n = 'Not Sure'	n = 'Maybe' (Only an Option in Phase Three)
Should children born through surrogacy be told they were born this way?	One	22 (88%)		3 (12%)	
	Two	20 (83%)	1 (4%)	3 (13%)	
	Three	5 (100%)			
Should children born through surrogacy know who their surrogate was?	One	21 (84%)		4 (16%)	
	Two	13 (54%)	2 (8%)	9 (38%)	
	Three	3 (60%)			2 (40%)
Should children born through surrogacy know whether the surrogacy was traditional or gestational?	One	15 (60%)	4 (16%)	6 (24%)	
	Two	16 (67%)	2 (8%)	6 (25%)	
	Three	3 (60%)			2 (40%)

children of surrogates and six were children without experience of surrogacy. Seven of these participants were teenagers (aged 13–16). This means that none of the participants born through surrogacy spoke of a right to know, and this kind of language was more prominent with older participants. This perhaps reflects the fact that all the participants who were born through surrogacy knew their surrogate and, therefore, had not considered the issue of such knowledge in a rights-based way. It may also reflect the fact that as children get older, they are more exposed to the concepts of rights/obligations and think more in these terms.[22]

A preference for openness was expressed in more colloquial terminology. Some participants simply stated that it would be 'good' or 'nice' to know, as seen in these quotes:

> It's just nice to know. (Ellie, 13, born through gestational surrogacy)

[22]Research on legal capability and human rights education shows low levels of awareness of human rights/children's rights amongst young people. See Struthers (2016; 2017) and Watkins et al. (2018).

> It would be nice if they did know. (Louisa, 13, child of surrogate)

> They might just feel. . .like. . .good that they know who gave birth to them. (Annabelle, 10)

Others framed their preference for openness around the fact that there was nothing shameful about knowing about one's birth through surrogacy, i.e., there was no reason *not* to tell, and there could be no harm from doing so, as can be seen in these quotes:

> I think yes, because I think it is an important part of their history and I don't think it is anything to be ashamed of. So, I don't see why they shouldn't be told. (Christina, 14, born through gestational surrogacy)

> I think that being born through surrogacy is nothing to be ashamed of. I think it is actually a cool way of being born. So, I put yes, because . . . other like children they should know, em, and yeah, like I said it is nothing to be ashamed of. I think it is quite cool actually. (Evalynn, 11, born through gestational surrogacy)

Such answers reveal that surrogacy is a positive experience for these participants; they already know about the manner of their birth, do not consider themselves harmed by knowing, nor do they see it as something shameful. In this regard, openness was a reality for participants with experience of surrogacy; all Phase One participants knew who their surrogate was and had contact with her; and in Phase Three, all participants knew and had met their surrogate, and three of the five also knew their egg donor. In line with this, positive experiences of surrogacy were also powerfully portrayed in the artwork of children born through surrogacy and children of surrogates (Wade & Mills, 2025), the prompt for which was: what surrogacy means to me? Artwork portrayed joy, pride and excitement, through bright colours, smiling faces and balloons, for example. One artwork simply stated 'no affect on me' [*sic*] which reflects the idea, above, that children should be told about surrogacy on the basis that it is not concerning information. This is also reflected in a UK-based study with 35 young adults born through egg donation, sperm donation or surrogacy, which found that for 40% of them, their conception made them feel special or unique, and for 60% it made them feel neutral or unconcerned (Jadva et al., 2023). These emotions about surrogacy are also explored in Chapter 5.[23]

While the term 'identity' was never used, the idea of identity came through in more colloquial language. Twins born through surrogacy said that children should know about surrogacy because it was 'an important part of their history' (Christina, 14, born through gestational surrogacy), and 'a big part at the beginning of their lives' (Jane, 14, born through gestational surrogacy). Anna

---

[23]See the theme: Disclosing Surrogacy: Pride and Openness in Chapter 5, pp. 148–153.

(16, cousin of a child born through surrogacy) said: 'they should know before going out into the world how they came into the world themselves'. Participants from Phase Two also mirrored such language, with Natalie (15) saying that children have a 'right to know' their surrogate as she 'is quite a big part of their existence', and Rose (13) saying that children 'deserve to know where they came from or like who they came from'. Some younger participants put this in simple terms, such as Lilly (9, child of surrogate), who said that children should know 'how they were made', and Jax (8), who said that they should know 'because that's the person who created them. . .sort of'. This idea was also expressed by Oliver (11, child of surrogate) in both a powerful and matter of fact way. He said:

> . . .[the surrogate] helped you be born, so I think it would be good if you knew the people. They basically made you alive.

Sometimes, knowing about surrogacy was framed more like knowing a 'story' that can help children understand surrogacy. For example, Camille (13, born through US gestational surrogacy and egg donation) said that knowing origin information would help children 'know and understand themselves a little better'. Aoife (10, child of surrogate) said that it would help children 'picture who did what and when'. Similarly, Christina (14, born through gestational surrogacy) explained that knowing her surrogate – seeing she was an actual person and being able to put a face to a name – helped her to understand that she carried her.

While the term 'identity' is not used in these accounts, it does appear that participants are talking about the idea of 'personal identity', in the sense that it is about attributes that make an individual unique (Olson, 2003, p. 352) and that it is something akin to a 'narrative' approach, whereby a person creates an 'integrated life story' (McAdams & McLean, 2013, p. 233). As McAdams & McLean (2013) note, '[t]hrough narrative identity, people convey to themselves and to others who they are now, how they came to be and where they think their lives may be going in the future' (p. 233). With these participants, there is an emphasis in knowing the start of one's story, that is, how one came to be and who was involved. However, participants did not go as far as to say that such information was *constitutive* of identity. It has been argued that in Euro-American cultures, information about reproduction has a 'constitutive character' (Strathern, 1999) and that such information has implications for both identity and kinship (Gilman & Nordqvist, 2018). However, while the participants supported openness, they did not seem to suggest that the absence of origin information would have devastating impacts on a child's sense of 'self' or 'identity'. As above, knowing about such information was seen as being 'good', 'nice' or 'better'.

Some participants were concerned that keeping secrets from children or children finding out inadvertently would lead to distress and negative outcomes in the family. For example, Tom (11, born through gestational surrogacy) commented that if children were not told and then inadvertently found out, they might feel 'betrayed'. Lucy (15, child of surrogate) also said children might feel 'betrayed' if they were to 'stumble across information later in life'. The issue of betrayal also came up in Phase Two. Some participants also noted the potential negative effects of finding out inadvertently. For example, Katie (10) mentioned the idea of children being 'angry', 'crying' and 'upset' in such circumstances, because they would be finding out that their parents are not their 'real parents'. These kinds of insights are in line with the trends outlined above in both law and sociological research, which indicate that openness is preferable to non-disclosure and that secret-keeping in families can be harmful (Nordqvist & Gilman, 2022; Smart, 2009, 2010).

Two participants who were born through surrogacy mentioned the issue of 'siblings' born to the same surrogate.[24] When answering the question about whether a child should know if the surrogacy was gestational or traditional, Jane (14, born through gestational surrogacy) said:

> I think they should know, because they could end up having siblings that they don't know of, and I think it's important that they know of these siblings. As long as everyone is, of course, comfortable with the knowledge.

When asked about whether children should know if they were born with the use of gamete donation, Scarlett (11, born through gestational surrogacy) said:

> I said "yes", because the children might want to know if they've maybe got like a half-brother or sister and they might, they'd know if they've got a family.

These participants born through surrogacy had clearly thought through the implications of traditional surrogacy and gamete donation, i.e., that a child may have genetic links with other children, and considered these 'lateral ties'[25] to also be meaningful, even though this did not apply to their situation.

Regarding reasons for openness about gamete donation, some participants attached importance to knowing about genetic links with others, as seen in the following quotes:

> I think they should know about their egg donor because they would technically be related to them. (Oliver, 11, child of surrogate)

> They're related to the donor, so they should know. (Ashley, 12, born through traditional surrogacy)

---

[24]However, it should be noted that the language of 'siblings' was not always used and, was sometimes objected to, when referring to children linked through surrogacy. See Chapter 5, pp. 164–167.

[25]See Nordqvist & Gilman (2024) for the use of this term to refer to donor siblings.

Table 4. Knowledge About Gamete Donors.

	Phase	**n = 'Yes'**	**n = 'No'**	**n = 'Not Sure'**	**n = 'Maybe' (Only an Option in Phase Three)**
If the surrogacy involves egg or sperm donation, should children born through surrogacy be told about this?	One*	15 (75%)	1 (5%)	4 (20%)	
	Two	10 (42%)	3 (13%)	11 (46%)	
	Three	4 (80%)			1 (20%)
Should children know who the egg or sperm donor is?	One**	N/A	N/A	N/A	
	Two	8 (33%)	3 (13%)	13 (54%)	
	Three	4 (80%)			1 (20%)

*Only 20 were asked this in Phase One.[26]
**This was not asked in Phase one.

It may be the case, that since she is born through traditional surrogacy and knows she is genetically related to her surrogate, Ashley is in support of others knowing the information that she herself knows. However, other participants seemed to attach less importance to genetic links, and said that children should only be told if they ask about these (Eliza, 11, child of surrogate; Aoife, 10, child of surrogate). Two participants born through gestational surrogacy (twins Scarlett and Evalynn, 11) said that while *they* would like to know, others may not, and so they were not sure whether children *should* know. Here, while genetics was seen as important, this information was not framed as something that was necessary for children to have. For example, in Phase Two, Lydia (16) said:

> I said that no, I don't think it's necessary, unless it's obvious. . .if it's a lone parent or a same-sex couple. . .but then if it's a male-female couple, then I don't think it's necessary, because I don't think that it would change anything.

Liam (18) pointed out the difficulties he thought disclosure could raise for the child in terms of attachment to the intended parents. He said that children should *not* be told about being donor conceived. He stated:

[26] As can be seen from Table 4, one focus group was not asked about donor conception at all, as we felt that there was not much engagement with the concept and because of timing. We did not ask: 'Should children know who the egg or sperm donor is?' in Phase One, as we wanted to keep the focus on surrogacy with this group who had experience of it.

> ...it could be hard for the child to see their intended parent or parents as their real parents, if that makes sense, especially if it's like a male and a female intended parent, then I think it could be hard for them to have that attachment with them if they know that they're almost not, they've not been involved in it.

On the other hand, some of the younger participants said that knowledge of donor conception could be a positive experience for children, as it might make them feel that there is a person who cares about them. Annabelle (10) brought up the idea of feeling special. She said:

> They might feel...like...special because they might be like, "Wow, somebody was... somebody actually donated an egg or sperm to make me".
>
> Similarly, Henry (10) said:
>
> I put "yes" because you would know then if they actually, like, cared about you, so much so that they...like what I said for [the previous question], because I would want to know if they cared about me so much so they gave up their sperm or egg to actually have me be born.

Another opinion expressed in Phase Two was that children should know this information in order to understand the nature and level of the intended parents' contribution, which they described as 'work' or 'care', as illustrated in the following quotes:

> I think "yes" because, well, I think you should know, if it was traditional, like, "Oh, so, my intended parents didn't really work that hard to help me be born". Or if it was a gestational, I think they'd be, like, very happy because, "Oh, my intended parents really cared for me. They really wanted me to be in their lives. They actually physically really, really wanted me so much that they actually went through that process". (Diego, 10)
>
> Like what Diego said, I would like to know if my parents actually cared about me that much to give them their own egg or sperm for me to be born. I wouldn't just, like, want to figure out that that's been kept a secret from me all my life. (Henry, 10)

This idea that the contribution of gametes in the conception of a child as 'care' or 'work' is an interesting insight into children's views on the role of genetics. Henry and Annabelle saw donation as a 'caring act' for the child, and Henry and Diego saw intended parents contributing gametes as being a 'caring' act or amounting to putting in 'work' to have a child. Why genetics or the physical act of donating gametes was linked to 'care' or 'work', was not explored. However, it could be argued that the requirement for a genetic link with one intended parent under s. 54 (1)(b) and s. 54A(1)(b) HFE Act 2008 for a parental order to be granted, reflects a version of this idea, namely, that such a link somehow legitimises a couple's or person's relationship with a child who is born through surrogacy.[27] It is also reflective of the above ideas that it is 'nice' to know about donation or surrogacy, and that learning about the intentions of the people involved can be a positive experience for children.

Respect for Children's Autonomy

Participants also framed knowing about origin information in terms of children's autonomy. However, this word was not used by any participants; the idea was expressed in more colloquial language. For example, participants stressed that disclosure of origin information to children depended on whether they 'want to know', 'ask questions' or 'show curiosity'. For example, when asked about whether children born through surrogacy should know if the surrogacy was traditional or gestational, two participants said the following:

> I put "yes", because if they were to ask the question, they should be told and it shouldn't be kept a secret from them. (Aoife, 10, child of surrogate).
>
> Well, I think if the child born through surrogacy asks their intended parents, their parents, if it was gestational or traditional then I think the intended parents should tell that child then if they straight ask. I don't think that really needs to be something they just blurt out. If they want to tell the child, then yeah, but if the child asks then definitely I think they should know. (Eliza, 11, child of surrogate)

Sometimes, participants who answered 'no' or 'not sure' as to whether parents should tell their children about origin information, caveated this with the idea that children should always be told if they asked. For example, Ivy (15) said:

> I think that if the child would ask the parent, their parents – the intended parents – if they wanted to know more about the surrogacy, then yes, but I don't think that the surrogacy, the different types of surrogacy, is that important to specify to the child. I think that if the child does want to know more about the surrogacy, then it can be mentioned, but they're not forced to tell the child about it.

[27]The policy reasons for the genetic link requirement in the current law, international stances and Law Commissions' proposals have not been clearly stated (see Park-Morton, 2024b, 2025).

Jasmine (11), in response to the question as to whether children should know if surrogacy involved egg or sperm donation, stated:

> I put "not sure", I guess, because, just like my last answer, it's only if they really want to know because if they're perfectly happy as they are, then only if they want to know. But, I'm not sure they need to be told.

In relation to telling children about who the surrogate is, Alison (12, born through US surrogacy and egg donation) took a similar approach and said:

> Maybe. If they want to know who it was they should definitely be told who it was or be able to know who it was. If it doesn't really affect them or if they don't really care about it then I don't think it matters if they know or not.

This approach of telling children 'if they want to know' or 'if they ask' was linked to the idea of not 'forcing' children to know information about surrogacy that they 'don't want to know'. This issue sparked a debate in one interview in Phase Two, with the group split into those who thought children should know (Alice, 13; Bella, 13) and those who said they should know 'if they want to know' or if they 'show curiosity' (Leonard, 12; Jasmine, 11). For example, Leonard (12) said that children should know information only if they want to know, and that no one should be forced to know something they might not want to know. However, Alice and Bella questioned how it could be known if children want to know origin information without telling them, since they would not know to ask about surrogacy unless they knew they were born this way. For example, Bella said: 'Yes, but they wouldn't...know...they're a part of that, you know, they wouldn't know that they were made like that'.

This debate reflects an ethical tension in this area of law. Some argue for disclosure of the manner of a child's birth to children to enable them to make their own decisions about accessing origin information (Ravitsky, 2012; Wade, 2020). Natalie (15) reflects this approach when asked if children should know the identity of their surrogate. She stated: 'I said "yes", so that the child could make an informed decision about whether or not perhaps they want to meet the surrogate, whether or not they care about it...'. On the other hand, it is questioned whether there is a 'right *not to know*', which appears to be what Leonard and Jasmine are referring to above.[28] Katie, from a different interview also seemed to reflect this view and said: '...say if you didn't want to know – you don't have to know, but if you really wanted to know then maybe ask your [intended parents]'.

Some participants gave suggestions about how a potential 'right not to know' could be respected. For example, Ivy (15) said:

[28]The 'right not to know' is more commonly used regarding knowledge of genetic disease. See Brownsword & Wale (2017); Laurie (2000).

> I think that, so, when the parent tells the child, if the child asked more questions about it, maybe when they are an older age, like 12 or above that, then the parents can tell them, if they ask questions about specifically, like, who was involved in the surrogacy, if the child asked questions similar to that, then yes, they can be told about it.
>
> ...you should save other things for whether the child wants to know. You can say, we can tell you this, or we can talk about this, if you want to know. And it's up to them to decide if that's something they want to hear.

Natalie (15) suggested the following:

> It's more you kind of explained to them, we love you very, very much. But perhaps if this is something you want to know more about, or you want to meet your surrogate, then we could facilitate that. It's just more about letting the children make a decision.

This is a nuanced response to the ethical tension of telling children information so that they can exercise their autonomy in relation to it. These approaches suggest telling children information incrementally in line with their wishes, but do seem to indicate that they would need to be told about the manner of their birth, as a starting point. This is in line with professional recommendations (Ethics Committee of the American Society of Reproductive Medicine [ECASRM], 2018; European Society of Human Reproduction and Embryology [ESHRE] Working Group on Reproductive Donation, 2022) guidance from donor conception support organisations[29] and from surrogacy organisations.[30] Research also shows that disclosure of donor conception leads to positive psychological outcomes for children (Golombok, 2015, 2017, 2020(b); Golombok et al., 2017, 2023), with studies demonstrating that families with disclosure of donor conception in pre-school years showed more positive psychological outcomes and more positive mother-child relationships when children reached middle school (Ilioi et al., 2017). It is interesting that this debate occurred in Phase Two, with children without experience of surrogacy. This kind of debate may not have occurred in Phase One and Three, since those children knew about their birth through surrogacy and knew their surrogate, and therefore, may not have considered this as an ethical dilemma. This shows the value of speaking to different groups of children with different lived experience when exploring law and policy reform, since those with lived experience may not

---

[29]See guidance from the Donor Conception Network: https://dcnetwork.org/telling-and-talking/why-openness-matters/and n. 18.

[30]See n. 8.

consider certain ethical or legal dimensions that have not arisen for them personally.

The second issue that was stressed by participants was that disclosure about origins should be child-dependent. Participants recognised that all children are different and, therefore, there can be no one approach to disclosure, as illustrated in the following quotes:

> I think it all depends on the situation and the circumstances and the type of child that they are, and because some children are more emotional. Some children are really, really good at understanding things and can take things and process them in their own way, whereas some children can't do that and so I think it all depends on the parents [and] on the child. (Lucy, 15, child of surrogate)

> ... every child is different. Parents will know when to tell them and how to tell them because people deal with things differently, and they could take it well or they couldn't, but I think it's best to tell them and so they understand. (Emily, 8, child of surrogate)

Jack (17, child of surrogate) noted how disclosure should not only be specific to children's understanding levels. He also recognised that different backgrounds in families may change how information disclosure is approached. He stated:

> Kids need to learn things at different ages and different people wanna teach in different ways and you know, depending on who they are and their family and their religion and background and all this kind of stuff.

In line with this, much was said about appropriate times and ages to tell children. It was stressed that disclosure must be at an age where they can understand. Leonard (12) indicated that a suitable age for disclosure was 16 or 18, giving the following reason:

> because, like, if you tell them when they're young, (a) they're going to forget it and (b) they might start worrying about it and think it's a big thing.

Similarly, Ivy (15) suggested disclosure over the age of 12 or 15. However, some participants suggested telling at a younger age, such as 'four or five' (Jasmine, 11), 'five' (Bella, 13), 'six or seven' (Alice, 13) and 'seven or eight' (Evalynn, 11, born through gestational surrogacy). Some participants did not specify an age for disclosure but said that it should be led by the child themselves, when they start to ask questions. For example, Aoife (10, child of surrogate) said: 'when they are ready' and 'when they start asking questions'; and Scarlett (11, born through gestational surrogacy) stated: 'when they start to get curious about how babies are born'. The views of the participants align with a longitudinal study with children born through donor conception (Ilioi et al., 2017). It was found that within families which disclosed the information, more positive family relationships and higher levels of well-being were evident among adolescents who had been told about the nature of their conception before the age of seven. Ilioi et al., therefore, argue that the earlier children are told, the more positive the outcomes are.

Other participants talked about not having one moment of disclosure, and said that information should be told to children incrementally throughout their childhood. For example, some said that parents should: 'dot it around a lot' (Valeria, 9, child of surrogate) or 'drip feed the idea of surrogacy and just normalise it' (Jane, 14, born through gestational surrogacy). Similarly, Jack (17, child of surrogate) stated:

> I think in an ideal situation they should be told as soon as possible, like, there shouldn't be a kind of sit down "OK, here is how you came to be." It just should, kind of, always be a known thing.

This method of disclosure was reflected in the experiences of those born through surrogacy. For example, Scarlett (11, born through gestational surrogacy) said that she could not remember when she was told; and Ellie (13, born through gestational surrogacy) said that she did not recall when she was told, as she 'always' knew. She said:

> I think, I can't really remember when we were told. I think we knew from pretty young. I don't really remember, it was always in the back of my mind, there wasn't really a shock really.

The approaches proposed by the participants suggest that disclosure should be led by children themselves. These insights are reflective of a recent study with donor-conceived young people aged 17–26, where it was found that the participants valued having control over the process of accessing donor information, having options and proceedings at their own pace (Maas et al., 2026).[31] The findings also align with a study by Gilman et al. (2025), in which parents of donor-conceived children felt that the decision to make contact with donor relatives was a decision for their children, to allow them to define kin in their own terms. However, participants did not think that questions about knowledge of, or access to, origin information was one for children alone, but also deferred to parents as decision-makers in this context, as explored in the next section.

[31]Research with young adults shows that the level of interest and motivations for accessing information donors vary considerably among donor-conceived people (Maas et al., 2026; Zadeh, 2024).

Deference to Parents

As outlined above, participants were concerned with openness and children's autonomy. However, in all Phases, there was also strong support for parental discretion. There was deference to parents in terms of whether children should know about their birth through surrogacy and how information should be disclosed. Therefore, while there was a strong support for disclosure of origin information to children, participants were not comfortable with the concept of force, as seen in the following quotes:

> I think it would be nice for them to know but they don't have to. (Louisa, 13, child of surrogate)
>
> I think the parents should decide if the child should know. (Steve, 9, born through US gestational surrogacy)
>
> Yes, I think it would be great to tell them. Again, like I've said for a lot of these it's not compulsory. It is not going to affect them hugely if they don't know but it would be quite nice again, to have that relationship with the donor if you can or to at least know and understand yourself a little bit better in that sense. (Camille, 13, born through US gestational surrogacy)

While it is not clear whether the above quotes refer to a lack of support for social/moral pressure or legal measures regarding disclosure, one participant directly engaged with the concept of law in this context. He said:

> I don't think there should be any specific laws on: "you must tell your child this point, you must tell your child at that point". I think it'd be good for kids to find out more if they want to...to have something in place for kids born through surrogacy to find out information about it if they want to, but I don't think there should be any rigid like "you must tell your child at this point", "you must not tell your child stuff like that", because it just doesn't seem fair. (Jack, 17, child of surrogate)

Jack also considered that disclosure of surrogacy may have negative consequences in some families, and said 'the [intended parents] might be in a situation where it's not safe for them, safe family-wise, to talk about how they've had a surrogate'. This shows that Jack is concerned with the entire family unit, and recognises that disclosure also impacts the intended parents, as well as the child. Anna (16, cousin of a child born through surrogacy) noted how in some families, the intended parents may not tell their own family about the surrogacy, making it harder to tell their child. This aligns with research in the area of donor conception, which emphasises how donation within a family has a wider impact than just the parent-child relationship, and this may impact whether and when parents disclose to their children (see Nordqvist & Smart, 2014, pp. 48–67).

Moreover, these views reflect the fact that stigma associated with infertility, child-bearing and reproduction, which can be influenced by cultural or religious beliefs, can affect how open certain families are about the use of assisted reproduction (Culley et al., 2006; Hudson & Culley, 2014).

The other way that this issue was expressed by participants was a concern that both intended parents and surrogates need to be 'comfortable' with disclosure, as can be seen in these quotes:

> I think if the parents didn't feel comfortable with it ... I'm not really sure, because in some cases, it might not necessarily matter, but I'm not sure. (Harry, 16). (In response to the question: should children know if the surrogacy was traditional or gestational?)

> I said "yes", because it will help the child ... like ... understand the surrogacy, and also they were such a big part of the beginning of their life, and I don't think they should just be cut out ... ehm ... But I don't think ... if anyone is uncomfortable with it, I don't think it should be a forced thing. (Jane, 14, born through gestational surrogacy) (In response to the question: should children know who the surrogate was?)

This need for everyone to be comfortable was also linked to the idea that disclosure of origins can lead to contact between the families. This was explained by Camille (13, born through US gestational surrogacy), in the following quote:

> I think if you still know who the surrogate was, you know where they are, you know who they are, introducing the surrogate child to that parent might be appropriate but only again if it is consensual on both party sides because the [intended parents] might not want that, the surrogate might not want that.

Another concern regarding contact related to parent-child bonding. Some participants felt that there should be parental discretion regarding disclosure of origin information because children might experience bonding with surrogates or donors, which might be inappropriate, as seen in the following quotes:

> I think they should know who their surrogate was because then they could get in contact with them and they're not going to ... they may prefer them to their actual Mum if they tell them the actual truth, but it really does depend if their parents don't want them to know and, if they're going to ever know... (Ava, 10, child of surrogate)

> I said "yes", but I think it depends on the relationship between the surrogate and the child. If they don't have a very strong

> relationship, then telling them something like that might make them drift apart even more. But if they have a strong relationship and they're close to each other, then I think that they'd be able to take it well. So, I think it's dependent on the relationship. (Lydia, 16)

These ideas are also reflected in research with adults in the area of donor conception, where it was found that parents who were opposed to establishing contact with donor relatives during childhood were concerned that such relatives may try to claim their child as kin and that this could be problematic (Gilman et al., 2025). The quotes above also seem to reflect their finding that childhood is often seen as a time when the making of kinship bonds may be intensified or heightened (Gilman et al., 2025).

Interestingly, one participant, whose cousin was born through surrogacy, noted that it might be difficult for the *surrogate* to have contact with a baby born through surrogacy. Anna (16) said:

> the surrogate might feel a bit like, it might be a bit hard for them, like to have too much contact because it might make them have a bond and a relationship with that baby, 'cause that's the only hard thing about being a surrogate, that relationship, trying not to build too much of a relationship with them.

Two participants in Phase One recognised a different concern for intended parents, to do with the difficulty in being open about infertility or in accepting a lack of gestational or genetic links with their child. Jack (17, child of surrogate) noted how it could be 'really hard to talk about', in the case of infertile parents who were not genetically related to a child born through assisted reproduction. Similarly, Lucy (15, child of surrogate) said that sometimes parents find infertility 'difficult to talk about it', as they may feel there is 'something wrong with them'. She also said:

> it might make situations difficult in. . .knowing that, although you wanted, if you want that child, it's not your child and that I feel like [disclosure] could hurt people.

This participant's view reflects the idea of 'genetic grief', which is described as an emotional response to being unable to have a genetically related child.[32] These views also recognise the stigma and shame that is often associated with infertility (Cosson et al., 2022a, 2022b; Culley & Hudson, 2006; Culley et al., 2006; Reissman, 2000). Lucy does not explain why parents may find the lack of a

[32]See a definition of genetic grief from Donor Conceived UK as: 'an emotional reaction experienced by individuals or couples who are unable to pass on their genetic material to their children'. See: https://donorconceiveduk.org.uk/genetic-grief/.

genetic connection with a child difficult; it is taken as self-evident. Interestingly, Lucy did not herself see parenthood as based on genetics, but she still recognised the role genetics can play for some people in this regard.[33]

The participants recognised the autonomy of children but also that of parents; there was recognition that parents should have some say over the disclosure of information about origins. Such approaches reflect a relational idea of autonomy, i.e., one which considers the social embeddedness of persons and the intersubjective and social dimensions of the self (Mackenzie & Stoljar, 2000).[34] Such accounts recognise that when people make decisions, they consider the impact on those with whom they are socially embedded. The participants' answers often reflected such an approach, in the sense that children's autonomy is seen as important, but as operating within a network of relationships. Participants were aware that knowing about or accessing information about surrogates or donors had implications for the entire family. This may reflect ideas about how such information can have a profound and sometimes 'disruptive' impact within families, in terms of relationships and ideas of relatedness (Haimes, 1990; Konrad, 2005; Smart, 2011).[35] Some participants did seem to recognise that such information may be difficult for parents, and were concerned that all those impacted needed to be 'comfortable' with disclosure. Such an approach is reflective of moral reasoning which is based on an 'ethics of care'. This approach is shaped by the centrality of relationships to people's ordinary moral experiences (Abbott, 2024, p. 185). It is recognised that relationships give rise to responsibilities and that conflict resolution can be addressed with communication (Gilligan, 1993, p. 3) and is, therefore, concerned with not causing hurt to both self and others (Bridgeman, 2025, p. 156).[36]

It should be noted, however, that such an approach is not always taken. For example, while Anna (16, cousin of a child born through surrogacy), Jack (17, child of surrogate) and Lucy (15, child of surrogate) recognised difficulties for parents regarding disclosure, they all said that, if children want to know, they should be told, with Lucy noting that children have a 'right to know', Jack saying that information should not be 'withheld from them', and Anna saying they 'deserve to know'. These older participants appear to be employing a more 'ethics of justice' style of reasoning, which is based on universal, detached reasoning

[33]When asked what makes someone a parent, Lucy referred to: 'constant commitment to the child' and 'responsibility'.

[34]This could also be said to reflect relational concepts of the self, whereby the 'self is created by our relationships with others'. For example, Herring (2019) argues that a focus on rationality underplays 'the worries, prejudices, unwanted desires, ambivalences and fears that are central to human experience' and that 'the self is constituted by and through our relationships' (p. 12).

[35]It has been argued that knowledge of genetic connectedness is not 'mere knowledge', but knowledge about kinship and self (Strathern, 1999, as cited in Smart, 2010).

[36]For arguments about the usefulness of a care-based approach in family law contexts, see Smart & Neale, 1999, pp. 193–195. They argue for principles of care, which would recognise that transitions in families must be handled slowly and sensitively, and that connectedness between family members should not be achieved through coercion.

about 'duties' or what is 'morally right' (Abbott, 2024, p. 160). In this sense, while balancing the interest of children and their parents, these participants recognised the potential difficulties for parents in disclosing information about origins, but reasoned that the children's interests in knowing information outweighs this.

Conclusion: Insights for Law, Policy and Practice

The first important insight for law, policy and practice is that the majority of these participants believe it is preferable to be open with children about surrogacy and gamete donation. The encouragement of openness is established practice in the United Kingdom; it is facilitated by the law in gamete donation (through the introduction of identity-release donors),[37] as well as by donor conception and surrogacy support organisations. The views of the participants in this project, therefore, support all measures that are taken in the United Kingdom to encourage openness. The creation of a new Surrogacy Register is also ideologically aligned with the views of the participants; it would allow children born through surrogacy to access information about genetic, gestational and 'intention-based' links, in circumstances where that information is not already known to them.[38] However, it should be noted that children talked about disclosure occurring within family units, while the proposed Register may be more to do with children accessing information that has not been available to them from their families. While the participants are not envisaging contact in this context, if the Surrogacy Register were to increase openness (through messaging about the importance of origin information) this would be a positive outcome, and one which these participants would likely support.

It must be noted, however, that notwithstanding support for openness in current law and policy, some studies in the United Kingdom show low levels of disclosure. In 21 embryo donation families, there was a disclosure rate of 2% (MacCallum et al., 2007), in 17 egg-donation families, 47% did not intend to disclose (Murray & Golombok, 2003). A study of 33 families involving traditional surrogacy showed 58% disclosed the use of the surrogate's egg (Jadva et al., 2012). The findings in this chapter lend support to the argument that openness with children about surrogacy and gamete donation is best practice. Therefore, we suggest that a summary of these findings, including the insights from the artwork (Wade & Mills, 2025), should be referenced in guidance that is given to intended parents when advising them on assisted reproduction, to demonstrate to them that children themselves are also encouraging of openness. This includes guidance by the HFEA and the British Infertility Counselling

---

[37]As noted, disclosure of information about surrogates is unregulated, but in the case of surrogacy, openness is likely as it is harder to conceal due to the friendship-based models of the surrogacy organisations.

[38]It should be noted that the Law Commissions do not suggest any punitive measures for intended parents who refuse to provide or cannot provide information for the Register (in the case of anonymous gamete donation used abroad for example). See Wade (2025).

Association,[39] who provide counselling to those undergoing fertility treatment in HFEA-licensed fertility clinics.[40] The project's findings could also be cited in the Department of Health and Social Care (DHSC) guidance on surrogacy for intended parents (Department of Health and Social Care, 2018a) which states that openness, confidence and transparency about surrogacy is best for children. Not all assisted reproduction involves clinics, and counselling is not mandatory. Therefore, it is important that the organisations who support those using surrogacy and/or gamete donation, such as SurrogacyUK (SUK), My Surrogacy Journey, Brilliant Beginnings, the Donor Conception Network, Donor Conceived UK and Paths to Parenthub, also continue to provide information on the importance of openness and could include this project's findings to support this.[41] A good example of such engagement with research is the HFEA webpage on 'Finding out about your Donor' which cites empirical research with those with experience of donor conception from the ConnecteDNA and the Young Adults Study.[42]

It should also be noted that openness, at least in relation to gamete donation, is also by no means the norm globally (Nordqvist et al., 2025), with some jurisdictions permitting anonymous gamete donation[43] and anonymous surrogacy.[44] Therefore, we also suggest that any international guidance on surrogacy and gamete donation (ECASRM, 2018; ESHRE Working Group on Reproductive Donation et al., 2022) should cite these research findings to show children's support for openness. This can be done in an engaging way through interviews and blogs. For example, international non-governmental bodies, namely, the International Social Service and the Child Identity Protection

---

[39]See the guidance at: https://www.hfea.gov.uk/donation/finding-out-about-your-donor and https://www.bica.net/browse.

[40]Licensed clinics should ensure that surrogates, any partner of the surrogate and intended parents should attend implications counselling (separately). See HFEA (2023a) paras. 14.7–14.14.

[41]The authors provided a blog post for SUK in Surrogacy Awareness Week in 2022, entitled Hearing from Children on Surrogacy Law: What are the important questions? See Surrogacy UK website https://surrogacyweek.co.uk/2022/08/03/hearing-from-children-on-surrogacy-law-what-are-the-important-questions/. We also provided a podcast called 'Children of Surrogacy'. See SUK podcasts: https://surrogacyuk.org/podcasts/.

[42]See https://www.hfea.gov.uk/donation/finding-out-about-your-donor. The leaflets created by the ConnecteDNA project on the HFEA website are also hosted on the websites of the British Fertility Society and the Association of Reproductive and Clinical Scientists. See Frith (2026). See also: https://sites.manchester.ac.uk/connecte-d-n-a/and https://www.youngadultsstudy.co.uk/.

[43]These include Spain and France. Denmark has a hybrid model where donors can be anonymous or identifiable (see Mulligan, 2022). For an overview of practices of American and Danish sperm banks, see Pennings, 2025.

[44]See n.12 above.

Network, have both engaged with the project in online written and video interviews.[45] A final point in this regard is that intended parents from the United Kingdom may undertake surrogacy in countries which allow anonymity in relation to gamete donors or surrogates. In this respect, the Law Commissions recommend that intended parents using clinics abroad should provide information regarding intended parents, surrogates and gamete donors to the Surrogacy Register, as a prerequisite for granting a parental order (Law Commission and Scottish Law Commission, 2023; para. 10.164). However, there are no penalties for being unable or unwilling to do so (Law Commission and Scottish Law Commission, 2023; para. 10.164). Given the participants' views on openness in this chapter and their positive experiences of contact with surrogates, incorporating disincentives, such as civil penalties, such as fines, could be considered in circumstances where origin information is not produced by intended parents (Wade, 2025).

A second insight for law and policy is that these participants considered that disclosure to children about their origins should be child-led, i.e., the process should be responsive to each individual child's understanding level and readiness to know. Some proposed a 'drip-feed' process whereby information is given to children in instalments, in which, at each stage, parents could assess their interest and readiness to receive information. It should also be noted that participants were clear that if children ask direct questions about their birth, they should be told the truth, again suggesting that what is important is the child's individual desire for information. This is a novel idea for information disclosure. The disclosure of information is not regulated in surrogacy, but such a disclosure method may already be used in practice and was reflective of some of the experiences of the children in this project who were born through surrogacy. Therefore, in this respect, such an approach should be included in the guidance for intended parents outlined above. As above, this project could be cited to explain that this approach to information disclosure is based on the views of children. In addition, the ages of disclosure proposed by the Law Commissions in relation to the Surrogacy Register would also allow for such an approach if the Register were used, since children could access information under this model under the age of 18, as outlined above.[46]

---

[45]The project team was interviewed by the International Social Service. See International Social Service (ISS) (2023). N° 267 – Children's voices in surrogacy law: an innovative UK research project aimed at putting children's views at the forefront. https://iss-ssi.org/resourcesiss/n-267-childrens-voices-in-surrogacy-law-an-innovative-uk-research-project-aimed-at-putting-childrens-views-at-the-forefront/. The PI conducted a video interview with Child Identity Protection (CHIP). See CHIP Website: https://www.child-identity.org/category/voices-chip-in/experts-chip-in/page/3/.

[46]It should be noted that the Surrogacy Register would seem to be more relevant for children who do not have information about an intended parent or surrogate, because a parent has not disclosed this information to them, meaning parental support for an application may not be present. Such circumstances would presumably be rare.

However, since surrogacy can also include gamete donation, the law on this issue is also relevant. A change in the law would be required to introduce a child-led disclosure model in gamete donation (in the context of HFEA-licensed clinics).[47] As explained above, non-identifying information about donors is accessible to children at age 16 and identifying information is available at age 18. This means that a gradual release of information about donors with oversight from parents is not possible. In this regard, the HFEA made recommendations to the DHSC to allow donor information to be available to donor-conceived children during childhood on request by parents (HFEA, 2023b). This has been prompted by advances such as direct-to-consumer DNA testing, which allows families to link with donors and donor siblings before the age of 18 (Gilman et al., 2025; Nordqvist et al., 2025). The HFEA has not set out details about how this information should be obtained. However, if different forms of information could be released with both parental and child consent or assent (Brown & Wade, 2024), this could facilitate the 'drip feed' model advanced above. Parents could tell their children about the nature of their birth through gamete donation, and if the child feels ready for information about the donor, this could be applied for together. The information applied for could be reflective of the child's wishes. This would be in line with views of the participants; both the autonomy of the child and that of the parent/s are seen as important, and therefore desires in relation to accessing origin information should be discussed between them. It should also be noted that if such a change were to occur, donors would need to be told that those born from their donation could find out their identity before they are aged 18.[48] In addition, any system of disclosing information to children about surrogacy and/or gamete donation would need to implement child-friendly application processes and child-friendly materials about origin information, in line with the ages and understanding of the applicants.

Third, regarding the issue of whether there must be an initial disclosure to a child conceived with surrogacy/gamete donation about the manner of their conception, models have been proposed that seek to (legally) ensure that children know they are born through surrogacy or gamete donation, either through notification systems or birth certificate annotations (Blyth et al., 2009; Wade, 2020). For example, it has been argued that children's interests, in relation to the exercise of their autonomy, should trump parental interests in not telling their children about the nature of their birth through surrogacy or gamete donation (Wade, 2020). Such birth certificate annotation systems have been introduced in

---

[47]For donors that are known to the family, this approach would not need a change to the law. Known donors can either donate in a HFEA-licensed clinic or donate through 'at-home' insemination. Known donation through at-home insemination is not likely in surrogacy, since a genetic link is required with one intended parent.

[48]The HFEA has proposed that if the law allowed for contact during childhood, clinics should be legally required to inform donors and recipient parents that children could discover their donor's identity before they are 18. (HFEA, 2023b, Proposal 9).

Victoria (Australia) and Ireland.[49] Similarly, as explained above, the Law Commissions suggest that birth certificates should be clear that children are born through surrogacy. In this respect, we did not directly ask participants about birth certificate notification; therefore, it cannot be known if this would be supported. On the one hand, participants did not support the idea of 'force', but on the other, the majority supported openness. Given that it would appear that initial disclosure of the fact of surrogacy/gamete donation would be needed to support openness and the child-led disclosure model advanced by many participants, it is possible that the birth certificate notification process recommended by the Law Commissions would have been supported by them. This is because such a notification would seek to ensure that openness would be the norm (on the assumption that parents would tell their children) and would still allow for the child-led disclosure system outlined above.[50] Since the certificate would only disclose the nature of the child's birth, it would still protect their interest not to find out information, since it would allow them to seek further information with support of their parents, if they wished. If birth certificate notification for surrogacy were introduced, birth certificates should also note if gamete donation was used, to ensure parity for children born through both forms of assisted reproduction (Wade, 2025). It is also essential that the wording on such birth certificates is written in child-friendly language (Wade, 2025).

A final implication for policy and practice is that a culture of openness about assisted reproduction is more likely to develop where there is social acceptance of the practice itself. If parents are open with their children about the nature of their birth, they cannot control who that child will tell. It would be preferable if both parents and children can feel comfortable telling those in their social circles about surrogacy and gamete donation in their lives. For example, telling a child that they must keep information about their origins through surrogacy or gamete donation a secret from their friends or other family members could have negative effects for children. It could make them feel shame or stigma attached to their manner of birth.[51] However, as will be shown in the next chapter, there is little knowledge of assisted reproduction practices among children and young people, meaning that for a culture of openness to flourish, education about different forms of family building for young people is needed. The issue of education is discussed in the next chapter.

---

[49]See Assisted Reproductive Treatment Act 2008 in Victoria; and s. 39(2) Children and Family Relationships Act 2015 (Republic of Ireland).

[50]However, it should be noted that children finding out purely through birth certificates without support from parents/carers is not the disclosure framework envisaged by children. Rather, the argument is that if birth certificate notification would potentially increase openness within families, this may be supported.

[51]It should be noted that none of the children with experience of surrogacy in this study felt shame about surrogacy, whether or not those around them understood it. See theme in Chapter 5: Disclosing Surrogacy: Pride and Openness, pp. 148–153. See also Wade & Mills (2025).

Chapter 5

Surrogacy in Children's Social Worlds

> 'Yeah, I'd rather tell people about it and be open about it. Then people can see, it's not some strange thing, it's just something that people do.'[1]

Introduction

This chapter explores understandings of surrogacy in children's social worlds. Despite the intensity of legal, policy and ethical debate surrounding surrogacy, there is a notable absence of empirical literature exploring children's own perspectives and lived experiences. Anti-surrogacy rhetoric often mobilises claims about children's welfare and best interests without reference to child-centred empirical data (Golombok, 2026; Horsey & Mahmoud 2025; Mahmoud, 2026b). For example, the 2025 UN Special Rapporteur's Report on global surrogacy asserted harms to children associated with surrogacy, with no direct evidence from children themselves (Horsey, 2025b; Jefford, 2025; Page, 2025). It simultaneously (2025, para. 17–18) dismissed evidence from the only longitudinal study into the psychological adjustment and well-being of surrogacy-born children, conducted by Golombok et al.,[2] describing this work as 'limited' (see Golombok, 2026).

This chapter addresses this gap by directly exploring children's views and discussing how they challenge prevailing assumptions within policy and academic debates. It explores how children with experience of surrogacy make sense of surrogacy in their everyday lives, focusing on how they feel about it, how they talk about it/who they talk about it to and how this is received by others. Further, it explores these children's experience of ongoing contact and connections formed during surrogacy. The chapter also examines the perceptions of children who do not have experience of surrogacy, including what they know (or do not

[1]Jack (17, child of surrogate).
[2]See Introduction, pp. 21–22, for a summary of the findings of this longitudinal study.

Children's Voices in Surrogacy Law, 147–177

doi:10.1108/978-1-83549-642-820261006

know/misunderstand), how they gain this knowledge and what they think they ought to know and why. It also discusses the extent to which children from both groups learn about surrogacy at school or elsewhere. The chapter concludes with lessons for policy and practice, drawn from the participants' insights. As mentioned in earlier chapters, it is important to note that participants in Phase One were recruited through domestic non-profit surrogacy organisations committed to altruistic surrogacy and those in Phase Three were recruited through a domestic non-profit surrogacy organisation that also specialises in international surrogacy in the United States; this may have shaped their views and the way they speak about surrogacy.[3]

In Phase One we asked: 'Do you tell people about surrogacy?' 'Do you have to explain it to people?' and 'Do you learn about surrogacy in school?' In Phase Three, we added: 'Is there anything you would like to add about your experience of being born through international surrogacy?' and 'Do you think children should be included in surrogacy law reform?' In Phase Two, the questions focused on participants' knowledge of surrogacy, what they learnt in school and whether they thought children should be included in law reform. While this chapter is mostly based on the responses to these questions, some of this chapter's findings draw on discussions related to the three substantive topics detailed in the previous chapters.

This chapter examines participants' experiences of and reflections on surrogacy, drawing out key patterns in how they understand, interpret and navigate these arrangements across six themes. The first theme, 'Disclosing surrogacy: pride and openness', captures how children perceive being born through surrogacy and how and when they discuss it with others. The second theme, 'Talking about surrogacy: misunderstandings and myths', highlights the persistence of inaccurate narratives surrounding surrogacy. Thirdly, 'Navigating surrogacy: the role of contact', explores how children understand ongoing relationships between families. The fourth theme, 'Navigating surrogacy: kinship and connections', examines how children make sense of familial roles and boundaries between biological, gestational and social forms of parenthood. The fifth theme, 'Educating about surrogacy: the need for surrogacy in schools', reflects participants' broader concern about social awareness and gaps in education. The final theme, 'Reforming surrogacy: the importance of engaging with young people', gives insights into the value children place on being included in conversations about law, policy and practice.

Disclosing Surrogacy: Pride and Openness

This section examines how surrogacy is portrayed, discussed and made sense of by children with experience of surrogacy. Amongst participants with experience of surrogacy in their lives, surrogacy is not a 'secret' and many expressed pride about being born through surrogacy or having a mother who acted as a

[3] See Chapter 1, p. 48.

surrogate. Among children born through surrogacy, in addition to feelings of pride, participants expressed happiness and gratitude, or said that surrogacy made them feel special. For example, Bill (11, born through US gestational surrogacy), explained:

> I am very proud... I think I am proud because it is a very special thing to be born by surrogacy and it is quite difficult in the UK so not very many people are in the UK.

His sister, Camille (13, born through US gestational surrogacy) agreed, describing surrogacy as:

> [a] hugely great solution to people who can't have kids, things like couples, single parents or maybe a fertility problem within the parents. It brings a connection. You still get to raise the child from a small baby rather than adopting as adopting doesn't always guarantee that but yes. I'm not sure how to go into detail about it but it is a great thing and I am very proud to be a child of surrogacy.

Camille also expressed pride extending beyond her own experience of being born through surrogacy to include vicarious pride in others who were involved. She highlighted the efforts made by her parents and the kindness of the surrogate and egg donor, as follows:

> My parents, ... They went through huge lengths to have us and the determination they put into that was amazing. I am proud of my surrogate because she was really kind. She didn't charge anything. She did that voluntarily completely, and my donor as well. She chose to help us out and that was really really sweet of her and I am so glad we are both in contact with them. They are really amazing people in our lives. They are amazing.

Similarly, participants whose mothers had been surrogates expressed pride in what she had done, as illustrated by the following quotes:

> Yeah, like all of my friends know... I've always been really open with it like because I'm really proud of my mum. ... like... for being a surrogate and for kind of helping these people in this way ... like... so with that like I've never hidden it. (Jack, 17, child of surrogate)

> I tell my friends about it and I said my mum's a surrogate, and they say "what's a surrogate?", and I say it's a person who carries for someone else probably because they probably have problems or can't carry anymore and then they understand me and say well that's very generous of your mum to do that, and I say "thank you". (Lilly, 9, child of surrogate)

Other participants were clear about surrogacy making them feel special in some way. Scarlett (11, born through gestational surrogacy) explained that telling her friends about being born through surrogacy elicited positive reactions, which made her happy. She said:

> My friends actually think it is really cool [to be born through surrogacy] and think it's a really nice way. And I completely agree. I think it is a really nice way to be created and just. . .yeah.

Her sister, Evalynn (11), agreed that it was 'a really nice way to be created' and that it made her special, linking this to the surrogate's 'kindness'. She said that:

> I enjoy being surrogacy born because it's something special about me and it makes me thankful for the kindness because if it was no kindness, I wouldn't, I probably wouldn't be here ... because my surrogate did it out of kindness.

Such positive perceptions of surrogates being 'nice' or 'kind' from children born through surrogacy has also been seen in other empirical studies (Jadva et al., 2012).

Likely because of these positive emotions, openness about surrogacy was prevalent: children are generally happy to tell others if they have been born through surrogacy or if their mother was a surrogate.[4] Most participants had told friends (and sometimes others) about how they were born or what their mothers had done, though the extent of this sharing varied.[5] Some confided only in their closest friends, others disclosed the information only when asked, while still others discussed it more openly, including with teachers. For example, Scarlett (11, born through gestational surrogacy) and Lilly (9, child of surrogate) described having told their 'friends'. Evalynn (11, born through gestational surrogacy) and Camille (13, born through US gestational surrogacy) said they told 'all my friends', while Anna (16, cousin of a child born through surrogacy) 'told everyone'. Among those whose mother had been a surrogate, Aoife (10) told her 'closest friend' and Louisa (13) told 'friends I've known for quite a while'.

Siblings Tom and Ellie (11 and 13, born through gestational surrogacy) explained that they only disclosed how they were born when specifically asked, or if the subject came up. Tom said:

---

[4]This corresponds with the findings produced from the artwork from the project, which depicted the themes love and positivity (Wade & Mills, 2025). It was clear that children were happy, positive and proud about surrogacy. This was depicted through smiling characters, bright colours and celebratory symbols like fireworks and balloons.

[5]This was also seen in Jadva et al.'s study (2023) with young adults born through surrogacy where there was a range of 'frequency of discussions' about how they were conceived, from 'very rarely' to 'fairly often' and none said they 'frequently' discussed it with others.

> If it comes up in conversation I don't try to hide it but I don't go around just saying it [as the] the first thing I tell people.

This may be because openness sometimes led to curiosity from others and the need to offer further explanation. For example, Ellie explained that after telling a teacher about it when younger, she was asked to talk about it in an assembly at school, which was 'quite a lot' for her.[6] She added:

> Now I don't tell many people because they don't need to know. If they're like "I heard from so and so you were born through this way" I would be like, "yeah". It's not a big secret, I just don't feel like people need to know.

Likewise, Christina (14, born through gestational surrogacy) said:

> So, I don't really introduce myself as ... a child born through surrogacy, but I think it comes up in a lot . . . because it is . . . like . . . part of me, it comes up in . . . some conversations, and obviously I am not going to . . . withhold that information like as if it is a secret.

Her sister, Jane (14), said that she doesn't 'just come out and say it' but talks about it if the subject arises, explaining that:

> [I]t's not that big, not that big a part of our life, and so, although people know about it, it's not . . . like ... the main thing that they know about us.

This was echoed by some children born through international surrogacy. For example, Alison (12, born through US gestational surrogacy) said 'I only tell them if they ask. I don't just go around telling people'. However, Bill (11) and Steve (9), both born through US gestational surrogacy, had not told their friends. Bill elaborated, as follows:

> I don't know why. There is no reason. I just haven't thought it necessary to tell them a random fact. I'm not ashamed of it. I'm not worried what anyone will think about it, [I] just haven't told them.

Later, he discussed having told 'all his friends' he was born in the United States; he said he thought this was 'cool', and that he disclosed his birth by surrogacy if asked. Steve said that talking about surrogacy 'makes me slightly

---

[6]She said this happened in Year 3, so she would have been aged 7–8 years old. The very fact of having been asked by a teacher to do this suggests limited coverage of surrogacy in schools, certainly before that age, as indicated in the fifth theme discussed in this chapter at pp. 168–173.

sad sometimes' but did not want to say why. Later, when discussing whether people should learn about surrogacy in school, he explained that he would feel less sad if this happened, as then everyone would know more about it:

> I wouldn't feel as sad so I would definitely feel happier telling people if more people knew about [surrogacy].

In further discussions, Steve's 'sadness' about telling appeared to be linked to the idea that others did not understand or *believe* him. When asked whether he felt sad about surrogacy 'in his life' (that is, the fact of being born through surrogacy), he said 'no'.

Overall, participants expressed pride and were open about surrogacy. This is despite the fact that they sometimes encountered curiosity, negative assumptions or myths about surrogacy, as we discuss below. Such negativity is often seen on social media and in news articles about surrogacy, from people who often base their comments on preconceptions, or from those deliberately seeking to spread mis/disinformation about surrogacy, often conflating issues that may arise in unregulated surrogacy destinations with surrogacy practice in the United Kingdom (Golombok, 2026; Horsey & Mahmoud, 2025; Mahmoud, 2026b). The participants' accounts of pride and being 'special' stand in sharp contrast to claims made by anti-surrogacy organisations, which argue that surrogacy invariably harms children by disrupting the bond between birth mother and child, resulting in a so-called 'primal wound' with lifelong consequences (Nordic Model Now, 2019b).[7] Such organisations claim that such separation can lead to mental health problems including depression, anxiety and behavioural problems, as well as likely difficulties in forming relationships (Nordic Model Now, 2019b). Although there are some accounts from adults who say they were harmed by discovering they were born through surrogacy – often in circumstances that were far from ideal (see, for example, Maurel, 2026; Stop Surrogacy Now UK, 2025a, 2025b),[8] there is no empirical evidence to support claims of systematic harm. On the contrary, empirical research points in the opposite direction, as seen in the longitudinal study of surrogate-born children followed from infancy through to adulthood discussed in the Introduction (see also Golombok et al., 2017, 2023; Jadva et al., 2023).[9] The experience of these participants also mirrors findings from a study with young adults born through surrogacy which found that they do not feel negatively about their birth, likely because of openness about how they were

---

[7]The concept of the 'primal wound' emerged from adoption literature, with its genesis in American author Nancy Verrier's 1993 book '*The Primal Wound: Understanding the Adopted Child*'. Verrier posits that a 'primal wound' is caused when a mother and child are separated by adoption shortly after childbirth. Anti-surrogacy groups have co-opted the term, assuming it to apply to the separation of a surrogacy-born child from the person who gave birth, despite the intentionality behind surrogacy arrangements.

[8]See also *R (on the application of Rose) v Secretary of State for Health & the HFEA* [2002] EWHC 1593 in relation to gamete donation (see Chapter 4, p. 125).

[9]Introduction, pp. 21–22.

conceived and the young age at which this became known to them (Jadva et al., 2023; see also Blake et al., 2014, pp. 257–258; Zadeh et al., 2018).

Talking About Surrogacy: Misunderstandings and Myths

Those who disclosed their connection to surrogacy to their peers were often faced with a lack of understanding. Children who did not have experience of surrogacy were generally unaware of what surrogacy means or what it entails. This was also reported by children born through surrogacy and by children of surrogates. Nearly every time the participants who had lived experience of surrogacy talked about surrogacy to their peers they found that they had to explain it to at least some extent. For example, Valeria (9, child of surrogate) said 'I told them that I'm... that my mum's done surrogacy and she's doing it again, but I don't really think they get it'. Similarly, Louisa (13, child of surrogate) said that:

> The friends I've known for quite a while, they know because they've come around my house and seen that my mum's pregnant and they think it's another sibling, but I've told them and explained to them what surrogacy is.

Like Louisa, others whose mothers were surrogates were asked questions about their relationship to the children that their mothers gave birth to. Jack (17, child of surrogate) said he had had to explain to 'multiple teachers' that 'no, mum isn't selling my brothers and sisters'.[10] Lucy (15, child of surrogate) said:

> A lot of people ask me all the time, like, when your mum has surrogate children, "do you feel like they're your siblings?" "Do you have a connection to them, do you?" "Umm do you love them like you would your sister?"

The language used by these participants indicates that they view the children their mothers had as surrogates differently from their own siblings, something we explore further later. Jack noted that people often misunderstand surrogacy and that he frequently found himself explaining it. He was happy to do so and viewed these conversations as a way of helping to normalise the practice. He said:

> Yeah, I'd rather tell people about it and be open about it. Then people can see, it's not some strange thing, it's just something that people do.

[10]Such a pervasive myth exists in part due to the conflation of UK surrogacy practices with international commercial surrogacy/unregulated surrogacy by anti-surrogacy activists (Horsey & Mahmoud, 2025; Mahmoud, 2026a).

Participants who were born through surrogacy also had to explain it. For example, Jane (14, born through gestational surrogacy) said that when surrogacy arose in conversation with others, she would 'tell them and explain it,' noting that this was often necessary because many people 'did not really understand' what it meant. Tom (11, born through gestational surrogacy) also said 'sometimes I have to explain'. Twins Evalynn and Scarlett (11, born through gestational surrogacy) also discussed that they had to explain surrogacy to friends. Scarlett said: 'I had to explain it because some of them, some of my friends didn't know'. Similarly, Alison (12, born through US gestational surrogacy) indicated that explaining was the default: 'Usually I just do explain it anyway. Most of the time they don't know what it means'.

When asked what their friends thought about surrogacy, once it was explained, children generally reported positive reactions:

> They think it is a really nice thing. Usually, when I tell them, they all go "Aw". (Jane, 14, born through gestational surrogacy)

> They all think it is really cool. (Christina, 14, born through gestational surrogacy)

> I think they think it is cool how I was born in such a... I think it is quite cool how science has brought us this far and everything. (Evalynn 11, born through gestational surrogacy)

Nevertheless, children often encountered misunderstandings about surrogacy, even after it was explained. Participants told us that sometimes people who had not come across surrogacy before equated it with adoption. For example, Louisa (13, child of a surrogate) explained that while some people understand a little about what surrogacy involves, others do not. She said:

> Others say "kinda like adopted", and I say "no".

Similarly, Alison (12, born through US gestational surrogacy) said that even after explaining, some of her friends remained confused. She added:

> When I say I have two dads – and there was a lady who had me in her tummy for nine months – they think that my parents adopted me.

Surrogacy is often portrayed as a form of assisted reproduction enabling a couple to have 'their own' child, with the practice sometimes understood as a form of pre-arranged adoption (Baron et al., 2024). For those who likened surrogacy to adoption in our participants' accounts, however, it may simply be that surrogacy was not known to them, and was therefore likened to adoption in the sense that the birth mother does not keep the child. This was also seen among some participants in Phase Two, where three participants from the same group – James, Katie and Diego (all aged 10) – appeared to frame it in this way. For example, Katie, seemingly referring to parental orders, remarked: 'It's like an adoption paper, but a bit different.'

Some participants had to explain surrogacy in the context of being born into different family forms. Alison and her brother, Bart (12, born through US gestational surrogacy) observed that they had to explain surrogacy because their family was visibly different from others.[11] Alison noted that there was an 'obvious' difference if children 'have two dads or two mums'.

Rarely, some participants were met with indifference or even negativity from peers, though this also tended to derive from a lack of understanding. For example, Aoife (10, child of surrogate) said:

> I haven't really told anyone, only the closest friends, but I don't think they're interested because I don't think half of them even know what it is. Like two of them were rude, saying that like: "Is your mum not able to afford a baby so she had to give it away?"

Participants born through surrogacy also encountered negative reactions at times. For example, as indicated earlier, it seems likely that some people simply did not believe Steve (9, born through US gestational surrogacy) when he told them he had been born by surrogacy in the United States. Alison (12, born through US gestational surrogacy) also said that some people did not believe her as she did not have an American accent, and sometimes did not believe she was born through surrogacy at all. Bill and his sister Camille (11 and 13, born through US gestational surrogacy) had an interesting exchange about negative reactions experienced by Bill, as follows:

> Bill: One of my friends does know but I don't know how he found out but he did. I didn't tell him but he found out. Then he started asking lots of questions about it so I've explained it really well to him. But sometimes when we fall out, me and that friend, he sometimes just...
>
> Camille: Holds it against him.
>
> Bill: Yes.
>
> Interviewer: Or would say something about it?
>
> Bill: Yes, that sort of stuff.

Bill also went on to explain that the same friend had told another about Bill's 'massive secret', but lied about what that secret was and made it something unconnected to surrogacy. Camille recounted having told people at her new school when she was 'quite little' that she was born through surrogacy, but that:

---

[11]These were the only children in our study whose family was headed by a same-sex (male) couple, though Steve's (9, born through US gestational surrogacy) parent was a solo father.

> It did affect some people's views on me though... I got people saying that God was angry with me, that God didn't like me because I wasn't born naturally.

Later, she went on to say she had 'learnt her lesson' from 'bragging about it in my junior school', which had led to her being more selective and telling only her friends. She explained that this was because, with others 'I am not sure how they are going to take it', suggesting that she had experienced other negative reactions in the past. Some reactions to or misunderstandings about surrogacy are linked to common surrogacy myths, as identified by Camille:

> A lot of them [think] it is quite cool. A lot of them are just "Oh yeah, thanks for saying. That's interesting". Other people say "Oh, that's kind of weird" and I have had to go into some detail to explain it to them because obviously there are myths going around. People don't always know the full extent of what it really is so I have had to explain the actual reality of it to some people.

When asked if she could tell us about the myths she had encountered, she answered:

> Myths like your [intended parents] are not your real parents, do you miss your surrogate family, do you see them as your real parents and was it illegal apparently.

At another point in the interview, she mentioned how she deals with one of those myths when explaining surrogacy to others:

> I just tell them someone else carried me for my parents who are my parents regardless of what myths may say.

Bill (11), Camille's brother, told us that sometimes people ask him 'really strange questions about it'. He could give no specific examples but the experience of this had clearly stuck with him, as he said: 'I don't remember any of them, but just weird questions.' This prompted Camille to remember that:

> I was asked once if my surrogate had sex with my dad, which was a bit uncomfortable.

When talking to children without experience of surrogacy in Phase Two, in the context of discussions about learning about surrogacy in schools or from popular culture, some participants told us about myths or misunderstandings of surrogacy that they had held. For example, it was apparent some had encountered myths about ongoing relationships, as demonstrated by Ivy (15), who said:

> I wasn't sure if like the law made it so that the surrogate could not have any contact with the intended parents and that family would just be with the child. I wasn't... so I kind of assumed that the surrogate couldn't have contact with the child.

Some children of surrogates were asked questions by their peers about payments, which seemed to assume a more commercial model of surrogacy. For example, Lucy (15, child of surrogate) noted that people assumed her mother was paid for surrogacy (and that the family would therefore be 'rich') and were shocked to find out this was not the case. Jack (17, child of surrogate) also told us that he had encountered questions based on this assumption.

Some participants, faced with lack of understanding or surrogacy myths, felt the need to advocate for surrogacy in some way. Two of the older participants talked about advocating to increase awareness about surrogacy. Lucy (15, child of surrogate) said that she likes it when friends and teachers ask her questions and that she enjoys answering them. She talked about wanting to dispel untrue messages about surrogacy, explaining to all her friends what surrogacy is and about giving a talk about it in one of her General Certificate of Secondary Education (GCSE) classes. She also noted that surrogacy is not talked about as much as it should be and that people often have the wrong idea about it. She said:

> So I tried to put in as many facts and ... answer as many questions ... and kind of really try and bring people's knowledge up because I know that it's really not talked about as much as it should be and people really do have the wrong idea about it sometimes.

Similarly, Anna (16, cousin of a child born through surrogacy) said she started to advocate about surrogacy when she found out her aunt was having a child through surrogacy. She said that she tried to have perceived stigma removed by explaining it to people in school and doing a project on it, as seen in this quote:

> I know there is such a big stigma and I don't like that my aunt was going through it by herself. So when I found out that she was going through surrogacy, I started, like trying to advocate for, like, the stigma to be removed.

Interestingly, of all the children, Anna was the only one who specifically mentioned 'stigma', though this is evidently something faced by Camille (13, born through US gestational surrogacy), as outlined above, where she described that some people's views about her were affected when they found out how she was born.

This section showed that participants with lived experience of surrogacy often had to explain it due to pervasive misunderstandings, and sometimes they encountered and felt compelled to challenge surrogacy myths. Only a small minority perceived that there might be stigma attached to surrogacy. As noted above, anti-surrogacy activists often circulate mis/disinformation, conflating poor practice in some international and unregulated surrogacy destinations with domestic practice (Golombok, 2026; Horsey & Mahmoud, 2025; Mahmoud, 2026b). Surrogacy is framed as a threat to women, children, families and society, rather than a regulated and accepted reproductive practice (see Birdy, 2026; Purves, 2026). Surrogates are positioned as violating a supposedly natural, sacred and nurturing role (Mahmoud, 2026b), while surrogacy itself is characterised as the state-sanctioned 'normalisation of for-profit baby-farming' (Harrington, 2023). Surrogate-born children are positioned as victims in need of protection, based on assertions that families created through surrogacy reflect a 'total ignorance of children's developmental needs,' particularly in relation to infant attachment (Harrington, 2024; Mahmoud, 2026b). These narratives contribute to a wider cultural context in which surrogacy is misunderstood and stigmatised.

It is within this context that the participants' accounts should be understood. The misunderstandings they faced arose from the interaction between non-normative family forms and a social environment shaped by limited knowledge and normative assumptions about family. For example, Steve's reflection that he 'would definitely feel happier telling people if more people knew about it' suggests his reticence is related to the social consequences of misunderstanding and lack of awareness, rather than to surrogacy itself. As explored later in this chapter, participants identified formal education about surrogacy as a key mechanism for addressing these gaps in knowledge and reducing stigma.

Navigating Surrogacy: The Role of Contact

This section explores the issue of contact between surrogates (and her family) and the child she had through surrogacy (and the child's family). It explores participants' views about the reality of such contact for those with experience of surrogacy, whether they think such contact is important and how contact is perceived by those without experience of surrogacy.

In Phases One and Three, all participants born through surrogacy knew their surrogate and had contact with her and her family.[12] Children of surrogates also spoke of different levels of contact with the family that had a child through surrogacy. Contact was framed positively, when personal experience was shared. For example, Scarlett (11, born through gestational surrogacy) said: '...I always

[12]We did not set out to collect personal information about contact from any group, as we were asking questions about what contact they think should happen. It was clear, however, that all children born through surrogacy, including those born in the United States, knew their surrogates.

want to stay in touch with my surrogate and her children and everything', and her sister, Evalynn (11, born through gestational surrogacy) said: 'It is a really nice relationship'. When describing meeting their surrogate, children born through surrogacy said it was 'really fun' (Steve, 9, born through US gestational surrogacy) and 'normal' (Bart, 12, born through US gestational surrogacy). Camille (13, born through US gestational surrogacy) said the following about knowing and meeting her surrogate and her family:

> I'm very, very happy I know who my surrogate is and I am very, very happy I know who my donor is and I love going to see them. I love going to visit them and talking to them about it because you get more information every time you talk to parents and every time you talk to the actual surrogate. It is just nice to know.

Examples of contact were given by participants who had experience of domestic surrogacy arrangements. These included visits to activity centres and leisure centres, wall-climbing, park visits, picnics, walks, having dinner, day visits and visiting each other at Christmas. Birthdays held special significance, with children mentioning visits or calls happening on their birthdays, or calling the surrogate on her birthday. The reason for such contact given by Scarlett (11, born through gestational surrogacy) was that she 'helped create the birthday'. Digital communication through calling, video-calling and texting was mentioned, as well as face-to-face contact. Children born through surrogacy in the United States described how their parents kept their surrogate's phone number and these children felt it was appropriate to be able to contact her by phone, video call or text message. All five had travelled to the United States to visit their surrogates and spoke enthusiastically about these trips, expressing happiness and excitement about the visits.

The prevalence of contact between families and positive attitudes towards such contact in Phases One and Three are not surprising, as maintaining ongoing relationships is the norm in the United Kingdom, particularly when surrogacy organisations are involved (Horsey, 2015, 2018b, 2025a, 2025c; Horsey et al., 2022, 2023; Pott & White, 2025). The artwork from the project also reflected the idea that contact between families was both commonplace and positive (Wade & Mills, 2025). For example, the art showed images including the surrogate and intended parents holding hands, which shows that surrogacy was perceived as a collaborative and relationship-based process between the intended parents and the surrogate.[13] The findings from the artwork and the interviews are in sharp contrast to accounts by anti-surrogacy organisations which portray surrogacy as transactional and exploitative (Nordic Model Now, 2019a, 2019b). The findings also do not reflect their critiques that children are 'ripped from the birth mother' (Nordic Model Now, 2020). Empirical work also does not support this. For

---

[13]See the themes 'connections' and 'love' from the artwork in Wade and Mills (2025), which includes the artwork on this book cover.

example, in a study of young adults born through surrogacy in the United Kingdom (Jadva et al., 2023), 60% remained in contact with their surrogate. Similarly, in a study with surrogates in the United Kingdom (Jadva et al., 2026), positive relationships were maintained in the longer term 'with over two-thirds of surrogates keeping in contact with the families they had helped 20 years later' (p. 243). Likewise, in studies with surrogates and parents through surrogacy in the United Kingdom ongoing contact between families was found to be common (Horsey, 2025a, 2025c; Horsey et al., 2022, 2023; Mahmoud, 2023).[14]

We asked participants in Phases One and Three whether maintaining contact between the child and the family who used surrogacy and the surrogate and her family is important.[15] Some participants said that maintaining contact between families is important as it recognises the significant role of the surrogate, as seen in the following quotes:

> I think it is good to remain in contact with each other because it is a huge thing you have done for someone when you decide to carry a baby for them. (Camille, 13, born through US gestational surrogacy)

> I think that they should keep in contact because the surrogate helped create the child. So, they should definitely keep in contact and meet a lot. I think that it's quite important to. Because she like she went through the stage with you... the least you can do is meet up with her and call her. (Evalynn, 11, born through gestational surrogacy)

> It is important because she helped create you and like went through the pregnancy with you... so she is like a second parent, if you think about it. So, keep in touch. It is a really nice relationship. (Evalynn, 11, born through gestational surrogacy)

Such views show that children born through surrogacy regard what the surrogate did as significant.[16] Camille refers to what surrogates do as a 'huge thing' you do for someone. Evalynn takes a very relational approach, saying that contact is important because she and her surrogate 'went through' pregnancy together.

---

[14]See also Horsey, 2015, where 83 of 111 surrogates surveyed maintained contact with the children/intended parents and 88 of 91 parents through surrogacy said they maintain contact with the surrogate, and Horsey, 2018b, where 71 of 85 surrogates and 94 of 104 parents through surrogacy said the same.

[15]We did not ask Phase Two this question, as they had no experience of such contact and we wanted to ask them more questions about their knowledge of surrogacy.

[16]In the context of parenthood, participants were less likely to acknowledge the surrogate's reproductive labour (see Chapter 2, p. 71), though were more likely to when discussing the financial contributions she should be able to receive (see Chapter 3, pp. 99–100).

Other reasons for maintaining contact included opportunities to learn more about the surrogacy arrangement (Bill, 11, and Camille, 13, siblings born through US gestational surrogacy), the surrogate (Bart, 12, born through US gestational surrogacy) and the surrogacy process (Christina, 14, born through gestational surrogacy). Participants also emphasised the relational value of contact, with Bart describing the surrogate as 'another person who cares for you'. Raven (9, child of surrogate) gave a different reason for contact and explained that knowing the surrogate would allow children to consider whether they might want to do it themselves in the future. She said:

> I think they should because they could have, like, a relationship with them, so they can ask what they felt like when having them and get to get know what it's like to be a surrogate in case they want to do that as their job as well.

Raven's reason for contact is more to do with finding out what it is like to experience surrogacy, which perhaps reflects that this is something she thinks about as a child of a surrogate, who, unlike most of those born through surrogacy, witnesses the process of surrogacy.[17]

The discussion by two participants regarding contact between families appeared to be shaped by the practice of the United Kingdom's non-profit organisations. One child (Oliver, 11, child of surrogate) said:

> ...we have a little group that my mum goes to, Surrogacy UK or something, they do loads of little meet ups in parks so it's like all the donors, the surrogates, they all just meet up to find people who they want to be surrogates for, so there was us, gay couples, lesbian couples, loads of people there.

This shows awareness of SurrogacyUK (SUK) events, known as 'socials', which are aimed at facilitating surrogacy journeys and ongoing contact (Pott & White, 2025). Similarly, Jack (17, child of surrogate) articulated an understanding of surrogacy as a 'journey' that is 'friendship-based'. His framing closely reflects the ethos associated with SUK, which promotes a 'friendship-first' and relationship-based model of surrogacy (Pott & White, 2025, p. 28), suggesting that engagement with such organisational discourses may shape the vocabulary used.

As with the findings relating to origin information disclosure, some participants said that maintaining contact between the surrogate (and her family) and the child/family created through surrogacy should not be 'compulsory' (Camille, 12, born through US gestational surrogacy), 'essential' (Lilly, 9, child of

[17]Children born through surrogacy do not ordinarily witness it, unless a sibling is born through surrogacy and they are old enough to understand. Even then, it will not be a comparable experience to a child whose parent is acting as a surrogate.

surrogate) or 'absolutely really essential' (Tom, 11, born through gestational surrogacy).[18] Jack (17, child of surrogate) said there should be no 'strict rigid things' around contact. Similar variability in contact, and similar reasoning, has been reported in empirical work with surrogates (Jadva et al., 2026; Horsey, 2025a; Horsey et al., 2022). The responses of the participants also suggest that they viewed maintaining contact with the surrogate as something that should be worked out on a case-by-case basis, as the following quotes illustrate:

> I don't think everybody in every situation you need it. (Ellie, 13, born through gestational surrogacy)

> It's nice to have a bit of a connection but it's not really important if they don't want to have it. (Louisa, 13, child of surrogate)

In line with findings regarding knowledge of origin information, participants emphasised that contact should remain a choice for both families (Alison, 12, born through US gestational surrogacy) and should depend on what each family is comfortable with (Scarlett, 11, born through gestational surrogacy). For example, Louisa said that there should be contact between the surrogate and the intended parents during pregnancy, but that while contact is 'nice' after the birth, it is up to the intended parents whether to continue this. She said:

> I think while the surrogate is pregnant there should be quite a lot of contact, keep up-to-date and stuff. But after the baby is born, then I think it's up to the intended parents but I think it's nice to have that connection and the baby to know who the surrogate is.

Bill (11, born through US gestational surrogacy), on the other hand, gave an example of child-led contact. He explained how he and his sister Camille (13) had wanted to know more; therefore, they asked their parents to plan a trip to the United States so that they could meet their surrogate and this was arranged.

One of the older participants recognised that maintaining contact may be difficult due to stigma associated with surrogacy. For example, Anna (16, cousin of a child born through surrogacy) said:

> There's still such a big stigma around surrogacy that a lot of intended parents don't tell a lot of people and then having this like random woman come into your life and all like. . .be there quite often. . .it can be hard to explain to other people, not that they should have to explain themselves, but like it can be really hard for intended parents to deal with that. So, it just depends on the intended parents, I think.

[18]See Chapter 4, pp. 127–128.

Therefore, for Anna, the reason why the issue of contact between families should be decided by *intended parents* is because contact may mean that they have to explain it to people and that might be difficult due to the stigma associated with surrogacy.

Some older participants with experience of domestic surrogacy explained how the non-profit organisations facilitate such family-led models of contact. For example, Lucy (15, child of surrogate) described how her mother was asked, via a surrogacy organisation, to indicate whether she would want to maintain contact with the intended parents and child after birth. Her mother later matched with intended parents who expressed similar preferences, enabling expectations around post-birth contact to be established prior to agreement. Her description illustrates how organisational mediation can support good practice including expectations of ongoing contact. In a similar vein, establishing boundaries was important for some participants, particularly in distinguishing surrogacy-related relationships from familial ones. This idea was summarised by Christina (14, born through gestational surrogacy) as follows:

> I think they should ... like ... have the same contact as you would ... like.... an aunt or a distant relative. I don't think that [the surrogate] should be a constant figure in their life because I think that would be maybe slightly overbearing, acting ... like ... more as a parent than a surrogate.

Christina's twin sister, Jane, said:

> I think, as well, that they should be like a relative or an aunt because they are such an important figure in their lives and I don't think that should just be cut off unless they are not comfortable with it. They shouldn't be ... like ... *always* there because they're ... like ... the surrogate ... and not the parent.

The issue of the way in which relationships through surrogacy are framed and navigated is dealt with in the section below.

Some children *without* experience of surrogacy imagined contact in a different way from those who had experience. Two participants in Phase Two questioned whether children should know about their surrogate at all, in case she was contacted but wanted nothing to do with the child's life (Ella, 14; Sienna, 13). James (10) pointed out the potential negative impacts of contact on the child and family. He imagined a scenario whereby the child wanted to spend more time with the 'biological' mother and less time with their intended parents, leading them to forget what their parents 'did to get them'. He also imagined that it would be negative if the child wanted care from the surrogate, but that was not forthcoming. These views are in contrast to the insights from those with experience of surrogacy. Contact between families was the norm among those participants and was valued. A different insight from a participant in Phase Two was that contact was important to reduce the chance of disagreement between intended parents and the surrogate. Natalie (15) said:

> . . .if you had contact between the two, then there might be fewer issues with a surrogate's rights over the child, because then you could say, well, you're not cutting out of their life completely. But I'm giving up my parental rights. And then you can have parental rights, but I can still see them.

This is an interesting insight, because disputes have arisen in circumstances where there were mismatched expectations and understandings between the surrogate and intended parents regarding her contact with the child (*Re C (Surrogacy: Consent)* [2023] EWCA Civ 16).[19] Natalie, who did not have experience of surrogacy, was able to foresee the kinds of complications that can arise, especially where expectations about contact are not clearly set out.

Navigating Surrogacy: Kinship and Connections

This section explores children's own interpretations and understandings of the kinship ties and other relational connections formed through surrogacy. Surrogacy formed extended kinship networks for participants, and these relationships were described using a variety of language and classificatory terms. Participants with experience of surrogacy variably foregrounded or downplayed genetic, biological and social relationships depending on context. Some drew on parental language to describe surrogates, without conflating this with legal or social/everyday parenthood. For example, Scarlett (11, born through gestational surrogacy) described a surrogate as 'like a second parent', while Lilly (9, child of surrogate) referred to her as 'kind of like a mum'.

Participants' accounts suggest that surrogacy creates relationships for which there is no established vocabulary and, therefore, children drew on existing kinship terms to make these connections understandable within familiar frameworks. Children frequently drew on extended kin terms (e.g. 'aunt', 'cousin') as linguistic resources, likely because these familiar labels make the relationship easier to explain to others while still signalling that the person is important (Jadva, 2021). For example, Lilly (9, child of surrogate) and Jack (17, child of surrogate) both used 'cousin' for the children their mothers had as a surrogate, and Jane (14, born through gestational surrogacy) explained that she

[19] In this case, the relationship between the intended parents and the surrogate deteriorated. The surrogate agreed to a parental order on the condition that she would have regular contact with the child. The order was granted but later appealed. The Court of Appeal held that the surrogate's consent was neither free nor unconditional as required under s. 54(6) HFE Act 2008 and the parental order was overturned, leaving the surrogate as the legal mother alongside the biologically related intended father. Child arrangements orders were issued, granting parental responsibility to the second male intended parent and placing conditions on all parties' parental responsibility (see Marsh, 2025).

calls her surrogate 'aunt', and sees her surrogate's children as 'cousins, distant cousins'.[20]

Camille (13, born through US gestational surrogacy) also referred to her surrogate as an 'aunt' (and the surrogate's partner as an 'uncle' and their children as 'cousins') and interestingly, used this term for the egg donor, with whom she also has contact. She added:

> I really love my parents. They are my parents. I love my surrogate as my aunt and I love my donor who is also an aunt. They are all family members and we are all really close with them.

Participants' responses also indicated that, for them, genetic connection does not automatically translate into kinship claims. Where genetic links existed (for example, in traditional surrogacy), they were often acknowledged but did not necessarily result in 'parental' or 'sibling' relationships. For instance, Alice (13) suggested that in cases of traditional surrogacy children have 'like a mother that they don't know', but also thought that they 'deserve to know that'. Eliza (11, child of a surrogate) distinguished between traditional and gestational surrogacy and used genetic connection as a way of deciding how close different relationships should be. She explained that in gestational surrogacy, it is important to 'maintain space', suggesting that 'you should still see your surrogate but not often' because 'too much can confuse a child'. However, with traditional surrogacy, she felt the surrogate should be treated more like extended family: 'as much as you see your cousin or auntie... a distant auntie', adding that 'you would obviously see them more if they're genetically related'. Her description shows how she used genetic relatedness to differentiate between types of surrogacy and to determine appropriate levels of contact and closeness. Her reasoning aligns with research showing that genetic ties can be meaningful without being determinative, and can shape expectations of closeness, responsibility and classification within reconfigured family forms (Nordqvist, 2014, 2019). Conversely, in gestational surrogacy, where no genetic link exists with the surrogate, Eliza viewed the surrogate's role as socially significant despite the absence of genetic ties. This supports the view that kinship in assisted reproduction is 'lived' and negotiated, rather than biologically fixed (Nordqvist, 2014, 2019).

Jack (17, child of a surrogate) similarly distinguished between genetic connection and relational experience when discussing the differences in the relationships he had with his own half-siblings and the children his mother carried as a traditional surrogate, as seen in this quote:

---

[20]In the longitudinal study led by Susan Golombok, some surrogates' children had made up their own terms to define children their mothers gave birth to as a surrogate, for example 'surrosister' or 'tummy sister' (Golombok, 2020, p. 111). Likewise, in Horsey, 2025a, one child whose mother acted as a surrogate for her sister, referred to his cousins as his 'womb mates' (p. 65).

> I can have the same biological relationship, but the actual relationship I have with them is completely different....Like with my little brother [...] I tell him off, if he did anything wrong. [...] Whereas, if it was like the baby that my mom had through surrogacy, if I was expected to watch her, I'd be like "what?" You know, I would never tell her off or anything, and it's just very different like relationship wise.

Jack also described enjoying visits with the children his mother had through both gestational and traditional surrogacy arrangements, while explicitly indicating he did not view either as 'another sibling'. His words reflect how genetic connections are 'lived', 'felt' and 'managed' in complex ways, rather than being self-evidently 'there' (Nordqvist, 2019). Lucy (15, child of surrogate) echoed this distinction, rejecting sibling categorisation despite genetic relatedness and instead describing the children her mother carried as a traditional surrogate as 'friends', in the following way:

> Since I was younger, I've always known that [the twins her mother had through surrogacy] like they're not, they're not our babies. They're not for us. They have different parents and their parents love them and they're not... while we are responsible while my mom was pregnant, they're not our full-time responsibility.

Like Jack, she was adamant that even though she shared a genetic connection with children her mother had through surrogacy, those children were not like siblings to her. Both conceptualised the relationship as different due to the circumstances of the conception, viewing the surrogate-born children as 'friends' and not 'siblings'.

In Phase Two, Ivy (15) said that the relationship between the surrogate and child may be similar to that of godparent and godchild. She also said:

> I think it'd be kind of interesting, like a third parent, like a godparent, kind of, but it's not really the same as godparents, but it's similar.

This shows that Ivy was grappling with the kind of language that should be used to describe a surrogate and also recognises that while a surrogate is similar to a godparent, the relationship is nonetheless distinct, and perhaps closer to a parent ('like a third parent'). Harry (16) reiterated the idea of 'third parent' in the same interview. This goes to the question of restricting legal parenthood to a maximum of two people, and conferring this on either the intended parents to the exclusion of the surrogate, or vice versa (McCandless, 2025). This kind of approach, where children were more flexible about parenthood than the law currently allows, was also seen in Chapter 2 when discussing parenthood.[21]

---

[21]See discussion at Chapter 2, p. 54.

Both Ivy and Harry spoke of the surrogate potentially 'being there' for the child and providing an outside perspective if the child needed advice. This is possibly because these were older children, who may have experienced the positive value of getting advice from people other than their parents in their adolescent years. In this respect, Jadva and Imrie (2014a, 2014b) noted the prevalence of surrogates formally taking on a godparent role for children born through surrogacy. It was argued that formalising the relationship not only reflects the closeness that can develop between surrogates and intended parents, but may also function as an effort to strengthen inter-family bonds and secure their lasting nature.

The participants' accounts demonstrate that genetic links are actively interpreted, managed and relationally positioned rather than automatically translated into kinship status (Nordqvist & Gilman, 2024). This aligns with broader donor conception research indicating that children often differentiate between genetic connection and lived family relationships (Golombok, 2021; Slutsky et al., 2016). With donor conception, donor-sibling networks are seen as special relations that are not disruptive to family life and hold the potential to become part of a new kind of family (Hertz, 2022; Hertz et al., 2013). The variability in participants' language is significant, offering insight into dominant and emerging meanings of kinship in the context of assisted reproductive technologies (ART), where 'kinship grammars play a crucial role in processes of connecting and disconnecting kinship relationships between adults and children' (Gunnarsson Payne, 2016, pp. 496–497). In this context, a central means of distinguishing among kinship connections involves negotiating third-party roles by identifying meaningful relationships that do not unsettle who are recognised as parents (Blell & Homanen, 2025). As with gamete donation, in surrogacy there is no settled social script for how surrogacy-generated relations should be interpreted or how children should conceptualise meaningful connectedness in these contexts (Nordqvist, 2021).

As discussed in Chapter 2, kinship language is flexible and context-dependent: relatedness may be understood at times through biology or genetics, and at other times as something that develops through lived relationships over time (Volkman, 2016). The data support this fluidity, showing that the distinction between biological and social understandings of family is not clear-cut in how participants talk about and make sense of kinship (Carsten, 2000, p. 21; see also Mason & Tipper, 2008). Their descriptions did not indicate confusion about parenthood; rather, they reflect the use of available linguistic resources to describe relationships that are meaningful yet non-parental (Mason & Tipper, 2008). Participants generally distinguished clearly between their parents in a legal and social sense on the one hand, and the distinct role occupied by surrogates on the other, using familiar terms to articulate relationships that are significant, but not equivalent to parenthood. In practice, participants typically located surrogates within extended or 'chosen' kin categories such as 'aunt', 'family friend' or 'someone important in our lives', reflecting accounts of kinship as simultaneously biological, gestational and social, with different dimensions emphasised depending on context. At the same time, participants' accounts indicate the continued cultural significance of shared biology, particularly through genetic connection (Nordqvist, 2017; Nordqvist & Gilman, 2024; Petersen, 2019). In some instances, genetic ties were treated as a decisive marker of relatedness, reflecting the 'geneticisation of family relationships' (Freeman & Richards, 2006, p. 80).

A further insight derived from children's experiences of international surrogacy was how participants in Phase Three articulated connections to the country in which they were born, particularly as this resulted in dual citizenship. These connections were not always framed in explicitly identity-based terms or kinship terms, but were nonetheless meaningful as part of how participants understood their backgrounds and future possibilities. Most participants described their birth in the United States as significant beyond the circumstances of the surrogacy arrangement itself, linking it to future opportunities related to education or work. For example, Steve (9) linked his birth in the United States directly to anticipated life opportunities, stating that he was 'happy he was born in the US', particularly in case he wanted to 'live in America', and noting his intention to do so in the future; he narrated his birthplace in the context of his future life, rather than viewing it solely as part of his past.

Like Steve, Alison (12) viewed her dual citizenship as favourable for the future, as it would alleviate some of the difficulties otherwise associated with immigration, while also referring to her future tax obligations:

> I think it lets me go and study in America or work in America. Also then I have to pay taxes from America.

Similarly, Bill (11) and Camille (13) described how being 'born in America' or having dual citizenship functioned as something notable in peer interactions. In fact, Camille described how this essentially functioned as 'clout'. She described how she would tell people that she has 'family in America', before disclosing to them that she was 'born through surrogacy in America'. Her narrative illustrated how she used her surrogacy birth in the United States as a form of social capital. She said: 'I think the first way I told people actually is that I've got dual citizenship; I'm special, I'm half American'. Bart (11), by contrast, described his American birth as 'normal', and stated that he did not 'think about it much', indicating that the fact of being born in another country holds different levels of significance for children born through international surrogacy, even within the same family. Their narratives suggest that international surrogacy can generate additional opportunities for work and travel that are positively valued by children.

Educating About Surrogacy: The Need for Surrogacy in Schools

There was general consensus among participants in all Phases that there is no clear part of the school curriculum that is dedicated to surrogacy. Some of the younger (primary school aged) children had not encountered it at all. In Phase Two, where there was no lived experience of surrogacy, James (10), Katie (10), Jax (8), Thomas (8) and Alan (8) all said they had only heard of surrogacy in the context of being invited to our interviews, when it had been briefly explained to them by a parent or a teacher before they participated. James said this was because he 'would actually have an idea of what questions [he] was answering'. When asked whether had ever learnt about surrogacy before the interview, Leonard (11) said 'no', adding:

> You would have said "surrogacy" to me and I would have been like, "I know that sounds like a word but I've got no clue what it means".

Some participants reported that surrogacy was mentioned briefly at school, usually within other topics, such as those covered in Personal, Social, Health and Economic Education (PSHE). PSHE (or otherwise-named similar modules) runs throughout school years and aims to provide age-appropriate 'knowledge for life', including on (physical and mental) health and relationships. While PSHE itself is not mandatory as a stand-alone subject, key elements within it became statutory in 2019. The Relationships Education, Relationships and Sex Education and Health Education (England) Regulations 2019, made under ss. 34 and 35 of the Children and Social Work Act 2017, introduced compulsory Relationships Education in primary schools, Relationships and Sex Education (RSE) in secondary schools and Health Education in all state-funded schools (sometimes combined as RSHE). Lucy (15, child of a surrogate) recalled that surrogacy was 'very, very briefly touched upon in PSE... like for half a lesson'; similarly, Bart (12, born through US gestational surrogacy) noted there had been 'not much' coverage in PSHE.

The differential coverage of relationships and sex education by age may explain why, for example, Scarlett (11, born through gestational surrogacy) said that:

> I think in our last PSHE lesson I think we did a tiny thing about it but I don't think ... I don't know if it was explained properly. I don't know if everybody in my class really gets it.

Even at secondary school level, some participants observed that there was a lack of detail or accuracy in any teaching of surrogacy. Lucy (15) said that after the brief coverage in PSHE (in the context of both avoiding pregnancy and different ways of having children, including adoption), other children, who knew about her situation, asked her about it. She explained:

> Because even the teacher couldn't fully explain everything because it's just not taught and it's not really on the curriculum. So the teachers don't know what to say and how to explain it well.

Others encountered surrogacy in the context of other subjects. Anna (16, cousin of a child born through surrogacy) described surrogacy as occupying 'a small place' within the Religious Studies syllabus, and Camille (13, born through US gestational surrogacy) described having 'a lesson which covered that a little bit'. Christina (14, born through gestational surrogacy) said:

> Yes. I think it was in Biology in Year 7. So, … like … 12 years old. We learned about it. It was kind of … like … one lesson where the topic was reproduction and I think one lesson where they were talking about IVF and surrogacy and things like that.

Her sister Jane (14) expanded on this, suggesting that any coverage there had been lacked depth:

> It's not that big of a topic. It's there. It's… kind of ... While we are learning about birth, there is a short part of the topic, it's about IVF, it's not really a main part, so, if we do learn about it, it is one of the topics which could easily be forgotten.

This lack of depth was also experienced by other participants, as illustrated by the following quotes:

> I think we covered it slightly in Biology, but that was just about, mainly it was brought up when we were talking about cloning. (Harry, 16)

> They kind of just go, "oh by the way, yes, these are some options you can have. Now let's talk about IVF, in more detail". (Ivy, 15)

However, Natalie (15) was not sure that surrogacy had been covered in Biology at all:

> I don't really remember, I remember talking about IVF and like, learning about it. But I don't think that we actually talked about actual, like real life situations with surrogacies and things like that.

Some Phase Two participants (Rose (13), Ella (14), Charlotte (14) and Sienna (13)), who took 'Childcare' as a subject, offered in some schools at GCSE or Business and Technology Education Council (BTEC) level (often within Health and Social Care), described how surrogacy was more explicitly discussed as a method of family formation. However, even here, coverage is likely to be constrained, as such courses tend to focus on pregnancy, neonatal care and child development, rather than the broader social and relational dimensions of surrogacy.[22]

Based on the participants' accounts, there appears to be limited coverage of surrogacy within the curriculum, despite recognition by the government of surrogacy as a legitimate form of family-building (DHSC, 2018a, 2018b; Law Commission and Scottish Law Commission, 2023). Surrogacy tended to appear

---

[22]Online searches for module content of Childcare at BTEC Level 1/Level 2 shows they are based around children's growth and development, with a focus on the role of play. See, for example: https://qualifications.pearson.com/en/subjects/childcare.html.

either alongside other forms of assisted reproduction, such as IVF, or within broader discussions of reproduction, contraception or adoption. Where surrogacy was included in the curriculum, it seems as though it was typically framed either in scientific terms, or covered briefly (e.g. within Biology), or as an ethical or moral issue (e.g. within Religious Studies), rather than as a social practice of family formation.

Outside of school education, children encounter surrogacy in other contexts. Some participants in Phase Two told us that they had derived some understanding of surrogacy from 'celebrities' (Carrie, 17) or representations in popular culture, particularly television programmes. Alice (13), for example, said:

> I mean, I knew what it is through watching like, you know, TV shows and stuff like that but we haven't had any lessons at school about it or anything.

Annabelle (10) similarly reported seeing surrogacy 'on a programme', *Fuller House*.[23] Harry (16) recalled encountering surrogacy in an episode of *It's Always Sunny in Philadelphia*, which prompted him to ask his parents about it because he 'was a bit curious'.[24] Ivy (15) suggested that her understanding was partial and shaped by media exposure:

> I think I watched the film *Genome* with my parents, this year, maybe early this year. That's kind of a little bit about, it's not really about surrogacy though is it? I kind of knew a little bit about it, but I didn't, I kind of assumed a lot of things.[25]

These accounts link to earlier discussion of surrogacy myths and misperceptions. Where knowledge is primarily derived from popular media, such as situation comedies or science fiction movies, representations may be inaccurate or sensationalised. The Phase Two participants' answers suggest an awareness that their understanding was incomplete or based on assumptions. This aligns with concerns in the literature about the role of media in shaping public perceptions of surrogacy (Golombok, 2026; Horsey & Mahmoud, 2025; Mahmoud, 2026b). Simultaneously, however, exposure through popular culture may

---

[23]*Fuller House* is an American sitcom following a large family occupying a house with other friends and their children. One character, Kimmy acts as a surrogate for her brother Jimmy and his partner Stephanie, who is infertile. Kimmy carries the baby via IVF using her Jimmy's sperm and Stephanie's egg, resulting in the birth of their daughter, Danielle.

[24]In the American sitcom *It's Always Sunny in Philadelphia*, character Dee Reynolds acts as a surrogate for Carmen (a transgender woman) and her husband, Nick. She carries an embryo created using Carmen's sperm and a donor egg. She is later shown to have received $30,000 for the arrangement. According to online reviews, the storyline highlights the show's dark humour, especially regarding Dee's unethical behaviour, including her financial motivations and disregard for the health of the foetus.

[25]*Genome* is a 2017 sci-fi feature film, which explores, amongst other things, gene editing.

introduce the idea of diverse family forms, even if in a limited or imperfect way, reflecting broader shifts in how family life is represented and understood. As Brown (2026) notes, 'social attitudes and family forms within UK society have continued to evolve in ways that suggest that the traditional 'nuclear family' possesses even less influence on people's actual choices about family life' (p. 30).

Several participants contended that there *should* be more coverage of the topic in schools. Anna (16), who mentioned some brief coverage in Religious Studies, said 'yeah, it should be in PSHE, but it's not'. Alison (12, born through US gestational surrogacy) said learning about surrogacy could be 'helpful' 'just to understand how people might be born', an idea echoed by her brother, Bart (12, born through US gestational surrogacy), who thought it important for children to know about surrogacy because: 'they'll come across people who've had it and they will know about it. It's a good thing to know'.

Other participants agreed that surrogacy should be taught at school, for similar reasons, as seen in these quotes:

> Because a lot of people will go through or could go through surrogacy. So it would be good to have a little bit of knowledge of it, I guess. (Liam, 18)

> It is a good option for anyone who wants to have a biological link with their children and doesn't want to adopt and can't give birth or that sort of stuff. (Bill, 11, born through US gestational surrogacy)

Carrie (17) thought that surrogacy was 'just something that everyone should know about', while Honey (16) thought that it was 'important to learn about' surrogacy. She said:

> Because people will be, if we're not learning about it in school then we're not really going to know how it works and if you'd want to do it. You wouldn't have an idea.

Natalie (15) thought that:

> It would be a very interesting part to add to the national curriculum, perhaps as part of PSHE, especially to educate people on that there are other kinds of methods of having children.

She justified this by reference to myths and misinformation, as follows:

> Obviously, when you kind of get to 15, 16, you do know that they're there. But it's not something you're explicitly taught. And it can be difficult because you form an opinion, based on perhaps media or things you've seen, and you don't really have all the facts

> available to you, or someone with expert knowledge who can tell you about it. You might see one thing that says surrogacy is awful. And another thing which says, surrogacy is great. And it's difficult to know who to believe and there's no one there to tell you, actually, these are some of the benefits and these are some of the disadvantages.

Some participants mentioned that 'enrichment days', which give opportunities to go beyond the curriculum, might be a good place for discussion of surrogacy. Ivy (15) thought assisted reproduction would be a good topic for an enrichment day, adding 'I think I'd quite like it to learn more about surrogacy in school'. Related to this, Harry (16), Natalie (15) and Ivy (15) in Phase Two recalled an 'enrichment day' held at their school connected to 'pregnancy', but explained that this had focused on avoiding unwanted pregnancies and the cost of raising children. When reflecting on this, Harry said 'that's something they should probably bring up, like different [family forming] options as well'.

At present, surrogacy appears only sporadically within existing subjects – most often as a brief reference within Biology, Religious Studies or PSHE – without sustained engagement as a form of family creation.[26] This fragmented coverage contributes to the misunderstandings discussed earlier. Participants consistently identified a lack of education about and an imperfect understanding of surrogacy, and the findings point towards the need for a more coherent approach to its curricular inclusion.

Reforming Surrogacy Law: The Importance of Engaging With Young People

We asked Phase Three participants whether children should be asked about surrogacy law and law reform. When we asked Alison (12, born through US gestational surrogacy) whether children and young people should have a say in the law, she said:

> Yeah, because they live here as well and they have to follow the law as well. Some things they might disagree on or not think are completely fair. I think they should listen or try to listen to what the children have to say.

A similar question was put to her brother Bart (12, born through US gestational surrogacy), eliciting the following exchange:

---

[26]Curriculum review based on analysis of Department for Education (2019) guidance for Relationships Education, Relationships and Sex Education (RSE) and Health Education (England) (for teaching until 31 August 2026). Search terms included 'surrogacy', 'assisted reproduction', 'family formation'; surrogacy was not consistently specified as a discrete topic within statutory guidance.

> Interviewer: Do you think that when people change the law that children and young people should be involved in that process like we're doing today?
>
> Bart: Yes because it's about them so their point of view is important and helps the decision.
>
> Interviewer: Why do you think it's important? Some people would say, "why ask children?"
>
> Bart: Because they can give you what it's actually like and tell you what they would like to be changed.

From this, we can see that these participants support the inclusion of children's views in law and policymaking, and see the value of them sharing their lived experience. As in other areas of law and society, including examples of criminal and family justice, education and healthcare,[27] the views of children and young people should be heard when reconsidering surrogacy laws in the United Kingdom and elsewhere. This is because their stories and experiences reveal the reality of surrogacy and should be included in the debate when reforming law and policy in this area.

Participants in Phase Two also said that it was important or desirable to consider the opinions of young people when making policy or law about surrogacy. They recognised that to be able to have any meaningful input into policy and law making, they would need to have more knowledge about surrogacy in the first place, including how it is regulated. For example, Harry (16), said:

> If you're making laws and things, then I feel like it would be good for people to know a bit more about it, so they can at least have the conversation and discuss it.

Harry also said that it would be important to specifically have young people's opinions included in the law-making process, as did Ivy (15) in the same group. When we asked others whether they agreed, this generated some thoughtful responses. Natalie (15) said:

> I think young people's opinions are really important because the law changing might not necessarily impact someone who's an adult in the same way, it might impact someone who wants to have [a] child through surrogacy in the future or who wants to become a surrogate.

This demonstrates an understanding of law reform in this area as something that may shape their own future reproductive choices (as someone who may

---

[27] Introduction, pp. 22–23.

want to have children in the future) rather than only those of existing adults (who may already have children).[28] She elaborated this further:

> Yes, because if [the law] changes, and in 10 years' time, I say to myself, I'd like a child and I go to a doctor and they're like, you can't have a child traditionally, then, I might think that I want to find a surrogate and have a child.

Liam (18) made this point in the following way:

> I suppose because a lot of people when they get to about 20 could possibly become surrogates, so it's quite good to have an impact on the law that could affect what their situation is if they do become a surrogate or are going to be parents from having a surrogate mother, it would be good to know the laws and have an impact possibly how it impacts them when they're going through that process.

Both Natalie and Liam framed surrogacy law as (potentially) shaping anticipated life-course decisions, whether in relation to becoming a parent or a surrogate, and as consequently relevant to younger people's current and future interests. Natalie's observation highlights the risk that legislation may embed values or ideologies that later no longer resonate with those governed by it, particularly when children's perspectives are excluded from law reform processes. This is not to argue that children's views should be decisive in shaping legal reform; there can be good reasons for giving greater weight to the reasoning of adults in assessing reform proposals. Nevertheless, it is imperative to incorporate children's perspectives alongside those of adults to help to reduce the likelihood of reforms (a) making assumptions about children's views and (b) overlooking issues that are important to children.

Conclusion: Insights for Law, Policy and Practice

This chapter focused on children's accounts of surrogacy as it is understood and navigated within their everyday social worlds. Their accounts provide an alternative to critiques of surrogacy, which frequently proceed on the basis of presumed/assumed harms, risks and ethical concerns, rather than being grounded in empirical evidence. The existing discourse – particularly as presented by anti-surrogacy activists – rests on assumptions that surrogacy is inherently harmful to children, using ideas such as disrupted attachment, identity confusion or commodification. However, the accounts presented in this chapter show that children express pride in being born through surrogacy, or in their mothers having acted as a surrogate. Participants were open about surrogacy with others

[28]This links back to the idea of generationing (Mayall, 2002): see Chapter 1, p. 36.

and only one overtly perceived stigma attached to it. This complements a substantial body of longitudinal empirical research demonstrating that children born through surrogacy show positive psychological adjustment and family relationships across childhood and into adulthood (Golombok, 2020a, 2020b; Golombok et al., 2017, 2023). Because surrogacy in the United Kingdom is predominantly practised within a regulated and ethical framework, arrangements are generally successful. This is reflected in participants' positive accounts of their experiences with surrogacy.

The findings discussed here provide strong evidence that, within domestic (and US-based) surrogacy arrangements, ongoing contact between families is common, valued and beneficial. Participants emphasised flexibility: contact should be available and facilitated but not mandated. The findings reflect the current practice of surrogacy in the United Kingdom, where ongoing contact is encouraged by the non-profit surrogacy organisations (Pott & White, 2025). The Law Commission and Scottish Law Commission (2023, para. 2.17) also observed that non-profit surrogacy organisations recognised by the Department of Health and Social Care (DHSC) support ongoing relationships between surrogates and the families they helped to create. Our findings indicate that the Law Commissions' proposal for a 'new 'pathway' to parenthood in surrogacy, overseen by Regulated Surrogacy Organisations (RSOs) should be supported. This would give State backing to a framework of regulated surrogacy support, that emphasises the importance of ongoing contact.

Any negativity experienced by the participants often stemmed from misunderstandings about surrogacy. Children born through surrogacy encountered confusion between surrogacy and adoption, disbelief about their own accounts and exposure to surrogacy myths (for example, that intended parents are not 'real' parents, or that UK surrogates are routinely paid). Importantly, children often took on the role of correcting these misconceptions, acting as informal educators for peers and even teachers. A striking finding across all Phases was the almost total absence of education about surrogacy. When it did appear in the curriculum, it was confined to brief references in Biology, Religious Studies or PSHE, typically framed either as a reproductive process or an ethical/moral issue. The children reported no systematic discussion of surrogacy as a route to family formation. Additionally, as some Phase Two participants noted, they may themselves engage with assisted reproduction in the future, including surrogacy, and would require knowledge to make decisions.

From September 2026, all schools were legally required to update their RSHE curriculum (UK Government Education Hub, 2025). The updated statutory RSE guidance outlines that 'teaching should illustrate a wide range of family structures in a positive way' (Department for Education, 2025, p. 7) and encourages inclusion of 'same-sex parents along with other family arrangements when discussing families' (Department for Education, 2025, p. 36). This is a welcome improvement over the previous guidance, given the explicit inclusion of family diversity. However, surrogacy is not consistently specified or developed as a standalone topic across key stages. A more coherent approach would be to situate surrogacy within a broader 'family forms' framework embedded in statutory RSE. We recommend that surrogacy should be taught in schools: not framed as a moral debate or contentious topic in Religious Studies or elsewhere, but as part of PHSE (or similar). Our findings could be presented to the Department for Education to show that surrogacy should be taught as part of factual, descriptive learning about how families are formed in contemporary society, alongside other routes such as IVF, adoption and donor conception. Such a recommendation aligns with broader educational policy debates about inclusive curricula and the recognition of diverse family forms (Ofsted, 2019). Education should be about family-building and contain information about different family forms to both help children understand infertility and to recognise that those around them might come from different family structures, thereby reducing any stigma and increasing peer understanding. It would also educate them about family-building in different ways, which would be beneficial if they needed to use such methods in the future.

Participants with experience of surrogacy thought that they should be included in law reform, as they could give insights into the reality of surrogacy. Participants without experience of surrogacy, especially older ones, demonstrated an awareness that legal frameworks governing surrogacy may affect their future reproductive choices. Importantly, they articulated principled reasons for their inclusion in law reform projects: they are the ones who will be potentially impacted by future law and, where they have lived experiences, this should feed into debates. Thus, we recommend that future law reform processes on surrogacy and assisted reproduction, more broadly, should incorporate children's perspectives. The involvement of children in such efforts should not be tokenistic, as their views enhance the legitimacy and empirical grounding of legal reform efforts. We suggest that where possible, law reform bodies and policymakers engage in child-friendly methods to involve children in consultative processes for those reasons. This could be done through commissioning research projects such as Children's Voices in Surrogacy Law, or by policymakers creating child-friendly consultation materials and/or meeting with children. This aligns with broader commitments in international and domestic law to children's participatory rights, including under Article 12 of the UNCRC, which emphasises the right of children to express views in matters affecting them, which includes law and policy development.[29]

[29]See discussion in Chapter 1, pp. 34–35.

Conclusion: Hearing From Children on Surrogacy Law Reform

Introduction

Law, policy and practice surrounding surrogacy in the United Kingdom have been shaped by assumptions about children. These have included how children born through surrogacy might be affected by knowing they were born through surrogacy, knowing about payments to surrogates and maintaining contact with the surrogate and her family. There have also been assumptions made about how children of surrogates might be impacted by experiencing their mother undertaking surrogacy. Some of these assumptions have shaped the existing law on surrogacy, particularly governing legal parenthood and contributions to surrogates. While access to origin information regarding surrogacy is not regulated, the law on gamete donation has been shaped by assumptions about the interests and needs of children. In recent years in the United Kingdom, there have been moves to reform the law on surrogacy, which were instigated, in part, by those with experience of surrogacy, drawing attention to the fact that the current law is unfit for purpose. The most recent development in this regard has been the Law Commissions' 5-year project considering surrogacy law reform. Support for the inclusion of this project was evident, given that the consultation on whether to include surrogacy in the 13th Programme of Law Reform received a significant number of favourable responses. The project included direct consultations with stakeholders, including intended parents, surrogates, non-profit surrogacy organisations, counsellors, social workers, lawyers and academics, alongside a 4-month public consultation period which received over 680 responses. The Law Commissions published a comprehensive Final Report making recommendations for surrogacy law reform, alongside a draft Surrogacy Bill in March 2023 (Law Commission and Scottish Law Commission, 2023). However, one set of views was notably absent in this process: those of children.

Children's Voices in Surrogacy Law, 179–193

doi:10.1108/978-1-83549-642-820261007

The Children's Voices on Surrogacy Law (CVSL) project was designed to address this gap in the consultation process and in the existing empirical research. The research questions were:

- What do children think of the current law and law reform on surrogacy?
- What are children's experiences and perceptions of surrogacy in the United Kingdom?
- What do these insights mean for current and future law and policy?

We engaged with 54 children through group and one-to-one interviews, which involved card games, follow-up questions and artwork. The methods were designed to be inclusive, child-friendly and engaging for the participant age range, which was 8–18 years old. The project engaged with two distinct cohorts of children. The first cohort had experience of surrogacy, by being born through surrogacy, being the child of a surrogate or being a relative of a child born through surrogacy (Phases One and Three). The second group did not have experience of surrogacy and were drawn from primary and secondary schools (Phase Two). There was significant value in speaking to both groups. Children born through surrogacy have experience of what it is like to be born through surrogacy, to know their surrogate and her family, and to navigate being born through surrogacy with friends and peers. Children whose mothers are surrogates or whose relatives are surrogate-born have direct experience of day-to-day surrogacy processes, interact with their mother/relative during the surrogacy journey and navigate this with peers and friends. Children without experience of surrogacy provide a different lens; they experience surrogacy as a social phenomenon with which they have no direct experience. Their views can tell us how surrogacy is perceived by this group, how much they know about surrogacy and how they approach issues in surrogacy without prior experience. Both cohorts provide insights that can enrich law and policy debates in surrogacy, both domestically and globally.[1] Children should be included in these debates, not only because their experiences and views can help us evaluate existing law and policy, but also because any reforms would impact them, if they were to be involved in surrogacy in the future.

This chapter sets out the main conclusions of each of this book's substantive chapters, with a focus on recommendations for law and policy and follows with some overarching conclusions and methodological reflections.

---

[1]It is recognised that these findings are reflective of social and historical settings of the United Kingdom and may not have the same significance in other time periods or social settings (Greene & Hill, 2005). Nonetheless, these findings can be used by other jurisdictions as an insight into children's views about the United Kingdom's framework and reform recommendations, which address the core issues in surrogacy that are the subject of debate globally.

Children's Insights on Parenthood in Surrogacy

The first insight is that participants recognised that being a parent is more about love and care and the day-to-day act of parenting than genetic or gestational connections. They therefore supported the idea that intended parents should be regarded in law as the parents of a child born through surrogacy. Largely, this was linked to intentionality, choice, the value of upholding agreements and assumed responsibility. In addition, across all Phases, most participants thought parental orders unnecessary and/or that the process should be changed. The findings suggest that participants would likely support the Law Commissions' recommendation to create a new 'pathway' to parenthood or even a presumption in favour of parenthood for intended parents.

The second insight is that participants believe that people should abide by the agreements they make. In this respect, the Law Commissions also propose the creation of Regulated Surrogacy Organisations (RSOs) which would facilitate and oversee agreements and support the parties to them, including via a Regulated Surrogacy Statement (RSS). Our participants, who saw the value in keeping to agreements, would likely support such a system.[2] Nonetheless, a minority of participants did think the surrogate should be able to change her mind and have parental rights or contact with the child. Therefore, the mechanisms in the proposed pathway, which facilitate changes of mind by surrogates, would possibly be supported by these participants. However, it should also be noted that some participants proposed the recognition of more than two parents (particularly in the case of traditional surrogacy). This could be considered in law reform by (a) allowing three (or more) parents to enter the new pathway; and/or (b) in case of a dispute or the withdrawal of the surrogate's consent, allowing courts to assign parenthood to multiple people.

A third insight is that the development of a 'recognised list' of suitable overseas surrogacy jurisdictions should be reconsidered for jurisdictions (or individual agencies), the practices of which are recognised as ethical by the regulator. There could also be a lighter touch process for parental orders for such countries. This is because of the positive insights we heard from all five children born through surrogacy in the United States in this project, as were explored in Chapters 4 and 5. However, in this respect, it would be important to ensure that any country placed on such a list makes origin information about surrogates and donors available. In this respect, all five participants born through surrogacy in the United States had contact with their surrogate and viewed this contact and connection with their country of birth positively.

A fourth insight is that most participants did not consider that a genetic link is necessarily material to the concept of *being* a parent. Currently, to obtain a

---

[2]Participants also indicated that there should be more education around surrogacy (Chapter 5), to avoid misunderstandings and myths. The creation of State-regulated RSOs should assure the public that surrogacy can be practised ethically, in the interests of all parties, including children. This could help to dispel myths and encourage surrogates and intended parents to choose this regulated model.

parental order, at least one intended parent must have a genetic link to the child. The Law Commissions recommend that this position should be maintained for both the new 'pathway' and residual parental order cases. Our participants would likely not support this recommendation. Some noted the disproportionate effect this could have on solo intended parents. One pointed out that even where there is no genetic connection, the intention could be proved with an agreement. Therefore, at least in the context of surrogacy arrangements undertaken on the pathway and overseen by a RSO, perhaps the genetic link requirement should be reconsidered, possibly by allowing 'double donation' based on the concept of 'medical need', a proposal initially included in the Law Commission and Scottish Law Commission (2019a, 2019b) consultation paper. If parental orders are retained, we would also recommend a reconsideration of this provision.

A final insight derives from our observations of participants' use of language such as 'proper', 'real' or 'actual' parent, or 'mum'. Mostly this was used in the context of genetic contributors rather than who gave birth. It was clear that genetics, though not viewed as determinative of parenthood, has a strong hold on participants' understanding of kinship (this was also noted in Chapter 5). This may suggest that participants would support a more radical reconsideration of legal parenthood in the context of assisted reproduction more generally, recognising their inclusive understanding of family forms. Though they did not explicitly say so, children might support measures to increase inclusive measures to recognise more diverse families. Law and policy makers could consider removing gendered terminology ('mother' and 'father') from the legislation and from birth registration. While children would be free to name their parents in any way they chose (e.g. 'mum', 'dad'), legislation and neutral birth certificates could simply define people (whatever number is allowed) as 'parents'. In addition, since the use of some of this terminology to refer to surrogates and gamete donors could be hurtful or confusing for children born through surrogacy, we suggest that is important to introduce education on alternative family forms in schools, to expand children's understandings of parenthood, as discussed in Chapter 5.

Children's Insights on Contributions to Surrogates

This chapter found two overarching insights about contributions to surrogates. The first is that participants assessed contributions to surrogacy arrangements through a relational and contextual framework rather than through a formal altruism/payment binary, the latter of which is reflected in current law and the Law Commissions' Final Report (2023). Across all Phases, participants were concerned with whether contributions preserved rather than displaced altruistic motivation, prevented financial disadvantage to the surrogate and intended parents, and reflected genuine agreement between the parties. Their reasoning was grounded in fairness, proportionality and sensitivity to coercion, rather than fixed categories. The second insight is that participants' reasoning challenged the assumption that payment is *inherently* commodifying for surrogates and/or children born through surrogacy. Participants generally focused on whether payment introduced coercion into the arrangement. This distinction was drawn across all Phases, though was most clearly articulated by Phase Three participants, whose interpretive framework may have reflected their personal experience and knowledge of being born through (commercial) surrogacy in the United States. For these participants, payment was understood as recognition of commitment and effort and as a signal of the intended parents' intentionality and desire, rather than as the 'purchase of gestational services'. This finding suggests that altruism/commercialisation distinction (as reflected in current and proposed UK law) should be replaced with a regulatory approach that attends to the meaning and function of particular contributions, rather than reliance on strict categorisation. Regulatory approaches that allow for this, rather than the assignment of formal labels to contributions, would more accurately reflect the range of ethical reasoning that the empirical findings present.

These overarching insights have the following implications for law and policy. The Law Commissions' recommendations, specifying 10 categories of permissible payments and four categories of prohibited payments, and introducing RSOs to oversee arrangements (Law Commission and Scottish Law Commission, 2023; para. 12.22, paras. 12.81–12.110), are a step towards greater clarity. However, the findings do not support the categorical prohibition of payments for 'gestational services', without any mechanism for assessing the relational context or function of an agreed payment. Rather, a framework in which the reimbursement of expenses remains central, while modest additional payments may be permissible, would seem more aligned with participants' views. Such payments should be clearly understood, agreed by all parties to the arrangement, clearly outlined in the RSS and overseen by an RSO. They should not be inducements to the surrogate or put pressure on intended parents. In this regard, if the Law Commissions' proposal to establish RSOs was introduced, they could be tasked with seeking to ensure that all payments outlined in the RSS are consistent with the non-commercial principles of the proposed new pathway. While an approval process is already envisaged in the Law Commissions' proposals, this covers consideration of the welfare of any child that would be born, medical and criminal checks, implications counselling, separate legal advice for intended parents and surrogates, and ensuring life and critical illness insurances are in place for the surrogate. We propose that this process could also include a requirement to check the financial terms of the agreement, what payments are proposed and whether they contravene the non-commercial underpinnings of the pathway. We also suggest that this oversight function of RSOs should be introduced into draft legislation and that, through a Code of Practice, RSOs should be empowered to develop their own guidance for assessing payments. Intended parents who would be ineligible for the new pathway would still need, under the existing recommendations, to apply for a parental order. This would include those who enter 'independent' domestic arrangements and international surrogacy arrangements. The Law Commissions' draft Surrogacy Bill still envisages that payments could be retrospectively authorised by the court in such situations (clauses 18(11) (b), 19(8) (b), 20(1)). However, the Commissions have also set out an option, conferring power on courts or RSOs to 'refer the intended parents to the enforcing authority for the imposition of a civil (financial) penalty' if they made impermissible payments. Such a system of oversight should be considered, given participants' concerns with ensuring agreements, including contributions within them, are fair but also flexible.

A final insight is that a minority of Phase Two participants moved beyond the private-ordering model entirely, suggesting that certain surrogacy-related costs should in principle be met through public provision by the state rather than allocated between the parties. This finding is a significant departure from the private ordering approach as practised in the United Kingdom. We suggest that exploration of an alternative framework for surrogacy regulation, beyond the private ordering approach currently adopted, deserves attention in future law and policy reform, even if it falls outside the scope of the Law Commissions' current recommendations.

Children's Insights on Origin Information

The first important insight is that most participants believed that being open about the manner of a child's birth and the people involved is preferable to secrecy. While there was some variability in responses to questions about access to information about donors, knowing about and having information about surrogates was very much supported. There was also support for children knowing if the surrogate was genetically related to them. In terms of surrogacy in the United Kingdom, it is common for there to be an ongoing relationship between the surrogate and her family and the surrogate-born child's family, at least when the arrangements are supported by the not-for-profit surrogacy organisations (Pott & White, 2025). However, studies in the United Kingdom show low levels of disclosure regarding gamete donation (MacCallum et al., 2007; Murray & Golombok, 2003) and the use of traditional surrogacy (Jadva et al., 2012). In this regard, the Law Commissions' Final Report (2023) proposed the establishment of a Surrogacy Register to allow children access to genetic, gestational and 'intention-based' information.[3] While participants would likely be supportive of measures to increase openness in surrogacy, it should be noted that the proposed Register may be more applicable for children who have *not* been told information by their parents. We did not ask participants what they thought of the Register proposal, or the idea of children applying for information that is not available to them from their family. However, participants did not envisage the disclosure process outside of the family setting. Therefore, it can be deduced that they would not consider that finding out information from the Register to be an ideal approach to disclosure. This means that all measures that are taken in the United Kingdom to encourage openness with children about surrogacy and/or gamete donation within families are in line with the participants' views. All ongoing efforts to encourage openness about donor conception and surrogacy should be continued. In this respect, we recommend including a summary of this research in any guidance given to intended parents by the Human Fertilisation and Embryology Authority (HFEA), the British Infertility

[3]The latter phrase is not used in the Report (see Brown & Wade, 2024; Wade, 2025). However, the Report refers to those intended parents without a genetic link who 'played a role in the formation of the agreement which led to the surrogacy agreement' and as part of the 'narrative of the surrogacy agreement'. See Law Commission and Scottish Law Commission (2023), para. 13.104.

Counselling Association and the Department of Health and Social Care and by support organisations such as SurrogacyUK (SUK), My Surrogacy Journey, Brilliant Beginnings, the Donor Conception Network, Donor Conceived UK and Paths to Parenthub. Since openness is not the norm globally, at least in relation to gamete donation, we also suggest that international guidance on surrogacy and gamete donation (ESHRE, 2022; Ethics Committee of the American Society for Reproductive Medicine, 2018) and instruments developed by international bodies should cite these research findings to show children's support for openness, as has been done by non-governmental organisations such as the International Social Service and the Child Identity Protection Network. This would draw the attention of law and policymakers to these first empirical insights into children's views on the law on origin information and potentially instigate further engagement with children's views in other jurisdictions. In addition, if the proposed Surrogacy Register were introduced and intended parents who used international surrogacy, for example, were unwilling or unable to provide origin information for the Register, a system of civil penalties could be introduced to disincentivise this practice.

A second insight for law and policy is that these participants supported a child-led and parent-supported approach to disclosure of origins and information about the people involved. They thought that disclosure should be led by children asking questions or showing curiosity about their origins and that parents should provide information in line with their questions and their understanding levels. There was respect for child autonomy, but also deference to adults' autonomy and a concern that everyone involved, including the surrogate, should be comfortable with information sharing. This is a novel idea for information disclosure. In terms of surrogacy in the United Kingdom, this would be relatively easy to implement and is likely to already be happening, since ongoing relationships between families is common, at least when the arrangements are supported by the not-for-profit surrogacy organisations (Pott & White, 2025). Nonetheless, such an approach should be included in the guidance for intended parents outlined above, and this research could be cited to show that this model of disclosure is based on children's views. However, to introduce such an approach for access to information about gamete donors would require a change in the law. Currently, donor-conceived children can access non-identifying donor information at age 16 and identifying information at age 18. Therefore, recent recommendations (HFEA, 2023b) to allow release of donor information during childhood would be more in line with the approach the participants envisage. To fully allow for this, however, the best approach would be for different types of information to be released with both parental consent and child consent/assent (Brown & Wade, 2024). If such a change were to occur, both the application system and the information released would need to be child-friendly in terms of usability and language.

One issue that is more difficult to discern is whether participants would support a mandatory disclosure system for origin information. For example, the Law Commission and Scottish Law Commission (2023, para. 13.216) proposed that birth certificates should be clear that a child's birth was through surrogacy. Some insights from participants would seem to go against such an approach:

participants said such information was not 'necessary' or 'essential'; many argued that children should not be forced to know information they did not want to know and there was also deference to parents' desires about disclosing information. At the same time, openness did seem to be the preferable approach; participants felt that children's autonomy should be respected if they asked/showed curiosity about their origins. In relation to the latter idea, it did seem that, when participants spoke about children asking their parents questions about origin information, these participants pre-supposed that such children knew *the fact* of their birth through surrogacy. While it cannot be known for certain, these participants may have supported birth certificate notification, but only if its function was to increase openness within families. They would be very unlikely to think that is how children should find out about their origins, given their ideas for a child-led and parent-supported model, outlined above.

A final insight for policy and practice is that a culture of openness regarding surrogacy and donor conception is more likely to flourish if there is social acceptance of the practice. While there may be a much more accepting attitude to assisted reproduction now than there was when it was first introduced,[4] this does not mean that children's social networks have been influenced by this. In Chapter 5, it was shown that there was very little knowledge about surrogacy among children who had no direct experience of it, and participants with experience of surrogacy encountered myths and misunderstandings in their peer networks. Therefore, while openness within families born through surrogacy and donor conception may be preferable, if children encounter ignorance or misunderstandings when speaking about this with their peers, this may lead to negative experiences for them. Therefore, as discussed in the next section, education about different forms of family-building for children and young people is needed.

Surrogacy in Children's Social Worlds

The findings show that children with experience of surrogacy often express pride about the way they were born or the role of their mother as a surrogate and they are open about surrogacy with their peers. This was evident from accounts from both children born through surrogacy and children of surrogates. This aligns with the findings in the project artwork, which depicted surrogacy as forging connections and eliciting positive emotions, such as joy and excitement (Wade & Mills, 2025). Such findings go against anti-surrogacy arguments that surrogacy is inherently harmful to children, and complement a substantial body of longitudinal empirical research demonstrating that children born through surrogacy show positive psychological adjustment and family relationships (Golombok, 2020a, 2020b; Golombok et al., 2017, 2023; Jadva et al., 2023). We therefore recommend that in other jurisdictions, where such arguments are used to restrict

[4]For societal reactions to IVF and gamete donation, see Richards (2016). For early attitudes to surrogacy, see the Warnock Report (Department of Health & Social Security, 1984).

surrogacy, there should be attempts to engage with children born through surrogacy (though this may be difficult in any context where surrogacy is illegal). However, other jurisdictions should at least consider these findings, as well as longitudinal research from the United Kingdom with children who have experience of surrogacy.

Another insight was that within children's peer networks, misunderstandings and myths about surrogacy are common. The participants highlighted the persistence of inaccurate narratives surrounding surrogacy, which led to some taking on the role of informal educators for peers and even teachers about surrogacy. Participants described the need to actively correct peers or navigate awkward social interactions shaped by misunderstandings. Some encountered confusion between surrogacy and adoption, disbelief about their own accounts and exposure to surrogacy myths (e.g., that surrogacy is illegal, that intended parents are not 'real' parents, that surrogates in the United Kingdom are paid or that surrogacy involved sexual intercourse between an intended father and the surrogate). Linked to this, another striking finding across all Phases was the almost total absence of education about surrogacy, with only brief references included in Biology, Religious Studies or Personal, Social, Health and Economic Education (PSHE). We recommend, therefore, that, as part of PSHE, there should be education in schools about assisted reproduction, including surrogacy and gamete donation. We do not recommend that this is taught in other areas of the curriculum, where it may be presented as a divisive ethical debate. This is to ensure that assisted reproduction is taught in an inclusive way, and is presented as a way to build a family, with the aim to reduce misunderstandings. Not only would this be important for increasing understanding; but some older participants also noted how they would need to have knowledge about surrogacy in case they needed to use such methods of family-building in the future.

Another important insight is that in surrogacy in the United Kingdom, families created through surrogacy typically have ongoing contact and relationships with the surrogate and her family. All of the participants born through surrogacy knew and had contact with their surrogate, including those born through international surrogacy arrangements in the United States. This contact was viewed positively, a finding which is also clear from the children's artwork, which depicted connections between intended parents, surrogates and children (Wade & Mills, 2025).[5] However, it was also noted by participants that there should be no fixed rules around contact. While some emphasised the importance of ongoing contact, others regarded limited or no contact as equally valid, depending on the circumstances and expectations established within families. In this regard, there was an emphasis on ensuring that there is agreement at the outset about the kind of contact that families are comfortable with. The participants' views align with the practice that is encouraged by non-profit

[5]See: https://childrensvoices.bristol.ac.uk/childrens-artwork/. A striking example of this positive depiction of the relationship and collaboration between intended parents and surrogate is displayed on this book's cover.

surrogacy organisations in the United Kingdom, i.e., that surrogacy should be based on friendship and collaboration (Pott & White, 2025). The findings also indicate that greater support for these organisations would be welcome, suggesting that the Law Commissions' proposal to create RSOs should be taken forward.[6] These findings lend support for such a model of surrogacy, based on friendship, collaboration and agreement about contact, for other jurisdictions that are considering introducing surrogacy law and policy or instigating reform.

We also explored insights into how children make sense of familial roles and boundaries in surrogacy. We found that surrogacy formed extended kinship networks for participants, which were described by them with a variety of language and classificatory terms. Participants often engaged in nuanced reasoning to distinguish between biological, gestational and social forms of parenthood, as well as other extended relationships created by surrogacy, revealing flexible yet deliberate constructions of kinship. For example, participants with experience of surrogacy variably foregrounded or downplayed genetic, biological and social relationships, depending on context. We also found that there was no established vocabulary for relationships created through surrogacy, which led participants to draw on existing kinship terms within the familiar 'family' framework, such as 'aunt' or 'cousin', to refer to surrogates or children their mother had through surrogacy. Again, these findings go against arguments that surrogacy may be confusing for children or cause them to question legal parenthood or their identity, as is sometimes advanced by anti-surrogacy organisations.

Finally, participants thought that their views should be heard in law and policy reform. For children with experience of surrogacy, they recognised that it was important that their views were heard, since they had direct experience. Children without experience said that they should be involved in law reform, since they would be impacted by any future law and policy. This aligns with the commitment in international law under Article 12 of the United Nations Convention on the Rights of the Child (UNCRC), which emphasises the right of children to express views in matters affecting them including in the context of law and policy development. Therefore, we recommend that any future law reform of surrogacy should seek to incorporate children's perspectives, both in the United Kingdom and globally, by engaging with these findings and/or consulting further with children on any changes to law and policy. Since the Committee on the Rights of the Child has interpreted States Parties' legal obligations under the UNCRC to include children in public decision-making more broadly (Byrne & Lundy, 2019; Committee on the Rights of the Child, 2009), the methods used in this project could be drawn on to involve children in other areas of law and

[6]The creation of a new Surrogacy Register is also ideologically aligned with the idea that contact between families is important. However, the contact that children talked about was contact facilitated between families during childhood, whereas the Register may be more to do with children accessing information that has not been available to them from their families. While the participants are not envisaging contact in this context, if the Surrogacy Register were to increase openness, this would be a positive outcome, and one which these participants would likely support.

policy. The next section sets out reflections on how the CVSL method is an effective way of engaging with children on research on law and law reform.

Engaging With Children on Surrogacy Law Reform: Reflections on Methods

The methodology in this project was based on the premise that children are social agents and holders of rights whose perspectives on law and policy are valuable and significant. The methods of data collection involved group and one-on-interviews, which involved 'speaking' (interview questions), 'playing' (card games) and 'creating' (artwork). The methods were based on the Lundy model of participation (Lundy, 2007), which is centred around the concepts of space, voice, audience and influence, and the Mosaic approach (Clark, 2017), which uses a variety of methods to capture different ways in which children express themselves. We had several aims when we designed the project. First, we aimed to listen to children's views, not merely as providing feedback on already established legal frameworks, but as a primary source of insight. In order to do this, we did not generally frame the questions in legal terms and did not present the current legal position. While we did address the law on parental orders, this was after a more open discussion and brainstorming exercise about parenthood. This approach sought to ensure that participants' views were not shaped by being presented with the status quo. In this sense, the research does not take a 'law first' approach (Watkins et al., 2018); it focuses on children's perspectives rather than foregrounding the research with abstract legal concepts or specific laws. Second, the data collection methods needed to be inclusive of our broad age range (8–18). Participants needed to be able to understand what was being asked and be able to engage in a meaningful way. In this respect, we used 'explanation cards' to define important concepts in surrogacy. Following the Mosaic approach and focusing on the 'voice' element of the Lundy model, we used different methods to capture children's insights, including through card games, follow-up questions and the creation of artwork. We also adapted the language and explanations for the age-group, and spent longer on explanations with younger age groups, for example. Our third aim was for the methods to be engaging. Since the topic was about complex legal issues, a way to maintain participants' attention was required. In this respect we paid attention to both 'voice' and 'space' under the Lundy model, providing participants with a 'play-space' including Post-its for brainstorming, and card games which included voting, sorting into categories and circling answers. They were also provided with an 'art space' to make any type of creative contribution on open topics about surrogacy.[7] This tactile, play-orientated method, along with the creative element of artmaking, was effective in maintaining participants' attention for the duration of the interviews.

---

[7]These were: What surrogacy means to me? (Phases One and Three) and What I learned about surrogacy today? (Phase Two).

This method could be used by academic researchers, law reform bodies, such as the Law Commission of England and Wales/Scottish Law Commission, and any other organisations working in law and policy development both in the United Kingdom and globally. There are, however, challenges and additional issues to be considered. First, it can be difficult to recruit children as research participants, since they are often only accessible via parents/carers or organisations. Second, the informed consent process is more complex, since parental and child consent/assent procedures must be considered. For example, different child-friendly and adult consent and information forms need to be designed. Third, there are logistical challenges, since the interviews need to occur when children are either not in school, as was the case in Phases One and Three, or when they are in school, but available to be interviewed, as was the case for Phase Two. In contrast to most research with adults, the interview groups need to be organised into close age ranges (usually with no more than two years in the age gap between participants). Two to three researchers need to be present with the groups, in line with guidelines for ethical research with children and to facilitate the data collection activities. Fourth, researchers need to have skills in engaging with children in research, by ensuring that the group is well managed and that all children have a chance to participate (Hennessy & Heary, 2005). Some of this can be achieved by building rapport through relaxed interactive activities at the start of the interviews and in breaks, as was the case with the artwork creation in this project.

Fifth, in the data analysis phase, it is important to try not to impose adult conceptualisations or language into the coding phase of the theme development. Unless themes are co-produced with participants, these are inevitably constructed by the researchers, and adult terminology will inevitably be used in the interpretation of findings (Westcott & Littleton, 2005). Therefore, it is important that the codes which underpin the themes use authentic language and ideas from the data, thus ensuring that the views of the children have shaped the themes constructed (Dockett et al., 2009; Einarsdóttir et al., 2009). For example, if participants say that children should know who their surrogate is, because she 'gave birth' or 'made you alive', the code should represent this idea, rather than being translated into 'a right to identity'. Another measure which can reduce bias in the data analysis is to engage in group coding, so that researchers can see the codes produced by other researchers (Braun & Clarke, 2022, p. 285). In addition, providing examples of the children's words or artwork, through the inclusion of quotes and artwork samples, is also effective in allowing the reader to see the way in which the language of the children was interpreted (Greig et al., 2013). Sixth, the method can be adjusted in certain ways to address issues we encountered. While asking open questions was effective in gaining authentic insights, it can sometimes be difficult to ascertain the meaning of the participants' views for specific laws or reform ideas. This can be seen in relation to birth certificate notification, for example. Therefore, if views on a particular legal measure are desired, direct questions on this would be effective, after open questions are posed, as was the case for the way in which parental orders were addressed. Furthermore, if researchers wish to ask questions without legal content, it is important to consider whether the way in which the question is framed is already shaped by law. For example, we asked participants who the parents of a surrogate-born child should be and only allowed their answer to include one or two individuals, which follows the current legal position and could foreclose other ideas for parenthood. Therefore, considering which questions are exploratory and which are directly about established law, and the order in which these are asked, are important factors to consider for those planning projects with children on law reform.

It has been recognised that participation of children in public decision-making must not be tokenistic, but their views should be considered when laws and policies are developed (Byrne & Lundy, 2019; Committee on the Rights of the Child, 2009). Article 12 of the UNCRC states that children's views must be given 'due weight' in line with their age and understanding, meaning active efforts should be made by government and policymakers to create a space where children's views are considered in public decision-making (Forde et al., 2020). The Committee on the Rights of the Child has made it clear that barriers to such participation should be removed, meaning that training should be provided for those who work with children, and that legislative and administrative resources need to be put in place to allow for participation (Committee on the Rights of the Child, 2009; Forde et al., 2020). This can include children's parliaments, councils, child representatives, clubs, conferences, ad hoc consultations, politicians' 'surgeries' and social media (Forde et al., 2020). The Committee has recommended that participation in public decision-making should not be restricted to issues affecting children, but that children should be consulted any time that their perspectives can enhance the quality of solutions (Byrne & Lundy, 2019; Committee on the Rights of the Child, 2009). Therefore, this means that if the proposals by the Law Commission are taken forward by the government and reform to the law is considered, the findings of this project should be taken into account in considering legal changes, through engagement with this book, the project's preliminary reports[8] and the analysis of the artwork (Wade & Mills, 2025). If the law is to be changed, children should also be involved directly, where possible, for example through consultative meetings during the pre-legislative scrutiny phase of any new legislation. Children's views should also be included in briefing papers for MPs and Peers who will be debating any new legislation as it passes through parliament and child rights impact assessments of the new legislation should be conducted.[9]

---

[8]See Children's Voices in Surrogacy Law, 2023a, 2023b.

[9]No statutory duty exists in England for child rights impact assessments. For Child Rights and Wellbeing Impact Assessments in Scotland, see https://www.gov.scot/publications/child-rights-wellbeing-impact-assessment-external-guidance-templates/ and for Wales see https://www.gov.wales/childrens-rights-impact-assessments-2025. Such measures are duties under the United Nations Convention on the Rights of the Child (Incorporation) (Scotland) Act 2024 and the Rights of Children and Young Persons (Wales) Measure 2011.

Conclusion: Listening to Children About Law Reform

CVSL is the first research project to explore children's views on law and policy governing surrogacy. It therefore makes a significant contribution to the empirical literature regarding children in the context of assisted reproduction. Previous empirical work has addressed the psychological well-being of surrogate-born children with considerable rigour and to significant effect (Golombok, 2015, 2020b; Golombok et al., 2017, 2023). However, what was lacking was attention to children's perspectives about the law and policy that governs surrogacy, including the regulation of legal parenthood, contributions to surrogates and access to origin information, which have particular significance for children. This gap in the research became particularly relevant when the Law Commissions embarked on their law reform project on surrogacy. While there was extensive engagement from the Law Commission and Scottish Law Commission (2019a) with adults with direct experience of surrogacy, there was no direct engagement with children. This is notwithstanding the fact that many of the issues under examination by the Commissions were relevant to children and that current law was shaped by assumptions about them (Brazier et al., 1998; Department of Health & Social Security, 1984).

The book presents a new method for engaging with children about law reform. It has demonstrated that children can meaningfully participate in research about complex legal and ethical questions when methods are appropriately designed. The combination of playing, speaking and creating art captured the diversity of children's communicative styles and capacities, and thereby, produced rich data. It allowed us not only to explore their views on legal issues, but also to gain insights into how they perceive, experience and understand surrogacy. The book adds to a growing body of scholarship on child-inclusive methods in legal research and provides a new model for research on law reform which is adaptable to future projects and reform consultations. Such methods can be used in seeking to abide by the legal obligations imposed by Article 12 of the UNCRC in international law to take children's views into account in all matters affecting them, including in law and policy development.

At the level of substantive law, the book made specific contributions regarding the regulation of parenthood, contributions to surrogates and origin information, as detailed above. Overarching arguments can also be drawn out. First, children often think in a different way about issues that the law regulates and are often creative in their approaches. For legal parenthood, children welcomed intention-based models and proposed ideas regarding three-parent families; the latter is something which is not currently permitted by law and was not put forward as a reform proposal. There was also acknowledgement of wider kinship relationships created by surrogacy. Participants adopted a relational and contextual approach to contributions, moving beyond the formal altruism/payment binary. They considered that payments in surrogacy should be allowed, as long as they did not indicate coercion of the surrogate or unfairness to the intended parents. Some even suggested that certain surrogacy-related costs should in principle be met through public provision by the state. For disclosure of origins, participants proposed a disclosure model for origin information during childhood which would be led by questions and curiosity from the child. Such an approach was not proposed by the Law Commissions and is not currently supported by the law on gamete donation.

Second, because the research also gave insights into children's social worlds, it became clear that while certain legal reforms could improve the lives of adults, differing understandings and knowledge of surrogacy within children's social circles means that wider changes may be needed than law and policymakers may have so far considered. For example, there were low levels of understanding about surrogacy and legal parenthood among children, meaning that surrogacy may be confused with adoption. Regarding payments, some children of surrogates spoke of assumptions by peers that their mother was paid for surrogacy. Additionally, while openness about surrogacy and gamete donation might now be seen as best practice, children born through assisted reproduction may still be met with misunderstandings amongst their peer groups, which may have negative effects. Therefore, education in schools about different types of family-building, including through assisted reproduction, is needed. If law and policy reforms are only considered as being implemented with adult social interactions in mind, the need for such policy measures could be overlooked entirely. Therefore, this research demonstrates that children's reasoning about surrogacy laws were not merely reflective of adults' views, and instead, constituted an independent source of insight, which provided novel ideas about regulation and insights into the social worlds of children, into which any law and policy reforms would be implemented.

This book therefore makes the case for child-inclusive law reform in the field of surrogacy. We found that children have knowledge about their own lives that adults, including legislators and academics, do not. We cannot know how surrogacy impacts children unless we ask children themselves. Talking to adults with experience of surrogacy and donor conception is valuable, but it does not provide an authentic insight into how surrogacy is understood or experienced by children. Talking to adults about their childhood will provide only adult reflections on the past, interpreted through adult understandings. It should not be assumed that children will be unable to understand legal concepts or ethical dilemmas. Our research found that children reason about complex legal and ethical issues with greater sophistication and nuance than may be assumed by law and policymakers. Their views revealed rich and nuanced perspectives that can shape law and policy and gave us insights into their unique social worlds. It is hoped that this research and the novel method presented will encourage increased engagement with children in other areas of law and policy, and ultimately, greater awareness of the value of taking these views into account in future law and policy reform.

Appendix 1: Tables of Participants

Table 5. Phase One Participants.

Interview Group	Name	Age	Gender	Experience of Surrogacy	Relationship
1	Penelope	8	Female	Child of surrogate	
	Raven	9	Female	Child of surrogate	
	Emily	8	Female	Child of surrogate	
	Jenny	8	Female	Child of surrogate	
	Ava	10	Female	Child of surrogate	Sibling of Freya
2	Freya	12	Female	Child of surrogate	Sibling of Ava
	Emma	13	Female	Child of surrogate	
	Ashley	12	Female	Born through traditional surrogacy	
	Eliza	11	Female	Child of surrogate	
	Oliver	11	Male	Child of surrogate	
	Cassidy	11	Female	Child of surrogate	Sibling of Lucy
3	Evalynn	10	Female	Born through gestational surrogacy	Twins
	Scarlett	10	Female	Born through gestational surrogacy	
4	Jack	17	Male	Child of surrogate	
	Lucy	15	Female	Child of surrogate	Sibling of Cassidy
	Anna	16	Female	Cousin of a child born through surrogacy	

(Continued)

Table 5. *(Continued)*

Interview Group	**Name**	**Age**	**Gender**	**Experience of Surrogacy**	**Relationship**
5	Lilly	9	Female	Child of surrogate	
	Aoife	10	Female	Child of surrogate	
	Valeria	9	Female	Child of surrogate	
6	Tom	11	Male	Born through gestational surrogacy	Sibling of Ellie
	Ellie	13	Female	Born through gestational surrogacy	Sibling of Tom
	Bob	11	Male	Child of surrogate	Sibling of Louisa
	Louisa	13	Female	Child of surrogate	Sibling of Bob
7	Christina	14	Female	Born through gestational surrogacy	Twins
	Jane	14	Female	Born through gestational surrogacy	

Table 6. Phase Two Participants.

Interview Group	**Name**	**Age**	**Gender**	**Experience of Surrogacy**	**Relationship**
1	Diego	10	Male	None	
	Tim	11	Male	None	
	Katie	10	Female	None	
	Henry	10	Male	None	
	James	10	Male	None	
2	Jax	8	Male	None	
	Thomas	8	Male	None	
	Alan	8	Male	None	
	Annabelle	10	Female	None	
3	Alice	13	Female	None	
	Jasmine	11	Female	None	
	Bella	13	Female	None	
	Leonard	11	Male	None	

Table 6. *(Continued)*

Interview Group	Name	Age	Gender	Experience of Surrogacy	Relationship
4	Harry	16	Male	None	
	Natalie	15	Female	None	
	Ivy	15	Female	None	
5	Charlotte	15	Female	None	
	Rose	13	Female	None	
	Sienna	13	Female	None	
	Ella	14	Female	None	
6	Carrie	17	Female	None	
	Lydia	16	Female	None	
	Honey	16	Female	None	
	Liam	18	Male	None	

Table 7. Phase Three Participants.

Interview Group	Name	Age	Gender	Experience of Surrogacy	Relationship
1	Camille	13	Female	Born through US gestational surrogacy, egg donor	Sibling of Bill
	Bill	11	Male	Born through US gestational surrogacy, egg donor	Sibling of Camille
2	Steve	9	Male	Born through US gestational surrogacy, egg donor	
3	Alison	12	Female	Born through US gestational surrogacy, egg donor	Twins
4	Bart	12	Male	Born through US gestational surrogacy, egg donor	

Appendix 2: Contributions Comparison

Table 8. Comparison Table.

Contributions in the Card Game	Law Commissions' Category
Maternity clothes; vitamins; food (Phase Three)	Essential costs of pregnancy
Doctors' fees	Costs associated with a surrogacy
Spa voucher; holiday, car, gifts (Phase Three)	Gifts
Lost wages	Loss of earnings
Money	Compensation for being a surrogate

As part of Topic 2 (Contributions to Surrogates), participants were asked to categorise a set of illustration cards into bundles corresponding to cards with 'yes', 'no', 'not sure' and 'maybe' [Phase Three only] to explore what they thought intended parents should be allowed to give surrogates. These illustration cards were drawn from the Law Commissions' proposed payments in the infographic in Appendix 3.

Appendix 3: Law Commissions' Infographic

Law Commissions' Diagrammatic Representation of Proposed Payments. *Source:* Law Commission and Scottish Law Commission. (2019b). *Building families through surrogacy: A new law – summary of consultation paper* (p. 18). https://cdn.websitebuilder.service.justice.gov.uk/uploads/sites/54/2025/12/Surrogacy-summary.pdf

Appendix 4: Images From the Project

Fig. 1. Card Made by Phase One Participants: Aoife (10), Lilly (9) and Valeria (9), All Children of Surrogates.

Fig. 2. Sample 'Explanation Cards' Used for Parental Orders. The image on the right was developed after consultation with children, before Phase 3.

Fig. 3. Sample 'Illustration Cards'. These cards were used in the topic 'Contributions to Surrogates'. The image on the right was developed after consultation with children, before Phase 3.

This illustration card was used only during Phase Three.

Fig. 4. Sample 'Question Card'.

This is a sample question card used during the group interviews in all three Phases. It was used as part of Topic 3 (Origin Information). Participants circled their answers. A 'Maybe' option was added for Phase 3, after consultation with children.

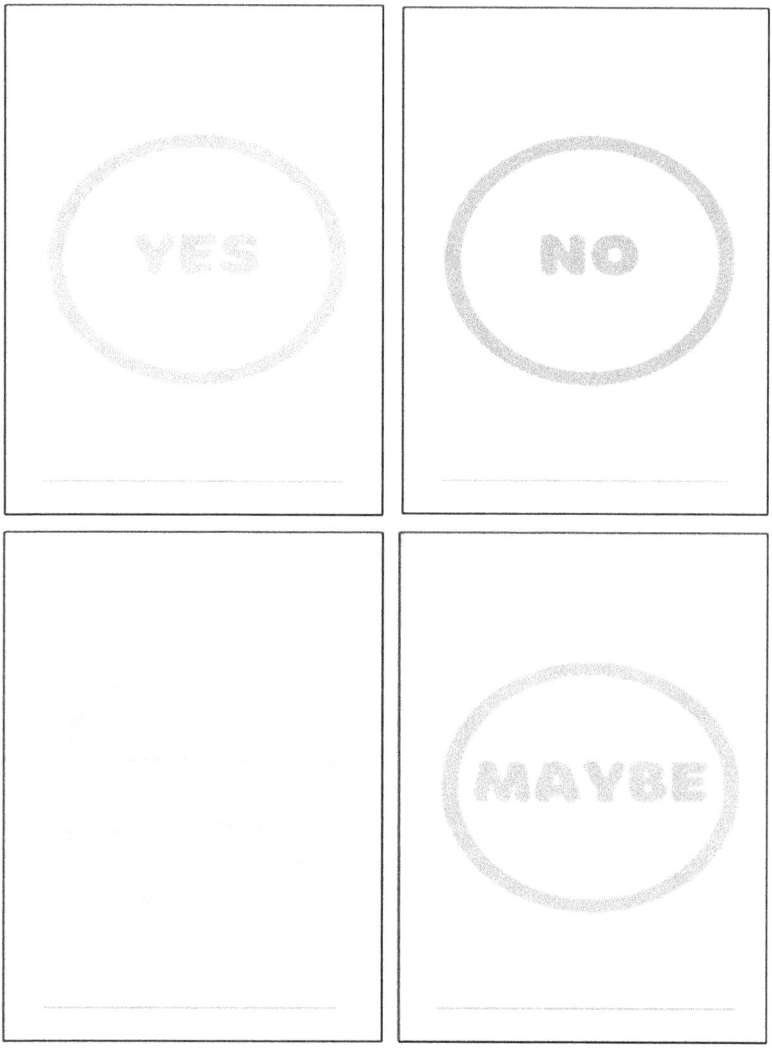

Fig. 5. Sample ‘Response Cards’.

During Topic 2 (Contributions to Surrogates), participants were asked to categorise various ‘illustration cards’ over these cards, as can be seen in Fig. 6. The ‘maybe’ card was added for Phase Three, following the consultation sessions with children held prior to Phase Three.

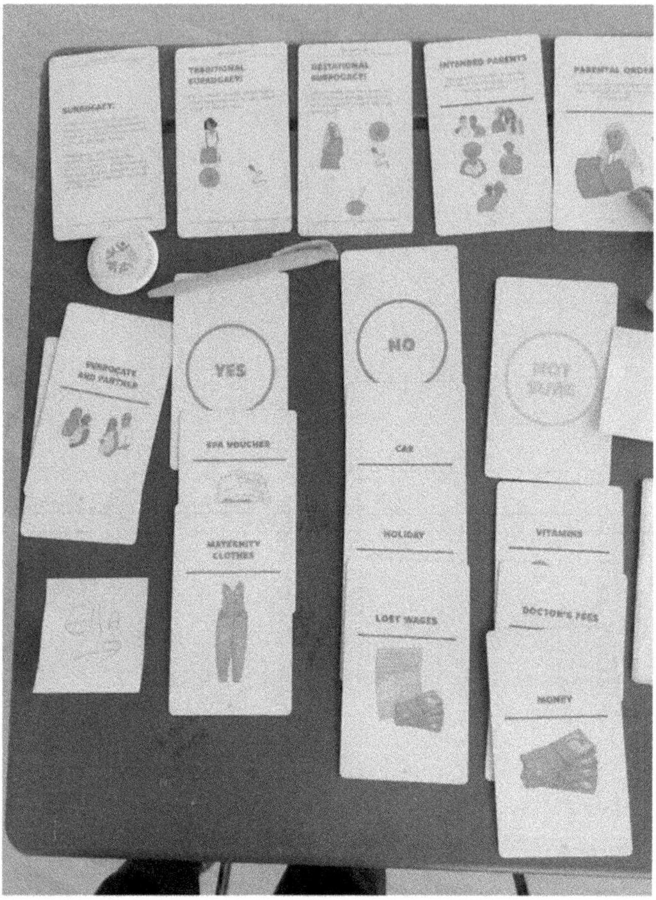

Fig. 6. Sample Set up of Part of the Card Game on the Topic: Contributions to Surrogates.

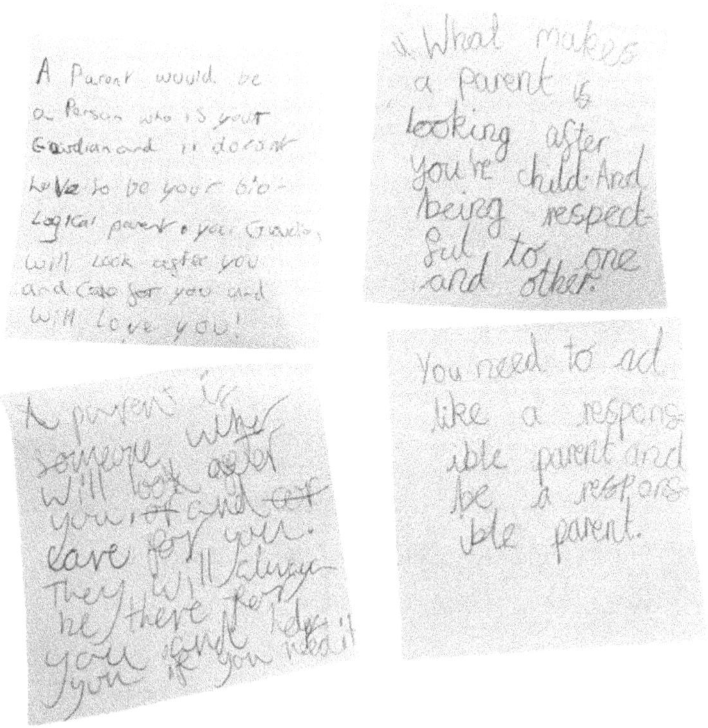

Fig. 7. Sample Post-Its From Participants Produced During Brainstorm Activity in Topic 1 (Parenthood). Participants Were Asked 'What Makes Someone a Parent?'.

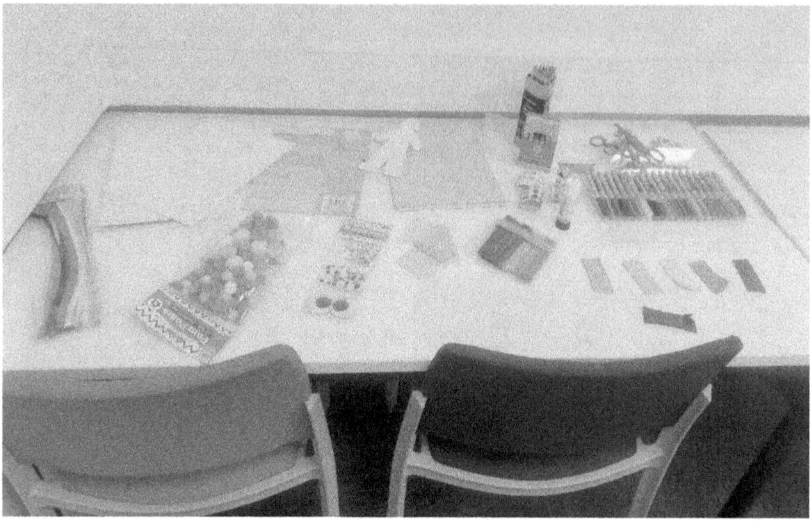

Fig. 8. Example of the Art Space.

Appendix 5: Semi-Structured Interview Questions

The wording of the questions/explanation of terms varied slightly by age group and perceived understanding.

Topic 1: Parenthood

(1) What makes somebody a parent?
(2) When a child is born through surrogacy, who do you think the parents should be?
(3) [Parental orders explained] What do you think of parental orders?
(4) One of the reasons for the rules that we have is to allow the surrogate to change her mind. What do you think of that?
(5) [Genetic link explained] In order to be able to apply to the judge to become the legal parents, one of the intended parents has to be genetically related to the child. What do you think of that?

Topic 2: Contributions to Surrogates

(1) What kinds of things do you think intended parents should be allowed to give surrogates? [Sort cards into categories] Cards in Phase One and Two: car, holiday, doctor's fees, maternity clothes, vitamins, money, spa voucher, lost wages. Added in Phase Three: gifts, food.
(2) Should intended parents be able to pay a surrogate?
(3) Some people think that surrogates should not be paid because children born through surrogacy would not want to know that their surrogate had been paid. What do you think of that?

Topic 3: Origin Information

(1) Should children born through surrogacy be told that they were born this way?
(2) Should children born through surrogacy know who their surrogate was?

(3) Should children born through surrogacy know whether the surrogacy was traditional or gestational?
(4) [Phase One only] Should children of women who act as surrogates know whether the surrogacy was traditional or gestational?
(5) If the surrogacy involves egg or sperm donation, should children born through surrogacy be told about this?
(6) Should children know who the egg or sperm donor is? (Some interviews)
(7) When/what age should children be told and who should them? (Some interviews)
(8) Is contact between the families important? (Some interviews)

Topic 4: Navigating Surrogacy

(1) Is there anything you would like to tell us about your experience of surrogacy?
(2) Do you tell people about surrogacy?
(3) Do you have to explain it to people?
(4) Do you learn about surrogacy in school?
(5) [Phase Three only] Is there anything you would like to add about your experience of being born through international surrogacy?
(6) [Phase Two and Three only] Do you think children should be included in surrogacy law reform?

References

Abbott, O. (2024). *Social theorists of morality: Essays on moral agency*. Palgrave Macmillan.

Åkerström, J., & Brunnberg, E. (2013). Young people as partners in research: Experiences from an interactive research circle with adolescent girls. *Qualitative Research, 13*(5), 528–545. https://doi.org/10.1177/1468794112451035

Akl, E. A., Khabsa, J., Petkovic, J., Magwood, O., Lytvyn, L., Motilall, A., Campbell, P., Todhunter-Brown, A., Schünemann, H. J., Welch, V., Tugwell, P., & Concannon, T. W. (2024). "Interest-holders": A new term to replace "stakeholders" in the context of health research and policy. *Cochrane Evidence Synthesis and Methods, 2*(11), e70007. https://doi.org/10.1002/cesm.70007

Alderson, P., & Morrow, V. (2020). *The ethics of research with children and young people: A practical handbook* (2nd ed.). Sage.

Alderson, P. (2001). Research by children. *International Journal of Social Research Methodology, 4*(2), 139–153. https://doi.org/10.1080/13645570120003

Alghrani, A., & Griffiths, D. (2017). The regulation of surrogacy in the United Kingdom: The case for reform. *Child and Family Law Quarterly, 29*(2), 165–168.

Allan, S. (2017). *Donor conception and the search for information: From secrecy and anonymity to openness*. Routledge. https://doi.org/10.4324/9781315568171

Allen, A. L. (1990). Surrogacy, slavery, and the ownership of life. *Harvard Journal of Law & Public Policy, 13*, 139–149.

Anderson, E. S. (2000). Why commercial surrogate motherhood unethically commodifies women and children: Reply to McLachlan and Swales. *Health Care Analysis, 8*(1), 19–26. https://doi.org/10.1023/A:1009477906883

Annelo, D. (2026). *First baby born through surrogacy celebrates her 40th birthday: "How lucky am I"*. People. https://people.com/first-baby-born-through-surrogacy-celebrates-40th-birthday-11953402

Annual Report of Council. (1973). Annual report of council: Appendix V. *British Medical Journal, 2*(5857), 3–5. https://www.jstor.org/stable/25425240

Armstrong, S. (2021). Surrogacy: Time we recognized it as a job? *Journal of Gender Studies, 30*(7), 864–867. https://doi.org/10.1080/09589236.2021.1915754

Armstrong, S. (2022). Labour is labour: What surrogates can learn from the sex work is work movement. *Journal of Law and Society, 49*(1), 170–192. https://doi.org/10.1111/jols.12350

Australian Law Reform Commission. (2025). *Review of surrogacy laws*. (Discussion Paper 89). https://www.alrc.gov.au/wp-content/uploads/2025/11/Surrogacy-Discussion-Paper.pdf

Bandelj, N., Morgan, P., & Sowers, E. (2015). Hostile worlds or connected lives? Research on the interplay between intimacy and economy. *Sociology Compass, 9*(2), 115–127. https://doi.org/10.1111/soc4.12242

Barlow, A., & Ewing, J. (2024). *Children's voices, family disputes and child-inclusive mediation: The right to be heard.* Bristol University Press. https://doi.org/10.51952/9781529228939

Barlow, C., Burton, M., Hunter, R., Richardson-Foster, H., & Scollay, C. (2026). *Policy briefing: Considerations for the national roll out of 'child focused courts'.* White Rose Research Online. https://eprints.whiterose.ac.uk/id/eprint/239700/1/Policy%20Briefing-%20Child%20focused%20courts.pdf

Baron, T., Svingen, E., & Leyva, R. (2024). Surrogacy and adoption: An empirical investigation of public moral attitudes. *Journal of Bioethical Inquiry, 21*(4), 671–681. https://doi.org/10.1007/s11673-024-10343-1

Barwick, J., Watkins, D., Kirk, E., & Law, E. L.-C. (2018). Adventures with Lex: The gamification of research? *The International Journal of Research into New Media Technologies, 24*(3), 229–250.

Baslington, H. (2002). The social organization of surrogacy: Relinquishing a baby and the role of payment in the psychological detachment process. *Journal of Health Psychology, 7*(1), 57–71. https://doi.org/10.1177/1359105302007001652

BBC. (1985). *On this day 4 January: Inquiry over 'baby-for-cash' deal.* http://news.bbc.co.uk/onthisday/hi/dates/stories/january/4/newsid_2495000/2495857.stm

Belliotti, R. A. (1988). Marxism, feminism, and surrogate motherhood. *Social Theory and Practice, 14*(3), 389–417. https://doi.org/10.5840/soctheorpract198814318

Berk, H. L. (2020). Savvy surrogates and rock star parents: Compensation provisions, contracting practices, and the value of womb work. *Law & Social Inquiry, 45*(2), 398–431. https://doi.org/10.1017/lsi.2019.52

Berthonnet, I., & Clos, C. (2024). Compensating a contested labour: The price of commercial surrogacy in the United States. *Economy and Society, 53*(4), 701–718. https://doi.org/10.1080/03085147.2024.2398948

Bessant, C., & Allsopp, R. (2024). Data-driven decision-making beyond COVID-19: Incorporating the voice of the child. In C. Redhead & M. Smallman (Eds.), *Governance, democracy and ethics in crisis decision-making: The pandemic and beyond* (pp. 94–123). Manchester University Press. https://doi.org/10.7765/9781526180056.00012

Bessant, J., & Broadley, K. (2014). Saying and doing child protective service and participation in decision-making. *The International Journal of Children's Rights, 22*(4), 710–729.

Bessant, C. (2022). Children, public sector data-driven decision-making and article 12 UNCRC. *European Journal of Law and Technology, 13*(2), Article 872.

Birdy, A. (2026). Surrogacy is exploitative, not altruistic. *Critic.* https://thecritic.co.uk/surrogacy-is-exploitative-not-altruistic/

Blaisdell, C., Arnott, L., Wall, K., & Robinson, C. (2019). Look who's talking: Using creative, playful arts-based methods in research with young children. *Journal of Early Childhood Research, 17*(1), 14–31. https://doi.org/10.1177/1476718X18808816

Blake, L., Zadeh, S., Statham, H., & Freeman, T. (2014). Families created through assisted reproduction: Children's perspectives. In T. Freeman, S. Graham, F. Ebtehaj, & M. Richards (Eds.), *Relatedness in assisted reproduction: Families, origins and identities* (pp. 251–269). Cambridge University Press. https://doi.org/10.1017/CBO9781139814737.017

Blank, R. H. (2004). The United Kingdom: Regulation through a national licensing authority. In I. A. Bleiklie, M. L. Goggin, & C. Rothmayr (Eds.), *Comparative biomedical policy: Governing assisted reproductive technologies* (pp. 120–137). Routledge. https://doi.org/10.4324/9780203358306

Blell, M., & Homanen, R. (2025). A haunted data "goldmine": Repropolitical anxieties and injustice in Finland. In S. Franklin & M. C. Inhorn (Eds.), *The new reproductive order: Technology, fertility, and social change around the globe* (pp. 273–290). New York University Press. https://urn.fi/URN:NBN:fi:tuni-202504284240

Blyth, E., Crawshaw, M., Haase, J., & Speirs, J. (2001). The implications of adoption for donor offspring following donor-assisted conception. *Child & Family Social Work*, *6*(4), 295–304. https://doi.org/10.1046/j.1365-2206.2001.00214.x

Blyth, E., Speirs, J., Frith, L., & Jones, C. (2009). The role of birth certificates in relation to access to biographical and genetic history in donor conception. *The International Journal of Children's Rights*, *17*(2), 207–233.

Blyth, E. (1993). Section 30—The acceptable face of surrogacy? *Journal of Social Welfare and Family Law*, *5*(4), 248–260.

Blyth, E. (1994). "I wanted to be interesting…": Interviews with surrogate mothers in Britain. *Journal of Reproductive and Infant Psychology*, *12*(3), 189–198.

Blyth, E. (2003). The United Kingdom: Evolution of a statutory regulatory approach. In E. Blyth & R. Landau (Eds.), *Third party assisted conception across cultures: Social, legal, and ethical perspectives* (pp. 226–245). Jessica Kingsley Publishers.

Borland, M., Hill, M., Laybourn, A., & Stafford, A. (2001). *Improving consultation with children and young people in relevant aspects of policy-making and legislation in Scotland: Guidelines for Scottish parliamentary committees* (SP Paper 365). Scottish Parliament, Education, Culture and Sport Committee.

Bowcott, O. (2015, May 18). Unregistered surrogate-born children creating 'legal timebomb', judge warns. *The Guardian*. https://www.theguardian.com/lifeandstyle/2015/may/18/unregistered-surrogate-born-children-creating-legal-timebomb-judge-warns

Bracken, L. (2021). The ECtHR's first advisory opinion: Implications for cross-border surrogacy involving male intended parents. *Medical Law International*, *21*(1). https://doi.org/10.1177/09685332211002592

Braun, V., & Clarke, V. (2022). *Thematic analysis: A practical guide*. Sage.

Braun, V., & Clarke, V. (2023). Toward good practice in thematic analysis: Avoiding common problems and be(com)ing a knowing researcher. *International Journal of Transgender Health*, *24*(1), 1–6. https://doi.org/10.1080/26895269.2022.2129597

Brazier, M., Campbell, A. V., & Golombok, S. (1998). *Surrogacy: Review for health ministers of current arrangements for payments and regulation (Cm 4068)*. Department of Health.

Brazier, M. (1999). Regulating the reproduction business? *Medical Law Review*, *7*(2), 166–193. https://doi.org/10.1093/medlaw/7.2.166

Bridgeman, J. (2025). Medical treatment refusals by teenagers and the law: Justice that is more caring? In L. Forsberg, I. Black, & A. Skelton (Eds.), *Consenting children: Autonomy, responsibility, well-being* (pp. 153–167). Liverpool University Press. https://doi.org/10.2307/jj.31510203.15

Brilliant Beginnings. (2020). *Who we are*. https://brilliantbeginnings.co.uk/who-we-are/

British Academy. (2022). *Reframing childhood: The final report of the childhood policy programme*. https://www.thebritishacademy.ac.uk/publications/childhood-policy-programme-final-report/

Brooks, M. (2009). Drawing, visualisation and young children's exploration of "Big Ideas". *International Journal of Science Education*, *31*(3), 319–341.

Brown, A., & Wade, K. (2022). The incoherent role of the child's identity in the construction and allocation of legal parenthood. *Legal Studies*, *43*(1), 29–46. https://doi.org/10.1017/lst.2022.21

Brown, A., & Wade, K. (2024). Reform of the legal framework for origin information in assisted reproduction. In C. Bendall & R. Parveen (Eds.), *Family law reform now* (pp. 77–97). Hart. https://doi.org/10.5040/9781509962211.ch-003

Brown, A. (2018). Two means two, but must does not mean must: An analysis of recent decisions on the conditions for parental orders in surrogacy. *Child and Family Law Quarterly*, *30*(1), 23–40.

Brown, A. (2019). *What is the family of law? The influence of the nuclear family*. Hart.

Brown, A. (2021). Surrogacy law reform in the UK: The ambiguous position of payments to the surrogate. *Child and Family Law Quarterly*, *33*(2), 95–114.

Brown, A. (2025). Reconsidering payments to the surrogate: Can the "ambiguities" be resolved? In K. Horsey, Z. Mahmoud, & K. Wade (Eds.), *Future directions in surrogacy law* (pp. 122–139). Bristol University Press. https://doi.org/10.2307/jj.18323798.12

Brown, A. (2026). The legal family. In A. Margaria & C. Fenton-Glynn (Eds.), *What is a family? Law and regulation in a transdisciplinary context*. Bristol University Press. https://doi.org/10.51952/9781529246360

Brownsword, R., & Wale, J. (2017). The right to know and the right not to know revisited. *Asian Bioethics Review*, *9*(1), 3–18. https://doi.org/10.1007/s41649-017-0012-1

Bucknall, S. (2014). Doing qualitative research with children and young people. In A. Clark, R. Flewitt, M. Hammersley, & M. Robb (Eds.), *Understanding research with children and young people* (pp. 69–84). Open University Press. https://doi.org/10.4135/9781526435637.n5

Busby, K., & Vun, D. (2010). Revisiting the handmaid's tale: Feminist theory meets empirical research on surrogate mothers. *Canadian Journal of Family Law*, *26*(1), 13–93.

Byrne, B., & Lundy, L. (2019). Children's rights-based childhood policy: A six-P framework. *International Journal of Human Rights*, *23*(3), 357–373.

Callus, T. (2012). A new parenthood paradigm for twenty-first century family law in England and Wales? *Legal Studies*, *32*(3), 347–368. https://doi.org/10.1111/j.1748-121X.2011.00224.x

Carone, N., Baiocco, R., & Lingiardi, V. (2017a). Italian gay fathers' experiences of transnational surrogacy. *Reproductive BioMedicine Online*, *34*, 181–190. https://doi.org/10.1016/j.rbmo.2016.10.012

Carone, N., Baiocco, R., & Lingiardi, V. (2017b). Single fathers by choice using surrogacy. *Human Reproduction*, *32*(9), 1871–1879. https://doi.org/10.1093/humrep/dex245

Carsten, J. (Ed.). (2000). *Cultures of relatedness: New approaches to the study of kinship*. Cambridge University Press.

Carsten, J. (2004). *After kinship*. Cambridge University Press. https://doi.org/10.1017/CBO9780511800382

Case, S., Hampson, K., & Nisbet, A. (2024). *Child first? Examining children's perspectives of their "effective" collaboration in youth justice decision-making*. Prifysgol Aberystwyth, Aberystwyth University. https://doi.org/10.17028/rd.lboro.27968766

Caulfield, M. (2023, November 8). *Review of surrogacy: Government interim response* [Letter to Sir Peter Fraser, Chair of the Law Commission of England & Wales]. Department of Health and Social Care. https://www.scotlawcom.gov.uk/files/9617/2830/6252/Letter_from_Maria_Caulfield_PUS_DHSC_8_November_2023.pdf

Centre for Health Ethics Law and Development. (2024). *The future of surrogacy in Nigeria: Arising issues and the surrogacy bills* [Policy brief]. CHELD. https://cheld.org/wp-content/uploads/2025/09/Surrogacy-Policy-Brief.pdf

Child Identity Protection Network. (2026a). *Launch of new tools for policy makers and practitioners to protect children's rights in third party reproduction and surrogacy*. https://www.child-identity.org/launch-of-new-tools-for-policy-makers-and-practitioners-to-protect-childrens-rights-in-third-party-reproduction-and-surrogacy

Child Identity Protection Network. (2026b). *Note for high-level policy makers: Ensuring respect for children's human rights in third-party reproduction including surrogacy*. https://www.child-identity.org/wp-content/uploads/2026/03/Recommendations-third-party-reproduction-including-surrogacy-ENG-1.pdf

Children and Family Court Advisory and Support Service (Cafcass). (2016). *Parental order reporters*. https://www.cafcass.gov.uk/sites/default/files/2023-06/Parental-Order-Reporters.pdf

Children and Family Court Advisory and Support Service. (2023, October 3). *Family justice young people's board*. https://www.cafcass.gov.uk

Children's Commissioner. (2025, September 26). *A new youth advisory board to help shape the future of childhood*. https://www.childrenscommissioner.gov.uk

Children's Voices in Surrogacy Law. (2023a). *Phase one preliminary report*. University of Leicester.

Children's Voices in Surrogacy Law. (2023b). *Phase two preliminary report*. University of Leicester.

Christensen, P., & James, A. (2008). *Research with children. Perspectives and practices* (2nd ed.). Routledge.

Christensen, P., & James, A. (Eds.) (2017), *Research with children* (3rd ed.). Routledge. https://doi.org/10.4324/9781315657349

Christensen, P., & Prout, A. (2002). Working with ethical symmetry in social research with children. *Childhood*, *9*(4), 477–497. https://doi.org/10.1177/0907568202009004007

Clark, A. (2010). *Transforming children's spaces: Children's and adults' participation in designing learning environments*. Routledge.

Clark, A., & Moss, P. (2008). *Listening to young children: The mosaic approach*. National Children's Bureau and Joseph Rowntree Foundation.

Clark, A., & Statham, J. (2005). Listening to young children: Experts in their own lives. *Adoption and Fostering*, *29*(1). https://doi.org/10.1177/030857590502900106

Clark, A. (2001). How to listen to very young children: The mosaic approach. *Child Care in Practice*, *7*(4), 333–341.
Clark, A. (2017). *Listening to young children: A guide to understanding and using the mosaic approach* (3rd ed.). Jessica Kingsley.
Committee on Human Artificial Insemination. (1960). *Report of the Departmental Committee on Human Artificial Insemination (Cmnd 1105)*. Her Majesty's Stationery Office.
Committee on the Rights of the Child. (1991). *General guidelines regarding the form and content of initial reports to be submitted by states parties under Article 44, paragraph 1 (a), of the convention* (CRC/C/5). United Nations.
Committee on Social Affairs, Health and Sustainable Development. (2016). *Children's rights related to surrogacy*. Council of Europe.
Committee on the Rights of the Child. (2003). *General comment no. 5: General measures of implementation of the convention on the rights of the child* (CRC/GC/2003/5). https://digitallibrary.un.org/record/513415?v=pdf
Committee on the Rights of the Child. (2005). *General comment no. 7: Implementing child rights in early childhood* (CRC/C/GC/Rev 1). United Nations.
Committee on the Rights of the Child. (2009). *General comment no. 12: The right of the child to be heard* (CRC/C/GC12). United Nations.
Committee on the Rights of the Child. (2021). *General comment no. 25 (2021) on children's rights in relation to the digital environment* (CRC/C/GC/25). United Nations. https://digitallibrary.un.org/record/3906061
Committee on the Rights of the Child. (2023). *General comment no. 26 (2023) on children's rights and the environment, with a special focus on climate change* (CRC/C/GC/26). United Nations. https://www.ohchr.org/en/documents/general-comments-and-recommendations/crccgc26-general-comment-no-26-2023-childrens-rights
Committee on the Rights of the Child. (2024). *Draft general comment no. 27 on children's right to access to justice and to an effective remedy*. Office of the United Nations High Commissioner for Human Rights. https://www.ohchr.org/sites/default/files/documents/hrbodies/crc/cfi-gc27/crc-gc27-public-consultation.docx
Cooper, D. (2023). Keeping prefigurative law in play: Utopianism, failure, and the not real. *Law & Social Inquiry*, *48*(2), 650–677. https://doi.org/10.1017/lsi.2022.1
Corea, G. (1985). *The mother machine*. HarperCollins.
Cosson, B., Dempsey, D., & Kelly, F. (2022). Secret shame - Male infertility and donor conception in the wake of retrospective legislative change. *Men and Masculinities*, *25*(3), 497–515. https://doi.org/10.1177/1097184X211038329
Costigan, C. L., & Cox, M. J. (2001). Fathers' participation in family research: Is there a self-selection bias? *Journal of Family Psychology*, *15*(4), 706–720. https://doi.org/10.1037/0893-3200.15.4.706
Cowden, M. (2012). "No harm, no foul": A child's right to know their genetic parents. *International Journal of Law, Policy and the Family*, *26*(1), 102–122. https://doi.org/10.1093/lawfam/ebr022
Cownie, F., & Bradney, A. (2017). Socio-legal studies. In D. Watkins (Ed.), *Research methods in law* (pp. 34–54). Routledge. https://doi.org/10.4324/9780203489352
Coyne, I., Mallon, D., & Chubb, E. (2021). Research with young children: Exploring the methodological advantages and challenges of using hand puppets and draw and tell. *Children & Society*, *35*(5), 813–830. https://doi.org/10.1111/chso.12452

Culley, L., & Hudson, N. (2006). Diverse bodies and disrupted reproduction: Infertility and minority ethnic communities in the UK. *International Journal of Diversity in Organisations, Communities and Nations*, *5*(2), 117–126.

Culley, L., Hudson, N., Rapport, F., & Katbamna, S. (2006). British South Asian communities and infertility services. *Human Fertility*, *9*, 37–45. https://doi.org/10.1080/14647270500282644

Daly, A., Purcell, N., Montesinos Calvo-Fernández, E., & Murray, E. M. (2025). Participation and postpaternalism: Youth climate action and the UN convention on the rights of the child. *The International Journal of Children's Rights*, *33*(2), 562–593. https://doi.org/10.1163/15718182-33030001

Daly, A. (2018). No weight for due weight? A children's autonomy principle in best interest proceedings. *The International Journal of Children's Rights*, *26*(1), 61–92. https://doi.org/10.1163/15718182-02601012

David, M. E. (2014). What were the lasting effects of Thatcher's legacy for families in the UK? In S. Farrall & C. Hay (Eds.), *The legacy of thatcherism: Assessing and exploring Thatcherite social and economic policies* (pp. 174–197). British Academy. https://doi.org/10.5871/bacad/9780197265703.003.0010

Declaration of Casablanca for the Universal Abolition of Surrogacy. (2023). *Declaration of Casablanca for the universal abolition of surrogacy.* https://declaration-surrogacy-casablanca.org

Department for Education. (2019). *Relationships Education, Relationships and Sex Education (RSE) and Health Education (for teaching until 31 August 2026).* https://assets.publishing.service.gov.uk/media/68b96b003f3e5483efdba9b4/Relationships_Education_RSE_and_Health_Education.pdf

Department for Education. (2025). *Relationships education, relationships and sex education (RSE) and health education (for introduction 1 September 2026).* https://assets.publishing.service.gov.uk/media/6970e7e67e827090d02d42e0/Relationships_education_relationships_and_sex_education__RSE__and_health_education__for_intro_1_September_2026_.pdf

Department of Children and Youth Affairs. (2015). *National strategy on children and young people's participation in decision-making, 2015–2020.* Government Publications.

Department of Health and Social Care. (2018a, updated 2025). *Having a child through surrogacy: Information for intended parents, surrogates and health professionals about the surrogacy process in England and Wales.* https://www.gov.uk/government/publications/having-a-child-through-surrogacy

Department of Health and Social Care. (2018b, updated 2025). *Care in surrogacy: Guidance for the care of surrogates and intended parents in surrogate births in England and Wales.* https://www.gov.uk/government/publications/having-a-child-through-surrogacy/care-in-surrogacy-guidance-for-the-care-of-surrogates-and-intended-parents-in-surrogate-births-in-england-and-wales

Department of Health and Social Care. (2018c, updated 2025). *The surrogacy pathway: Surrogacy and the legal process for intended parents and surrogates in England and Wales.* https://www.gov.uk/government/publications/having-a-child-through-surrogacy/the-surrogacy-pathway-surrogacy-and-the-legal-process-for-intended-parents-and-surrogates-in-england-and-wales

Department of Health and Social Care. (2023). *Review of surrogacy: Government interim response*. [Letter to Sir Peter Fraser, Chair of the Law Commission of England & Wales]. https://www.scotlawcom.gov.uk/files/9617/2830/6252/Letter_from_Maria_Caulfield_PUS_DHSC_8_November_2023.pdf

Department of Health and Social Care. (2025). *Letter from Baroness Merron: Review of surrogacy—Government response*. UK Government. https://cdn.websitebuilder.service.justice.gov.uk/uploads/sites/54/2025/04/Letter-from-Baroness-Merron.pdf

Department of Health and Social Security (The Warnock Report). (1984). *Report of the committee of inquiry into human fertilisation and embryology (Cm 9314)*. https://wellcomecollection.org/works/pxgeeqnf

Dewar, J. (1989). Fathers in law? The case of AID. In R. G. Lee & D. Morgan (Eds.), *Birthrights: Law and ethics at the beginnings of life* (pp. 115–131). Routledge. https://doi.org/10.4324/9780203393222

Dimopoulos, G., Hew, E., Vosz, M., & Walsh, H. (2025). "Talk to us, not about us": Children's understandings and experiences of participation in Australian family law. *Child & Family Social Work*. https://doi.org/10.1111/cfs.13275

Dockett, S., Einarsdóttir, J., & Perry, B. (2009). Researching with children: Ethical tensions. *Journal of Early Childhood Research*, *7*(3), 283–298. https://doi.org/10.1177/1476718X09336971

Douglas, G. (1994). The intention to be a parent and the making of mothers. *The Modern Law Review*, *57*(4), 636–641. https://doi.org/10.1111/j.1468-2230.1994.tb01965.x

Dow, K. (2018). "Now she's just an ordinary baby": The birth of IVF in the British press. *Sociology*, *53*(2), 314–329. https://doi.org/10.1177/0038038518757953

Dow, K. (2019). Looking into the test tube: The birth of IVF on British television. *Medical History*, *63*(2), 189–208. https://doi.org/10.1017/mdh.2019.6

Dunne, P. R., & Brown, A. (2024). Trans parenthood in the UK: The "unanswered questions" of the McConnell litigation. *The Cambridge Law Journal*, *83*(3), 490–518. https://doi.org/10.1017/S0008197324000461

Economic and Social Science Research Council. (2023, May 31). *What is social science?* UK Research and Innovation. https://www.ukri.org/who-we-are/esrc/what-is-social-science/social-science-disciplines/

Einarsdóttir, J., Dockett, S., & Perry, B. (2009). Making meaning: Children's perspectives expressed through drawings. *Early Child Development and Care*, *179*(2), 217–232. https://doi.org/10.1080/03004430802666999

Einwohner, J. (1989). Who becomes a surrogate. In J. Offerman-Zuckerberg (Ed.), *Gender in transition* (pp. 97–108). Springer. https://doi.org/10.1007/978-1-4684-5631-8_10

Espejo-Yaksic, N., Fenton-Glynn, C., & Scherpe, J. (Eds.). (2024). *Surrogacy in Latin America*. Intersentia. https://doi.org/10.1017/9781839703812

Ethics Committee of the American Society for Reproductive Medicine. (2018). Informing offspring of their conception by gamete or embryo donation: An ethics committee opinion. *Fertility and Sterility*, *109*(4), 601–605. https://doi.org/10.1016/j.fertnstert.2018.01.016

European Commission. (2022). *Proposal for a council regulation on jurisdiction, applicable law, recognition of decisions and acceptance of authentic instruments in matters of parenthood and on the creation of a European certificate of parenthood*

(COM(2022) 695 final). Publications Office of the European Union. https://eur-lex.europa.eu/legal-content/EN/TXT/?uri=CELEX%3A52022PC0695

European Commission. (n.d.). *The lundy model of child participation*. [Online]. https://ec.europa.eu/info/sites/default/files/lundy_model_of_participation.pdf. Accessed on April 22, 2026.

European Court of Human Rights. (2019). *Advisory opinion concerning the recognition in domestic law of a legal parent-child relationship between a child born through a gestational surrogacy arrangement abroad and the intended mother*. Request no. P16-2018-001, 10 April 2019.

European Parliament. (2023, December 14). *Recognition of parenthood: MEPs want children to have equal rights*. [Press release]. https://www.europarl.europa.eu/news/en/press-room/20231208IPR15786/recognition-of-parenthood-meps-want-children-to-have-equal-rights

European Society of Human Reproduction and Embryology Working Group on Reproductive Donation, Kirkman-Brown, J., Calhaz-Jorge, C., Dancet, E. A. F., Lundin, K., Martins, M., Tilleman, K., Thorn, P., Vermeulen, N., & Frith, L. (2022). Good practice recommendations for information provision for those involved in reproductive donation. *Human Reproduction Open*, *2022*(1), hoac001. https://doi.org/10.1093/hropen/hoac001

Ewick, P., & Silbey, S. (1998). *The common place of law: Stories from everyday life*. University of Chicago Press.

Fane, J., MacDougall, C., Jovanovic, J., Redwood-Campbell, L., & Bonamici, A. (2018). Exploring the use of emoji as a visual research method for eliciting young children's voices in childhood research. *Early Child Development and Care*, *188*(3), 359–374.

Farmer, D., & Cepin, J. (2017). Creative visual methods in research with children and young people. In R. Evans & L. Holt (Eds.), *Methodological approaches: Geographies of children and young people* (Vol. 2, pp. 303–333). Springer.

Feasey, R. (2019). *Infertility and non-traditional family building: From assisted reproduction to adoption in the media*. Springer. https://doi.org/10.1007/978-3-030-17787-4_3

Fenton-Glynn, C. (2019). Surrogacy in England and Wales. In J. M. Scherpe, C. Fenton-Glynn, & T. Kaan (Eds.), *Eastern and Western perspectives on surrogacy* (pp. 115–134). Intersentia. https://doi.org/10.1017/9781780688633

Finch, J., & Mason, J. (1993). *Negotiating family responsibilities*. Tavistock/Routledge.

Fineman, M. A. (1995). *The neutered mother, the sexual family and other twentieth century tragedies*. Routledge.

Fischer, L. R., Gamble, N., Horsey, K., Jackson, E., Seidelman, D. E., & Vaughn, R. (2024). Surrogacy needs to be regulated, not prohibited. *BMJ*, *386*, e079542. https://doi.org/10.1136/bmj-2024-079542

Fitzgerald, R., & Graham, A. (2011). The changing status of children within family law from vision to reality? *Griffith Law Review*, *20*(2), 421–448. https://doi.org/10.1080/10383441.2011.10854704

Flewitt, R. (2014). Interviews. In A. Clark, R. Flewitt, M. Hammersley, & M. Robb (Eds.), *Understanding research with children and young people* (pp. 136–153). Open University Press.

Forde, L., & Kilkelly, U. (2023). Children and police questioning: A rights-based approach. *Criminology and Criminal Justice*, *24*(3), 648–669.

Forde, L., Kilkelly, U., Lundy, L., & Kelleher, D. (2020). The right of children to participate in public decision-making processes. *Save the Children International*. https://resourcecentre.savethechildren.net/document/right-children-participate-public-decision-making-processes

Foster, M. (2025, March 4). *"I have finished the court case…" judges writing letters to children could become the norm*. Charles Russell Speechlys. https://www.charles-russellspeechlys.com/en/insights/quick-reads/102k2nd-i-have-finished-the-court-case-and-i-have-decided-that-now-is-not-the-right-time/

Fox, M. (2009). The Human Fertilisation and Embryology Act 2008: Tinkering at the margins. *Feminist Legal Studies*, *17*, 333–344. https://doi.org/10.1007/s10691-009-9129-2

Franklin, S., & Roberts, C. (2006). *Born and made: An ethnography of preimplantation genetic diagnosis*. Princeton University Press.

Franks, M. (2011). Pockets of participation: Revisiting child-centred participation research. *Children & Society*, *25*(1), 15–25. https://doi.org/10.1111/j.1099-0860.2009.00258.x

Fraser, S., Flewitt, R., & Hammersley, M. (2014). What is research with children and young people? In A. Clark, R. Flewitt, M. Hammersley, & M. Robb (Eds.), *Understanding research with children and young people* (pp. 34–50). Open University Press.

Freeman, T., & Richards, M. (2006). DNA testing and kinship: Paternity, genealogy and the search for the "truth" of our genetic origins. In F. Ebtehaj, B. Lindley, & M. Richards (Eds.), *Kinship matters* (pp. 67–95). Hart.

Freeman, M. (1989). Is surrogacy exploitative? In S. A. M. McLean (Ed.), *Legal issues in human reproduction* (pp. 164–184). Gower.

Frith, L. (2001). Gamete donation and anonymity: The ethical and legal debate. *Human Reproduction*, *16*(5), 818–824.

Frith, L. (2026). Conceptualizing reproductive donation: Developing models of egg and sperm donation and the implications for regulating information giving. *Journal of Law Medicine & Ethics*, *54*(1), 102–115. https://doi.org/10.1017/jme.2026.10243

Gamble, N. (2017, October 22). Top 5 UK surrogacy myths. *Fertility Road*.

Gamble, N. (2018, December 4). Surrogacy isn't about money. But the law must change to benefit women. *The Guardian*.

Gamble, N. (2019, August 19). Do proposals to reform UK surrogacy law go far enough? *BioNews, 1011*. https://www.progress.org.uk/do-proposals-to-reform-uk-surrogacy-law-go-far-enough/

Gamble, N. (2025). Why UK parents go overseas: The challenges, and what it means for UK law reform. In K. Horsey, Z. Mahmoud, & K. Wade (Eds.), *Future directions in surrogacy law* (pp. 78–96). Bristol University Press. https://doi.org/10.2307/jj.18323798.10

Gilligan, C. (1993). *In a different voice: Psychological theory and women's development* (Rev. ed.). Harvard University Press.

Gilman, L., & Nordqvist, P. (2018). Organizing openness: How UK policy defines the significance of information and information sharing about gamete donation.

International Journal of Law, Policy and the Family, *32*(3), 316–333. https://doi.org/10.1093/lawfam/eby014

Gilman, L., & Nordqvist, P. (2022). *Donors: Curious connections in donor conception*. Emerald. https://doi.org/10.1108/9781800435643

Gilman, L., Nordqvist, P., Hudson, N., & Frith, L. (2025). Exploring the generational ordering of kinship through decisions about DNA testing and gamete donor conception. *The Sociological Review*, *73*(3), 526–545. https://doi.org/10.1177/00380261241309488

Głos, A. (2024). Advancing children's participation rights in healthcare through play. *The International Journal of Children's Rights*, *32*(3), 799–830.

Goldberg, S. B. (2006). Constitutional tipping points: Civil rights, social change, and fact-based adjudication. *Columbia Law Review*, *106*(8), 1955–2022. https://www.jstor.org/stable/40041691

Golombok, S., Murray, C., Jadva, V., MacCallum, F., & Lycett, E. (2004). Families created through surrogacy arrangements: Parent–child relationships in the 1st year of life. *Developmental Psychology*, *40*(3), 400–411. https://doi.org/10.1037/0012-1649.40.3.400

Golombok, S., MacCallum, F., Murray, C., Lycett, E., & Jadva, V. (2006a). Surrogacy families: Parental functioning, parent–child relationships and children's psychological development at age 2. *Journal of Child Psychology and Psychiatry*, *47*(2), 213–222. https://doi.org/10.1111/j.1469-7610.2005.01453.x

Golombok, S., Murray, C., Jadva, V., Lycett, E., MacCallum, F., & Rust, J. (2006b). Non-genetic and non-gestational parenthood. *Human Reproduction*, *21*(7), 1918–1924. https://doi.org/10.1093/humrep/del039

Golombok, S., Readings, J., Blake, L., Casey, P., Marks, A., & Jadva, V. (2011). Families created through surrogacy. *Developmental Psychology*, *47*(6), 1579–1588. https://doi.org/10.1037/a0025292

Golombok, S., Blake, L., Casey, P., Roman, G., & Jadva, V. (2013). Children born through reproductive donation. *Journal of Child Psychology and Psychiatry*, *54*(6), 653–660. https://doi.org/10.1111/jcpp.12015

Golombok, S., Ilioi, E., Blake, L., Roman, G., & Jadva, V. (2017). A longitudinal study of families formed through reproductive donation. *Developmental Psychology*, *53*(10), 1966–1977. https://doi.org/10.1037/dev0000372

Golombok, S., Blake, L., Slutsky, J., Raffanello, E., Roman, G. D., & Ehrhardt, A. (2018). Parenting and the adjustment of children born to gay fathers through surrogacy. *Child Development*, *89*(4), 1223–1233. https://doi.org/10.1111/cdev.12728

Golombok, S., Jones, C., Hall, P., Foley, S., Imrie, S., & Jadva, V. (2023). A longitudinal study of families formed through third-party assisted reproduction. *Developmental Psychology*, *59*(6), 1059–1073. https://doi.org/10.1037/dev0001526

Golombok, S. (2015). *Modern families: Parents and children in new family forms*. Cambridge University Press.

Golombok, S. (2017). Parenting in new family forms. In M. van IJzendoorn & M. Bakermans-Kranenburg (Eds.), *Parenting* (pp. 76–80). Elsevier.

Golombok, S. (2020a). The psychological wellbeing of ART children: What have we learned from 40 years of research? *Reproductive BioMedicine Online*, *41*(4), 743–746. https://doi.org/10.1016/j.rbmo.2020.08.012

Golombok, S. (2020b). *We are family: What really matters for parents and children.* Scribe Publications.

Golombok, S. (2021). Love and truth: What really matters for children born through third-party assisted reproduction. *Child Development Perspectives, 15*(2), 103–109. https://doi.org/10.1111/cdep.12406

Golombok, S. (2026). When research challenges belief: Surrogacy families in the political crossfire. *BioNews, 1334*. https://www.progress.org.uk/when-research-challenges-belief-surrogacy-families-in-the-political-crossfire/

Government Office for Science. (2025, June 26). *Future of childhood and adolescence.* https://www.gov.uk/government/publications/future-of-childhood-and-adolescence/future-of-childhood-and-adolescence

Graham, A., Simmons, C., & Truscott, J. (2017). "I'm more confident now, I was really quiet": Exploring the potential benefits of child-led research. *International Journal of Qualitative Studies in Education, 30*(2), 190–205. https://doi.org/10.1080/09518398.2016.1242803

Green, C. (2017). Four methods for engaging young children as environmental education researchers. *International Journal of Early Childhood Environmental Education, 5*(1), 6–19.

Greene, S., & Hill, M. (2005). Researching children's experience: Methods and methodological issues. In S. Greene & D. Hogan (Eds.), *Researching children's experience: Approaches and methods* (pp. 1–21). Sage Publications. https://doi.org/10.4135/9781849209823.n1

Greig, A., Taylor, J., & MacKay, T. (2013). *Doing research with children: A practical guide* (3rd ed.). Sage.

Groundwater-Smith, S., Dockett, S., & Bottrell, D. (Eds.). (2015). *Participatory research with children and young people.* Sage. https://doi.org/10.4135/9781473910751

Gruben, V., Cattapan, A., & Cameron, A. (Eds.). (2018). *Surrogacy in Canada: Critical perspectives in law and policy.* Irwin Law.

Grupo de Información en Reproducción Elegida, A.C.. (2017). *Surrogacy in Mexico: The consequences of poor regulation.*

Guichon, J., Mitchell, I., & Giroux, M. (Eds.). (2012). *The right to know one's origins: Assisted reproduction and the best interests of children.* Academic and Scientific Publishers.

Gunnarsson Payne, J. (2016). Grammars of kinship: Biological motherhood and assisted reproduction in the age of epigenetics. *Signs: Journal of Women in Culture and Society, 41*(3), 483–506. https://doi.org/10.1086/684233

Haimes, E. (1988). Secrecy: What can artificial reproduction learn from adoption? *International Journal of Law and the Family, 2*, 46–61.

Haimes, E. (1990). Recreating the family? Policy considerations relating to the new reproductive technologies. In M McNeil (Ed.), *The new reproductive technologies.* Macmillan.

Haimes, E. (1992). Gamete donation and the social management of genetic origins. *Sociology, 26*(4), 693–710. https://doi.org/10.1177/0038038592026004011

Haimes, E. (1998). The making of 'the DI child': Changing representations of people conceived through donor insemination. In K. Daniels & E. Haimes (Eds.), *Donor insemination: International social science perspectives.* Cambridge University Press. https://doi.org/10.1017/CBO9780511557804.004

Hardach, S. (2022). What it's like to raise a child in a new family. *BBC Future*. https://www.bbc.co.uk/future/article/20220215-the-pioneers-remaking-the-modern-family

Hargreaves, C., Cusworth, L., Alrouh, B., Broadhurst, K., Griffiths, L. J., Cowley, L., & Doebler, S. (2024). *Uncovering private family law: How often do we hear the voice of the child?* Nuffield Family Justice Observatory. https://www.nuffieldfjo.org.uk/wp-content/uploads/2024/02/Child_participation_08-02-24.pdf

Harrington, M. (2023). Kill the mother part 2: Babies to order. *Mary Harrington*. https://www.maryharrington.co.uk/p/kill-the-mother-part-2-babies-to

Harrington, M. (2024). Camus part 3: Globo homo economicus: Transhumanism, mothers, and replacism of the body. *Mary Harrington*. https://www.maryharrington.co.uk/p/camus-part-3-globo-homo-economicus

Hart, R. A. (1992). *Children's participation: From tokenism to citizenship*. UNICEF.

HC Deb vol. 170, col. 945. (1990, april 2). *Hansard*. https://hansard.parliament.uk/Commons/1990-04-02/debates/2d7e7002-19b7-4514-b5d7-6c6edea9c918/HumanFertilisationAndEmbryologyBillLords

HC Deb 14 October 2014, vol 586, col 2WG. *Hansard*. https://hansard.parliament.uk/Commons/2014-10-14/debates/14101451000001/Surrogacy

HC Deb 7 February 2017, vol 621. *Hansard*. https://hansard.parliament.uk/Commons/2017-02-07/debates/6FD93322-A48E-4AA2-88C8-B0AF602826E1/Surrogacy

HC Deb 21 Jan 2020 vol 670, col 69WH. *Hansard*. https://hansard.parliament.uk/Commons/2020-01-21/debates/925AF06F-A059-4093-90B9-073C4ACC326C/SurrogacyGovernmentPolicy

HCCH Working Group on Parentage/Surrogacy. (2025). *Final report of the working group on parentage/surrogacy on the feasibility of a possible convention on the recognition of judgments on legal parentage*. https://assets.hcch.net/docs/09215fe7-6f22-4777-9fd4-ad292efd00b9.pdf

Hendricks, H. (1997). *Children, childhood, and English society, 1880–1990*. Cambridge University Press.

Hennessy, E., & Heary, C. (2005). Exploring children's views through focus groups. In S. Greene & D. Hogan (Eds.), *Researching children's experience: Approaches and methods* (pp. 236–252). Sage Publications. https://doi.org/10.4135/9781849209823.n13

Hennink, M., Hutter, I., & Bailey, A. (2020). *Qualitative research methods* (2nd ed.). Sage.

Herring, J. (2019). *Law and the relational self*. Cambridge University Press.

Hertz, R., Nelson, M. K., & Kramer, W. (2013). Donor conceived offspring conceive of the donor: The relevance of age, awareness, and family form. *Social Science & Medicine*, *86*, 52–65. https://doi.org/10.1016/j.socscimed.2013.03.001

Hertz, R. (2022). Sociological accounts of donor siblings' experiences: Their importance for self-identity and new kinship relations. *International Journal of Environmental Research and Public Health*, *19*(4), Article 2002. https://doi.org/10.3390/ijerph19042002

Hill, M., Laybourn, A., & Borland, M. (1996). What children and young people say they want from social services. *Social Work in Europe*, *3*(1), 16–21.

Hill, M. (2006). Children's voices on ways of having a voice: Children's and young people's perspectives on methods used in research and consultation. *Childhood, 13* (1), 69–89.

Hill, J. (2024). Does contract surrogacy undermine gender equality? *Bioethics*, *38*(8), 702–708. https://doi.org/10.1111/bioe.13337

Hirst, L. (2026). Our surrogacy fight to become our child's legal parents. *BBC News*. https://www.bbc.co.uk/news/articles/cn4p9kde0zyo

Horsey, K. (2010). Challenging presumptions: Legal parenthood and surrogacy arrangements. *Child and Family Law Quarterly*, *22*(4), 449–474.

Horsey, K. (Ed.). (2015). *Revisiting the regulation of human fertilisation and embryology*. Routledge.

Horsey, K. (2015). *Surrogacy in the UK: Myth-busting and reform*. Surrogacy UK.

Horsey, K. (2016). Not withered on the Vine: The need for surrogacy law reform. *Journal of Medical Law and Ethics*, *4*(3), 181–196. https://doi.org/10.7590/221354016X14803383336888

Horsey, K. (2018a). Surrogacy 2.0: What can the law learn from lived experience? *Contemporary Issues in Law*, *14*(4), 305–324. https://kar.kent.ac.uk/id/eprint/59741

Horsey, K. (2018b). *Surrogacy in the UK: Further evidence for reform*. Surrogacy UK.

Horsey, K. (2024). The future of surrogacy: A review of current global trends and national landscapes. *Reproductive BioMedicine Online*, *48*(5), Article 103764. https://doi.org/10.1016/j.rbmo.2023.103764

Horsey, K. (2025a). How UK surrogates navigate arrangements, processes and the law. In K. Horsey, Z. Mahmoud, & K. Wade (Eds.), *Future directions in surrogacy law* (pp. 51–77). Bristol University Press. https://doi.org/10.2307/jj.18323798.9

Horsey, K. (2025b). The UN Special Rapporteur's report on surrogacy: Biased from the outset. *BioNews, 1306*. https://www.progress.org.uk/the-un-special-rapporteurs-report-on-surrogacy-biased-from-the-outset/

Horsey, K. (2025c). *Surrogacy in the UK: Myth-busting and reform 10 years on*. Surrogacy UK.

Horsey, K. (2026). Surrogacy in the UK. In T. Vidalis & I. Kriari (Eds.), *Surrogacy today. A European legal overview*. Trivent Publishing.

Horsey, K., Arian-Schad, M., Macklon, N., & Ahuja, K. (2022). UK surrogates' characteristics, experiences, and views on surrogacy law reform. *International Journal of Law, Policy and the Family*, *36*(1), ebac030. https://doi.org/10.1093/lawfam/ebac030

Horsey, K., Arian-Schad, M., Macklon, N., & Ahuja, K. (2023). UK intended parents' characteristics, experiences, and views on surrogacy law reform. *International Journal of Law, Policy and the Family*, *37*(1), ebad004. https://doi.org/10.1093/lawfam/ebad004

Horsey, K., & Avery, S. (2016). Meeting Mary Warnock. *BioNews, 837*. https://www.progress.org.uk/meeting-mary-warnock/

Horsey, K., & Jackson, E. (2023). The human fertilisation and embryology act 1990 and non-traditional families. *Modern Law Review*, *86*(6), 1472–1488. https://doi.org/10.1111/1468-2230.12818

Horsey, K., & Mahmoud, Z. (2023). Surrogates' and intended parents' experiences of surrogacy arrangements: A systematic review. *Reproductive Biomedicine Online, 46* (1), 7–9. https://doi.org/10.1016/j.rbmo.2022.09.017

Horsey, K., & Mahmoud, Z. (2025). It's time to call out surrogacy misinformation. *Bio News, 1275*. https://www.progress.org.uk/its-time-to-call-out-surrogacy-misinformation/

Horsey, K., Mahmoud, Z., & Wade, K. (Eds.). (2025). *Future directions in surrogacy law: Law and policy reform in the UK and beyond*. University of Bristol Press. https://doi.org/10.56687/9781529238785

Horsey, K., & Sheldon, S. (2012). Still hazy after all these years: The law regulating surrogacy. *Medical Law Review*, *20*(1), 67–89. https://doi.org/10.1093/medlaw/fwr039

Hudson, N., & Culley, L. (2014). Infertility, gamete donation and relatedness in British South Asian communities. In T. Freeman, S. Graham, F. Ebtehaj, & M. Richards (Eds.), *Relatedness in assisted reproduction: Families, origins and identities* (pp. 79–96). Cambridge University Press. https://doi.org/10.1017/CBO9781139814737.016

Human Fertilisation and Embryology Authority. (2016, June 17). *Donor sibling link (DSL)*. https://www.hfea.gov.uk/donation/finding-out-about-your-donor/donor-sibling-link-dsl/

Human Fertilisation and Embryology Authority. (2023a). *Code of practice* (9th ed.). https://portal.hfea.gov.uk/media/yrkn55xa/2024-10-01-hfea-code-of-practice-v9-4.pdf

Human Fertilisation and Embryology Authority. (2023b). *Modernising fertility treatment*. https://www.hfea.gov.uk/about-us/modernising-the-regulation-of-fertility-treatment-and-research-involving-human-embryos/modernising-fertility-law/

Human Fertilisation and Embryology Authority. (2025). *Fertility treatment 2023: Trends and figures*. https://www.hfea.gov.uk/about-us/publications/research-and-data/fertility-treatment-2023-trends-and-figures/

Huxtable, R. (2017). Friends, foes, flatmates: On the relationship between law and bioethics. In J. Ives, M. Dunn, & A. Cribb (Eds.), *Empirical bioethics: Practical and theoretical perspectives* (pp. 84–102).

Iliadou, M. (2025a). Surrogacy in Europe: The findings of the ECtHR and the Law Commissions' reform proposals. In K. Horsey, Z. Mahmoud, & K. Wade (Eds.), *Future directions in surrogacy law* (pp. 191–211). Bristol University Press.

Iliadou, M. (2025b). Surrogacy: Reproductive rights enabling 'biological colonialism'. In E. Wicks & N. Papadopoulou (Eds.), *Research handbook on human rights law and health* (pp. 137–158). Edward Elgar Publishing. https://doi.org/10.4337/9781803928036.00015

Ilioi, E., Blake, L., Jadva, V., Roman, G., & Golombok, S. (2017). The role of age of disclosure of biological origins in the psychological wellbeing of adolescents conceived by reproductive donation: A longitudinal study from age 1 to age 14. *Journal of Child Psychology and Psychiatry*, *58*(3), 315–324. https://doi.org/10.1111/jcpp.12667

Imrie, S., & Golombok, S. (2018). Long-term outcomes of children conceived through egg donation and their parents. *Fertility and Sterility*, *110*(7), 1187–1193. https://doi.org/10.1016/j.fertnstert.2018.08.040

Imrie, S., Jadva, V., & Golombok, S. (2019). Psychological well-being of identity-release egg donation parents with infants. *Human Reproduction*, *34*(11), 2219–2227. https://doi.org/10.1093/humrep/dez201

Institute for Children's Futures. (2024). *Our research*. Manchester Metropolitan University. https://www.mmu.ac.uk/institute-for-childrens-futures/research

International Social Service–General Secretariat. (2021). *Verona principles for the protection of the rights of the child born through surrogacy*. https://iss-ssi.org/storage/2023/03/VeronaPrinciples_25February2021-1.pdf

International Social Service (ISS). (2023). *N° 267 – Children's voices in surrogacy law: An innovative UK research project aimed at putting children's views at the forefront*. https://iss-ssi.org/resourcesiss/n-267-childrens-voices-in-surrogacy-law-an-innovative-uk-research-project-aimed-at-putting-childrens-views-at-the-forefront/

Isard, H. (2025). Gestational labour as affective labour. *Studies in the Maternal*, *15*(1), 1–21. https://doi.org/10.16995/sim.23946

Ives, J., Damery, S., & Redwood, S. (2018). Standards of practice in empirical bioethics research. *BMC Medical Ethics*, *19*, Article 68. https://doi.org/10.1186/s12910-018-0304-3

Jackson, E. (2001). *Regulating reproduction: Law, technology and autonomy*. Hart.

Jackson, E. (2008). The Human Fertilisation and Embryology Bill 2007. *Expert Review of Obstetrics & Gynecology*, *3*(4), 429–431. https://doi.org/10.1586/17474108.3.4.429

Jackson, E., Millbank, J., Karpin, I., & Stuhmcke, A. (2017). Learning from cross-border reproduction. *Medical Law Review*, *25*(1), 23–46.

Jackson, E. (2016). UK law and international commercial surrogacy. *Journal of Medical Law and Ethics*, *4*(3), 197–214.

Jacobson, H. (2016). *Labor of love: Gestational surrogacy and the work of making babies*. Rutgers University Press. https://doi.org/10.36019/9780813569529

Jadva, V. (2021). Sibling relationships across families created through assisted reproduction. In A. Buchanan & A. Rotkirch (Eds.), *Brothers and sisters: Sibling relationships across the life course* (pp. 171–184). Palgrave Macmillan/Springer Nature. https://doi.org/10.1007/978-3-030-55985-4_10

Jadva, V., & Imrie, S. (2014a). Children of surrogate mothers: Psychological well-being, family relationships and experiences of surrogacy. *Human Reproduction*, *29*(1), 90–96. https://doi.org/10.1093/humrep/det410

Jadva, V., & Imrie, S. (2014b). The significance of relatedness for surrogates and their families. In T. Freeman, S. Graham, F. Ebtehaj, & M. Richards (Eds.), *Relatedness in assisted reproduction: Families, origins and identities* (pp. 162–177). Cambridge University Press.

Jadva, V., Imrie, S., & Golombok, S. (2015). Surrogate mothers 10 years on. *Human Reproduction*, *30*(2), 373–379. https://doi.org/10.1093/humrep/deu339

Jadva, V., Jones, C., Hall, P., Imrie, S., & Golombok, S. (2023). 'I know it's not normal but it's normal to me, and that's all that matters': Experiences of young adults conceived through assisted reproduction. *Human Reproduction*, *38*(5), 908–916. https://doi.org/10.1093/humrep/dead048

Jadva, V., Murray, C., Lycett, E., MacCallum, F., & Golombok, S. (2003). Surrogacy: The experiences of surrogate mothers. *Human Reproduction*, *18*(10), 2196–2204. https://doi.org/10.1093/humrep/deg397

Jadva, V., Prosser, H., & Gamble, N. (2018). Cross-border and domestic surrogacy in the UK context. *Human Fertility*, *24*(2), 93–104. https://doi.org/10.1080/14647273.2018.1540801

Jadva, V., Prosser, H., & Gamble, N. (2021). Cross-border and domestic surrogacy in the UK context: An exploration of practical and legal decision-making. *Human Fertility*, *24*(2), 93–104. https://doi.org/10.1080/14647273.2018.1540801

Jadva, V., Shaw, K., Hall, P., Ross, S., & Imrie, S. (2026). Surrogates 20 years on: Long-term psychological health, contact with surrogacy families, and thoughts and feelings about post-birth contact. *Human Reproduction, 41*(12), 239–245. https://doi.org/10.1093/humrep/deaf234

Jadva, V., Blake, L., Casey, P., & Golombok, S. (2012). Surrogacy families 10 years on: Relationship with the surrogate, decisions over disclosure and children's understanding of their surrogacy origins. *Human Reproduction, 27*(10), 3008–3014. https://doi.org/10.1093/humrep/des273

James, A. (1999). Researching children's social competence. In M. Woodhead, D. Faulkner, & K. Littleton (Eds.), *Making sense of social development* (pp. 232–250). Routledge.

James, A. (2001). Ethnography in the study of childhood. In P. Atkinson, A. Coffey, S. Delamont, J. Lofland, & L. Lofland (Eds.), *Handbook of ethnography* (pp. 246–257). Sage.

Jefford, S. (2025). *Response to the UN Special Rapporteur report.* https://sarahjefford.com/response-to-the-un-special-rapporteur/

Jones, M. (2009). *Legal capability.* Public Legal Education Network (Plenet). https://plenet.org.uk/what-is-public-legal-education/

Jones, C., Jadva, V., Zadeh, S., & Golombok, S. (2023). Single fathers' experiences of using egg donation and surrogacy. *Human Reproduction, 38*(10), 1981–1990. https://doi.org/10.1093/humrep/dead152

Jones, R., Pert, H., Diaz, C., & Westlake, D. (2026). *Young people meeting judges: What we learnt from a pilot with young people in care proceedings.* Nuffield Family Justice Observatory.

Just Futures Collaborative. (2025). *"Valorized, but not compensated": Reproductive labour and bodily autonomy in the criminalisation of surrogacy.* https://freight.cargo.site/m/B2578236107193730279491366082347/Valorize-but-not-Compensated_JFC_DIGITAL.pdf

Karlidag-Dennis, E., Maher, M., Paterson-Young, C., Cin, M., & Giroletti, T. (2025). Towards research with children: Assessing participatory methods in England and Wales. *Global Studies of Childhood, 15*(2). https://doi.org/10.1177/20436106251341215

Kellett, M., & Ding, S. (2004) 'Middle childhood' in Fraser, S., Lewis, V., Ding, S., Kellett, M. and Robinson, C. (Eds.). *Doing research with children and young people.* Sage, 161–175.

Kellett, M. (2010). Small shoes, big steps! empowering children as active researchers. *American Journal of Community Psychology, 46*(1), 195–203. https://doi.org/10.1007/s10464-010-9324-y

Kellett, M. (2011). Empowering children and young people as researchers. *Child Indicators Research, 4*(2), 205–219. https://doi.org/10.1007/s12187-010-9103-1

Kelly, F. (2014). Multiple-parent families under BC's new family law act. *UBC Law Review, 47*(2), 565–597.

Kilkelly, U., & Forde, L. (2020). *Children's rights and police questioning: A qualitative study of children's experiences of being interviewed by the Garda Síochána.* Policing Authority.

Kilkelly, U., Lundy, L., & Byrne, B. (Eds.). (2021). *Incorporating the UN convention on the rights of the child into national law.* Intersentia. https://doi.org/10.1017/9781839701764

Klotz, M. (2014). *(K)information: Gamete donation and kinship knowledge in Germany and Britain* (Vol. 32). Campus Verlag.

Kluger-Bell, K. (2012). *The pea that was me: An egg donation story*. CreateSpace.

Kneebone, E., Beilby, K., & Hammarberg, K. (2022). Experiences of surrogates and intended parents. *Reproductive BioMedicine Online*, *45*, 815–830.

Konrad, M. (2005). *Nameless relations*. Berghahn Books.

Križ, K., & Petersen, M. (Eds.). (2023). *Children and young people's participation in child protection*. Oxford University Press. https://doi.org/10.1093/oso/9780197622322.001.0001

Lamba, N., Jadva, V., Kadam, K., & Golombok, S. (2018). Psychological well-being and prenatal bonding of gestational surrogates. *Human Reproduction*, *33*(4), 646–653. https://doi.org/10.1093/humrep/dey048

Laurie, G. (2000). Protecting and promoting privacy in an uncertain world: Further defences of ignorance and the right not to know. *European Journal of Health Law*, *7*(2), 185–195.

Law Commission and Scottish Law Commission (The Law Commissions). (2019a). *Building families through surrogacy: A new law*. (Law Com Consultation Paper No. 244/Scottish Law Com Discussion Paper No. 167). https://webarchive.nationalarchives.gov.uk/ukgwa/20250109121307mp_/https://cloud-platform-e218f50a4812967ba1215eaecede923f.s3.amazonaws.com/uploads/sites/30/2019/06/Surrogacy-consultation-paper.pdf

Law Commission and Scottish Law Commission (The Law Commissions). (2019b). *Building families through surrogacy: A new law—Summary of consultation paper*. https://cdn.websitebuilder.service.justice.gov.uk/uploads/sites/54/2025/12/Surrogacy-summary.pdf

Law Commission and Scottish Law Commission (The Law Commissions). (2023). *Building families through surrogacy: A new law*. (Law Com No. 411/Scot Law Com No. 262). https://lawcom.gov.uk/project/surrogacy/

Lee, R. G., & Morgan, D. (2001). *Human fertilisation and embryology: Regulating the reproductive revolution*. Blackstone Press.

Lee, J. Y. (2023). Surrogacy: Beyond the commercial/altruistic distinction. *Journal of Medical Ethics*, *49*(3), 196–199. https://doi.org/10.1136/medethics-2021-108093

Leitch, R. (2008). Creatively researching children's narratives through images and drawings. In P. Thompson (Ed.), *Doing visual research with children and young people* (pp. 37–58). Routledge.

Levron, Y., Dviri, M., Segol, I., Yerushalmi, G. M., Hourvitz, A., Orvieto, R., Mazaki-Tovi, S., & Yinon, Y. (2014). The "immunologic theory" of preeclampsia revisited: A lesson from donor oocyte gestations. *American Journal of Obstetrics and Gynecology*, *211*(4), 383.e1–383.e5. https://doi.org/10.1016/j.ajog.2014.03.044

Lewis, J., & Cannell, F. (1986). The politics of motherhood in the 1980s. *Journal of Law & Society*, *13*(3), 321–342.

Lewis, S. (2017). Defending intimacy against what? *Signs*, *43*(1), 97–125. https://doi.org/10.1086/692518

Lewis, S. (2019). *Full surrogacy now: Feminism against family*. Verso.

Lima, D. (2024). Legal parenthood in surrogacy. *Journal of Social Welfare and Family Law*, *46*(2), 245–266. https://doi.org/10.1080/09649069.2024.2344935

Literat, I. (2013). A pencil for your thoughts": Participatory drawing as a visual research method with children and youth. *International Journal of Qualitative Methods*, *12*(1), 84–89.

Little, S., Raine, H., Choo, A., Joshi, R., Qarni, S. J., Sukri, A., Horton, G., & Pakravesh, S. (2023). "The power to SAY what I want to and it gets written down": Situating children's and adults' voices and silence in participatory research. *British Educational Research Journal*, *50*(2), 964–980. https://doi.org/10.1002/berj.3963

Lundy, L., McEvoy, L., & Byrne, B. (2011). Working with young children as co-researchers: An approach informed by the United Nations Convention on the Rights of the Child. *Early Education & Development*, *22*(5), 714–736. https://doi.org/10.1080/10409289.2011.596463

Lundy, L., Tobin, J., & Parkes, A. (2019). Article 12: The right to respect for the views of the child. In J. Tobin (Ed.), *The UN Convention on the Rights of the Child: A commentary* (pp. 397–434). Oxford University Press. https://doi.org/10.1093/law/9780198262657.003.0013

Lundy, L., Byrne, B., Lloyd, K., Templeton, M., Brando, N., Corr, M.-L., Heard, E., Holland, L., MacDonald, M., Marshall, G., McAlister, S., McNamee, C., Orr, K., Schubotz, D., Symington, E., Walsh, C., Hope, K., Singh, P., Neill, G., & Wright, L. H. V. (2021). Life under coronavirus: Children's views on their experiences of their human rights. *The International Journal of Children's Rights*, *29*(2), 261–285. https://doi.org/10.1163/15718182-29020001

Lundy, L. (2007). "Voice" is not enough: Conceptualising article 12 of the United Nations Convention on the rights of the child. *British Educational Research Journal*, *33*(6), 927–942.

Luo, Y. (2026). Navigating structural tensions: Australian surrogacy facilitators' understanding on children's rights in cross-border surrogacy. *Asian Bioethics Review*, *18*, 135–156. https://doi.org/10.1007/s41649-025-00364-2

Maas, J. B. M., de Kever, G. M. M., van den Boom, L., & Bolt, S. H. (2026). Donor-conceived adolescents accessing donor information in the Netherlands: Their needs, motivations, experiences and available support. *Human Fertility*, *29*(1), Article 2646883. https://doi.org/10.1080/14647273.2026.2646883

MacCallum, F., Golombok, S., & Brinsden, P. (2007). Parenting and child development in families with a child conceived through embryo donation. *Journal of Family Psychology*, *21*(2), 278–287. https://doi.org/10.1037/0893-3200.21.2.278

MacCallum, F., Lycett, E., Murray, C., Jadva, V., & Golombok, S. (2003). Surrogacy: The experience of commissioning couples. *Human Reproduction*, *18*(6), 1334–1342. https://doi.org/10.1093/humrep/deg253

Mackenzie, C., & Stoljar, N. (Eds.). (2000). *Relational autonomy: Feminist perspectives on autonomy, agency, and the social self*. Oxford University Press.

Mahmoud, Z., & Romanis, E. C. (2023). On gestation and motherhood. *Medical Law Review*, *31*(1), 109–140. https://doi.org/10.1093/medlaw/fwac030

Mahmoud, Z. (2023). *Surrogates across the Atlantic* [Doctoral dissertation]. University of Exeter.

Mahmoud, Z. (2024). Comparing surrogacy regulation in the UK and California. In H. Zagel (Ed.), *Reproduction policy in the twenty-first century* (pp. 167–182). Edward Elgar.

Mahmoud, Z. (2025a). Comparing surrogates' healthcare provision in the UK and California. In K. Horsey, Z. Mahmoud, & K. Wade (Eds.), *Future directions in surrogacy law* (pp. 167–190). Bristol University Press.

Mahmoud, Z. (2025b). Mandatory (m)othering. In R. Brione, A. Brown, & Z. Mahmoud (Eds.), *Reproduction, narratives of consent and invisible women* (pp. 211–239). Routledge.

Mahmoud, Z. (2026a). Surrogacy in England. In A. Kaur & M. E. Hickman (Eds.), *The Palgrave handbook on the sociology of reproduction in England*. Palgrave Macmillan.

Mahmoud, Z. (2026b). Surrogacy's sensationalised scandals. In G. Halden & Z. Mahmoud (Eds.), *Radical narratives of assisted reproduction: Perspectives from law, social sciences, and humanities*. Palgrave Macmillan.

Mandell, N. (1988). The least-adult role in studying children. *Journal of Contemporary Ethnography*, *16*(4), 433–467.

Marsh, R. (2025). Non-traditional families and the tenacity of motherhood: *Re C (Surrogacy: Consent)* and *Re Z (Surrogacy: Step-parent Adoption)*. *The Modern Law Review*, *88*(3), 598–619. https://doi.org/10.1111/1468-2230.12950

Martínez-López, J. A., & Munuera-Gómez, P. (2024). Surrogacy in the United States. *Reproductive BioMedicine Online*, *49*(4), Article 104302.

Mason, J., & Tipper, B. (2008). Being related: How children define and create kinship. *Childhood*, *15*(4), 441–460. https://doi.org/10.1177/0907568208097201

Mason, J. (2008). Tangible affinities and the real life fascination of kinship. *Sociology*, *42*(1), 29–45. https://doi.org/10.1177/0038038507084824

Maurel, O. (2026). *In search of my mother*. Spinifex Press.

Mayall, B. (Ed.). (1994). *Children's childhoods: Observed and experienced*. Falmer Press.

Mayall, B. (2002). *Towards a sociology for childhood*. Open University Press.

McAdams, D. P., & McLean, K. C. (2013). Narrative identity. *Current Directions in Psychological Science*, *22*(3), 233–238.

McCandless, J., & Sheldon, S. (2010a). The Human Fertilisation and Embryology Act (2008) and the tenacity of the sexual family form. *The Modern Law Review*, *73*(2), 175–207. https://doi.org/10.1111/j.1468-2230.2010.00790.x

McCandless, J., & Sheldon, S. (2010b). "No father required"? The welfare assessment in the Human Fertilisation and Embryology Act 2008. *Feminist Legal Studies*, *18*(2), 201–224.

McCandless, J. (2025). Regulating parenting through legal parenthood: The case of surrogacy. *Child and Family Law Quarterly*, 137–144.

McCoy, D. E., Haig, D., & Kotler, J. (2024). Egg donation and gestational surrogacy: Pregnancy is riskier with an unrelated embryo. *Early Human Development*, *196*, Article 106072. https://doi.org/10.1016/j.earlhumdev.2024.106072

McMellon, C., & Tisdall, E. K. M. (2020). Children and young people's participation rights: Looking backwards and moving forwards. *The International Journal of Children's Rights*, *28*(1), 157–182.

McWhinnie, A. (2001). Gamete donation and anonymity: Should offspring from donated gametes continue to be denied knowledge of their origins and antecedents? *Human Reproduction*, *16*(5), 807–817.

Merron, G. (2025). *Letter: Review of surrogacy: Government position*. Department of Health and Social Care.

Mills, C., Watkins, D., Magkafa, D., & George, A. M. (2026). Beyond yes or no: Navigating consent and assent in research with children and young people. *Research Ethics*. Advance online publication. https://doi.org/10.1177/17470161261437470

Ministry of Justice. (2026, June 25). *Family court statistics quarterly: January to March 2026*. https://www.gov.uk/government/collections/family-court-statistics-quarterly

Mohnke, M., Christmann, U., Roos, Y., & Thomale, C. (2022). Do metaphors make opinions? An empirical study on the effect of metaphorical framing on the opinion on surrogacy. *International Journal of Law, Policy and the Family*, *36*(1), Article ebab025. https://doi.org/10.1093/lawfam/ebab025

Montgomery, J. (1986). Constructing a family—After a surrogate birth. *The Modern Law Review*, *49*(5), 635–640.

Morgan, D. (1986). Who to be or not to be: The surrogacy story. *The Modern Law Review*, *49*(3), 358–368. https://doi.org/10.1111/j.1468-2230.1986.tb01693.x

Morgan, D. (2001). Focus group interviewing. In J. Gubrium & J. Holstein (Eds.), *Handbook of interview research* (pp. 141–160). Sage.

Morrow, V. (2001). Using qualitative methods to elicit young people's perspectives on their environments: Some ideas for community health initiatives. *Health Education Research*, *16*(3), 255–268.

Mulcahy, L. (2017). Eyes of the law: A visual turn in socio-legal studies? *Journal of Law and Society*, *44*(S1), S111–S128.

Mulligan, A. (2022). Anonymous gamete donation and Article 8 of the European Convention on Human Rights: The case for incompatibility. *Medical Law International*, *22*(2), 119–146. https://doi.org/10.1177/09685332221096210

Murray, C., & Golombok, S. (2003). To tell or not to tell: The decision-making process of egg donation parents. *Human Fertility*, *6*(2), 89–95. https://doi.org/10.1080/1464770312331369123

Nardi, F., Dragnic, L., & Pappier, G. (2025). Surrogacy under scrutiny: A conservative shift in legislative debates. *Sexual and Reproductive Health Matters Blog*. https://www.srhm.org/news/surrogacy-under-scrutiny-a-conservative-shift-in-legislative-debates/

National Health Service. (n.d.). *Vitamins, supplements and nutrition in pregnancy*. https://www.nhs.uk/pregnancy/keeping-well/vitamins-supplements-and-nutrition

National Institute for Health and Care Research. (2024). *Guidance on co-producing a research project*. https://www.learningforinvolvement.org.uk/content/resource/nihr-guidance-on-co-producing-a-research-project/. Accessed on January 23, 2026.

Nebeling Petersen, M. (2018). Becoming gay fathers through transnational commercial surrogacy. *Journal of Family Issues*, *39*(3), 693–719.

Nelson, J. L. (1992). Genetic narratives: Biology, stories, and the definition of the family. *Health Matrix*, *2*(1), 71–83.

NGA Law. (n.d.). *Surrogacy disputes in UK law*. https://www.ngalaw.co.uk/knowledge-centre/surrogacy-disputes-uk-law/

Nielsen, L. B. (2010). The need for multi-method approaches in empirical legal research. In P. Cane & H. M. Kritzer (Eds.), *The Oxford handbook of empirical legal research* (pp. 952–979). Oxford University Press. https://doi.org/10.1093/oxfordhb/9780199542475.013.0040

Nordic Model Now. (2019a). *The Law Commission's surrogacy consultation: How to bamboozle through a dangerous new law.* https://nordicmodelnow.org/2019/08/15/the-law-commissions-surrogacy-consultation-how-to-bamboozle-through-a-dangerous-new-law/

Nordic Model Now. (2019b). *Surrogacy consultation questions template.* https://nordicmodelnow.org/wp-content/uploads/2019/09/surrogacy-consultation-responses-pdf-2.pdf

Nordic Model Now. (2020, February 14). *Surrogacy: A human rights violation.* https://nordicmodelnow.org/2020/02/14/surrogacy-a-human-rights-violation/

Nordqvist, P., & Gilman, L. (2022). *Donors: Curious connections in donor conception.* Emerald Publishing Limited. https://doi.org/10.1108/9781800435643

Nordqvist, P., & Gilman, L. (2024). A sense of connectedness in reproductive donation: Contrasting policy with donor and donor kin lived experience. *Journal of Family Issues*, *45*(8), 1973–1996. https://doi.org/10.1177/0192513X231194285

Nordqvist, P., & Smart, C. (2014). *Relative strangers: Family life, genes and donor conception.* Palgrave Macmillan.

Nordqvist, P., Gilman, L., Redhead, C., Fox, M., Hudson, N., MacCallum, F., & Frith, L. (2025). Relational dynamite: Engagements with kinship at the interface of donor conception and DNA testing. *Social Science & Medicine*, *382*, Article 118354. https://doi.org/10.1016/j.socscimed.2025.118354

Nordqvist, P. (2014). Bringing kinship into being: Connectedness, donor conception and lesbian parenthood. *Sociology*, *48*(2), 268–283. https://doi.org/10.1177/0038038513477936

Nordqvist, P. (2017). Genetic thinking and everyday living: On family practices and family imaginaries. *The Sociological Review*, *65*(4), 865–881. https://doi.org/10.1177/0038026117711645

Nordqvist, P. (2019). Un/familiar connections: On the relevance of a sociology of personal life for exploring egg and sperm donation. *Sociology of Health & Illness*, *41*(4), 601–615. https://doi.org/10.1111/1467-9566.12862

Nordqvist, P. (2021). Telling reproductive stories: Social scripts, relationality and donor conception. *Sociology*, *55*(4), 677–695.

Nuffield Council on Bioethics. (2013). *Donor conception: Ethical aspects of information sharing.* https://cdn.nuffieldbioethics.org/wp-content/uploads/Donor_conception_report_2013.pdf

Nuffield Council on Bioethics. (2015). *Children and clinical research: Ethical issues.* https://cdn.nuffieldbioethics.org/wp-content/uploads/Children-and-clinical-research.pdf

Nuffield Council on Bioethics. (2023). *Surrogacy law in the UK: Ethical considerations.* [Briefing paper]. https://cdn.nuffieldbioethics.org/wp-content/uploads/Surrogacy-law-in-the-UK-ethical-considerations.pdf

Office for National Statistics. (2025). *Births in England and Wales: 2024 (refreshed populations).* https://www.ons.gov.uk/peoplepopulationandcommunity/birthsdeathsandmarriages/livebirths/bulletins/birthsummarytablesenglandandwales/2024refreshedpopulations

Ofsted. (2019). *Education inspection framework: Equality, diversity and inclusion statement.* Office for Standards in Education, Children's Services and Skills. https://assets.publishing.service.gov.uk/government/uploads/system/uploads/

attachment_data/file/821069/Education_inspection_framework_-_equality__diversity_and_inclusion_statement.pdf

O'Kane, C. (2000). The development of participatory techniques: Facilitating children's views about decisions which affect them. In P. Christensen & A. James (Eds.), *Research with children: Perspectives and practices* (pp. 136–159). Falmer Press.

Okin, S. M. (1990). A critique of pregnancy contracts: Comments on articles by Hill, Merrick, Shevory, and Woliver. *Politics and the Life Sciences, 8*(2), 205–210.

Olajoku, F. (2026, April 24). Why Nigeria needs urgent surrogacy regulation. *The Cable*. https://www.thecable.ng/why-nigeria-needs-urgent-surrogacy-regulation/

Oliver, K. (1989). Marxism and surrogacy. *Hypatia, 4*(3), 95–115. https://doi.org/10.1111/j.1527-2001.1989.tb00594.x

Olson, E. (2003). Narrative identity. In S. Stich & T. Warfield (Eds.), *The Blackwell guide to philosophy of the mind* (pp. 274–292). Blackwell.

Overall, C. (1987). *Ethics and human reproduction: A feminist analysis*. Routledge.

Padilla-Walker, L. M., & Memmott-Elison, M. K. (2020). Family and moral development. In L. A. Jensen (Ed.), *The Oxford handbook of moral development: An interdisciplinary perspective*. Oxford University Press.

Page, S. (2025). *UN Special Rapporteur calls for the "eradication" of all surrogacy*. Page Provan. https://pageprovan.com.au/un-special-rapporteur-calls-for-eradication-of-all-surrogacy/

Pande, A. (2014). *Wombs in labor: Transnational commercial surrogacy in India*. Columbia University Press.

Parker, A., & Tritter, J. (2006). Focus group method and methodology: Current practice and recent debate. *International Journal of Research and Method in Education, 29*(1), 23–37. https://doi.org/10.1080/01406720500537304

Parker, P. J. (1983). Motivation of surrogate mothers: Initial findings. *American Journal of Psychiatry, 140*(1), 117–118.

Parkes, A. (2013). *Children and international human rights law: The right of the child to be heard*. Routledge. https://doi.org/10.4324/9780203797808

Park-Morton, L. (2024a). Using (and refusing) adoption orders following surrogacy. *Child and Family Law Quarterly, 36*(3), 255–270.

Park-Morton, L. (2024b). The role of non-genetic parents in a surrogate-born child's identity: An argument for removal of the genetic link requirement. *Medical Law Review, 32*(1), 61–80. https://doi.org/10.1093/medlaw/fwad032

Park-Morton, L. (2025). The genetic link requirement: Reconsidering the arguments for double donation. In K. Horsey, Z. Mahmoud, & K. Wade (Eds.), *Future directions in surrogacy law: Law and policy reform in the UK and beyond* (pp. 99–121). Bristol University Press. https://doi.org/10.2307/jj.18323798.11

Park-Morton, L. (2026). The tension between competing statutory obligations in the granting of parental orders: A systematic review of the case law. *Common Law World Review*. https://doi.org/10.1177/14737795261434019

Parry, B. (2018). Surrogate labour: Exceptional for whom? *Economy and Society, 47*(2), 214–233. https://doi.org/10.1080/03085147.2018.1487180

Parsons, K. J., Halstead, F., Jones, L. M., & Harris-Smith, S. (2025). Crumbling cliffs and intergenerational cohesivity: A new climate praxis model for engaged community action on accelerated coastal change. *Geoscience Communication, 8*(3), 213–228. https://doi.org/10.5194/gc-8-213-2025

Parsons, S. (2018). Assent. In B. B. Frey (Ed.), *The SAGE encyclopedia of educational research, measurement, and evaluation* (Vol. 1, pp. 115–118). SAGE Publications.

Pateman, C. (1988). *The sexual contract*. Stanford University Press.

Paths to Parenthub. (n.d.). *Why telling matters: Talking to your child about donor conception*. [Webinar series]. https://pathstoparenthub.com/webinars/https://pathstoparenthub.com/donor-conception-webinars/

Pelegrino Toraño, L. A. (2025). The changes in the sources of filiation in Cuba with the implementation of the Family Code. *Actualidad Jurídica Iberoamericana*, *22*, 650–679. https://turia.uv.es/index.php/aji/en/article/view/33194

Pennings, G. (2025). The management of donor information, donor anonymity and family limits by international sperm banks. *Ethics, Medicine and Public Health*, *33*, Article 101153. https://doi.org/10.1016/j.jemep.2025.101153

Percy, A. M. P. (2020). *Report on understandings of the law and practice of surrogacy*. All-Party Parliamentary Group on Surrogacy.

Percy-Smith, B., Thomas, N. P., O'Kane, C., & Twum-Danso Imoh, A. (Eds.). (2023). *A handbook of children and young people's participation: Conversations for transformational change*. Routledge. https://doi.org/10.4324/9781003367758

Petersen, M. L. (2019). Finding the "appropriate distance" in egg donor kinship relations. *Lambda Nordica*, *24*(2–3). https://doi.org/10.34041/ln.v24.583

Pott, L., & White, A. (2025). From wilful neglect to progressive support: Surrogacy law and its human impact. In K. Horsey, Z. Mahmoud, & K. Wade (Eds.), *Future directions in surrogacy law* (pp. 25–50). Bristol University Press. https://doi.org/10.2307/jj.18323798.8

Powell, M. A., & Smith, A. B. (2009). Children's participation rights in research. *Childhood*, *16*(1), 124–142. https://doi.org/10.1177/0907568208101694

President of the Family Division. (2025, February 26). Writing to children – A toolkit for judges. *Courts and Tribunals Judiciary*. https://www.judiciary.uk/wp-content/uploads/2025/02/Writing-to-Children–A-Judges-Toolkit-V1.7-1.pdf

Priest, J. A. (1988). Assisted reproduction—Developments in England. *International and Comparative Law Quarterly*, *37*(3), 535–550. https://doi.org/10.1093/iclqaj/37.3.535

Prosser, H., & Gamble, N. (2016). Modern surrogacy practice and the need for reform. *Journal of Medical Law and Ethics*, *4*(3), 257–274.

Punch, S. (2006). Interviewing strategies with young people: The 'secret box', stimulus material and task-based activities. *Children & Society*, *16*(1), 45–56.

Purdy, L. M. (2018). Surrogate mothering: Exploitation or empowerment? In S. Brennan & R. Jaworski (Eds.), *Reproducing persons: Issues in feminist bioethics* (pp. 182–197). Cornell University Press.

Purves, L. (2026, April 27). Male surrogacy betrays our inability to say 'no'. *The Times*. https://www.thetimes.com/comment/columnists/article/male-surrogacy-betrays-mothers-rights-children-n05kklhsg

Quennerstedt, M., & Quennerstedt, A. (2014). Children's rights and physical education: An exploratory study. *European Physical Education Review*, *20*(2), 210–228.

Radin, M. J. (1987). Market-inalienability. *Harvard Law Review*, *100*(8), 1849–1937.

Radin, M. J. (1996). *Contested commodities*. Harvard University Press.

Ragoné, H. (1994). *Surrogate motherhood: Conception in the heart*. Westview Press.

Rap, S. (2019). *The participation of juvenile defendants in the youth court: A comparative study of juvenile justice procedures in Europe*. Routledge.

Ravitsky, V. (2012). Autonomous choice and the right to know one's genetic origins. *Hastings Center Report*, *44*(2), 36–43.

Reame, N. E., & Parker, P. J. (1990). Surrogate pregnancy: Clinical features of forty-four cases. *American Journal of Obstetrics and Gynecology*, *162*(5), 1220–1224.

Redman, S., Greenhalgh, T., Adedokun, L., Staniszewska, S., & Denegri, S. (2021). Co-production of knowledge: The future. *BMJ*, *372*, Article n434. https://doi.org/10.1136/bmj.n434

Reissman, C. K. (2000). Stigma and everyday practices: Childless women in South India. *Gender & Society*, *14*, 111–135.

Richards, M. (2016). A British history of collaborative reproduction and the rise of the genetic connection. In T. Freeman, S. Graham, F. Ebtehaj, & M. Richards (Eds.), *Relatedness in assisted reproduction: Families, origins and identities* (pp. 21–43). Cambridge University Press.

Robertson, J. A. (1983). Surrogate mothers: Not so novel after all. *Hastings Center Report*, *13*(3), 28–34.

Robinson, C. (2014). *Children, their voices and their experiences of school: What next?* Routledge.

Robinson, C. (2025). Ethical considerations of children's involvement in school-based research: Balancing children's provision, protection, and participation rights. *Research Ethics*, *21*(3), 480–502. https://doi.org/10.1177/17470161241272872

Robson, C., & McCartan, K. (2016a). *Real world research* (4th ed.). John Wiley & Sons.

Rogers, M., & Boyd, W. (2020). Meddling with Mosaic: Reflections and adaptations. *European Early Childhood Education Research Journal*, *28*(5), 724–739.

Rogers, A. G. (2005). Interviewing children using an interpretive poetics. In S. Greene & D. Hogan (Eds.), *Researching children's experience: Approaches and methods* (pp. 158–174). Sage Publications. https://doi.org/10.4135/9781849209823.n9

Rose, G. (2022). *Visual methodology: An introduction to researching with visual methods* (5th ed.). Sage.

Rothman, B. K. (1992). Reproductive technologies and surrogacy: A feminist perspective. *Creighton Law Review*, *25*(5), 1599–1607.

Saravanan, S. (2013). An ethnomethodological approach to examine exploitation in the context of commercial surrogacy in India. *Philosophy, Ethics, and Humanities in Medicine*, *8*, Article 10.

Satz, D. (2010). *Why some things should not be for sale: The moral limits of markets.* Oxford University Press.

Savin-Baden, M., & Major, C. H. (2013). *Qualitative research: The essential guide to theory and practice.* Routledge.

Scherpe, J. M., Fenton-Glynn, C., & Kaan, T. (Eds.). (2019). *Eastern and Western perspectives on surrogacy.* Intersentia. https://doi.org/10.1017/9781780688633

Schrama, W., Freeman, M., Taylor, N., & Bruning, M. (Eds.). (2021). *International handbook on child participation in family law.* Intersentia. https://doi.org/10.1017/9781839701726

Scotland National Records Office. (2025). *Vital events reference tables 2024.* https://www.nrscotland.gov.uk/publications/vital-events-reference-tables-2024/

Sevön, E., Rönkä, A., Malinen, K., & Tammelin, M. (2022). The daily negotiations of boundaries in Finnish families. In M. Järvinen & A. Vallgårda (Eds.), *Intimate relationships and social change: The Nordics in context* (pp. 145–164). Palgrave Macmillan.

Shanley, M. L. (1995). "Surrogate mothering" and women's freedom: A critique of contracts for human reproduction. In P. Boling (Ed.), *Expecting trouble: Surrogacy, fetal abuse and new reproductive technologies* (pp. 156–173). Westview Press.

Shaw, K., Imrie, S., Hall, P., & Jadva, V. (2024). "It's all settled on the right page": Surrogates' feelings and reflections of surrogacy two decades on. *Human Reproduction, 39*(12), 2734–2742. https://doi.org/10.1093/humrep/deae216

Sheldon, S. (2005). Fragmenting fatherhood: The regulation of reproductive technologies. *The Modern Law Review, 68*(4), 523–533. https://doi.org/10.1111/j.1468-2230.2005.00550.x

Shier, H. (2001). Pathways to participation: Openings, opportunities and obligations. A new model for enhancing children's participation in decision-making. *Children & Society, 15*(2), 107–117.

Sifris, R. (2024). Compensation in the context of surrogacy: A feminist perspective on the insistence on altruism. In B. Batagol, K. Seear, H. Askola, & J. Walwisch (Eds.), *The feminist legislation project: Rewriting laws for gender-based justice* (pp. 143–154). Routledge. https://doi.org/10.4324/9781003372462-16

Sills, E. S. (Ed.). (2016). *Handbook of gestational surrogacy: International clinical practice and policy issues.* Cambridge University Press.

Sinclair, R., & Franklin, A. (2000). *Young people's participation* (Quality Protects Research Briefing No. 3). Department of Health.

Sinclair, R. (2004). Participation in practice: Making it meaningful, effective and sustainable. *Children & Society, 18*(2), 106–118.

Slutsky, J., Jadva, V., Freeman, T., Persaud, S., Steele, M., Steele, H., Kramer, W., & Golombok, S. (2016). Integrating donor conception into identity development: Adolescents in fatherless families. *Fertility and Sterility, 106*(1), 202–208. https://doi.org/10.1016/j.fertnstert.2016.02.033

Smart, C., & Neale, B. (1999). *Family fragments?* Polity Press.

Smart, C. (2009). Family secrets: Law and understandings of openness in everyday relationships. *Journal of Social Policy, 38*(4), 551–567.

Smart, C. (2010). Law and the regulation of family secrets. *International Journal of Law, Policy and the Family, 24*(3), 397–413. https://doi.org/10.1093/lawfam/ebq007

Smart, C. (2011). Families, secrets and memories. *Sociology, 45*(4), 539–553.

Smietana, M. (2017). Affective de-commodifying, economic de-kinning: Surrogates' and gay fathers' narratives in U.S. surrogacy. *Sociological Research Online, 22*(2), 163–175.

Smith, L. (2010). Clashing symbols? Reconciling support for fathers and fatherless families after the Human Fertilisation and Embryology Act 2008. *Child and Family Law Quarterly*, 46–70.

Smith, N. (2016). Mapping out a future for the UK's law on surrogacy. *Journal of Medical Law and Ethics, 4*(3), 237–255.

Smithson, J. (2000). Using and analysing focus groups: Limitations and possibilities. *International Journal of Social Research Methodology, 3*(2), 103–117.

Söderström-Anttila, V., Wennerholm, U., Loft, A., Pinborg, A., Aittomäki, K., Romundstad, L. B., & Bergh, C. (2016). Surrogacy: Outcomes for surrogate mothers, children and the resulting families—A systematic review. *Human Reproduction Update, 22*(2), 260–276. https://doi.org/10.1093/humupd/dmv046

Speirs, J. M. (2012). Semen donors' curiosity about donor offspring and the barriers to their knowing. *Human Fertility*, *15*(2), 89–93. https://doi.org/10.3109/14647273.2012.658900

Spriggs, M. (2023). Clarifying consent and assent in medical and research settings. *British Medical Bulletin*, *145*(1). https://doi.org/10.1093/bmb/ldac038

Stoeckle, A. (2018). Rethinking reproductive labor through surrogates' invisible bodily care work. *Critical Sociology*, *44*(7–8), 1103–1116. https://doi.org/10.1177/0896920518766651

Stop Surrogacy Now UK. (2025a). *Law reform will not proceed!*. https://stopsurrogacynowuk.org/2025/05/08/law-reform-will-not-proceed/

Stop Surrogacy Now UK. (2025b). *Words from a surrogate mother (Parts 1–4)*. https://stopsurrogacynowuk.org/blog/

Strathern, M. (1999). *Property, substance and effect: Anthropological essays on persons and things*. Athlone Press.

Strathern, M. (2005). *Kinship, law and the unexpected: Relatives are always a surprise*. Cambridge University Press. https://doi.org/10.1017/CBO9780511614514

Struthers, A. E. C. (2016). Human rights: A topic too controversial for mainstream education? *Human Rights Law Review*, *16*(1), 131–162. https://doi.org/10.1093/hrlr/ngv040

Struthers, A. E. C. (2017). Teaching British values in our schools: But why not human rights values? *Social & Legal Studies*, *26*(1), 89–110. https://doi.org/10.1177/0964663916656752

Surrogacy Concern. (n.d.). *About*. https://surrogacyconcern.uk/

Surrogacy360. (2023). *Recommended principles and standards for engaging in international commercial surrogacy arrangements*. Center for Genetics and Society. https://surrogacy360.org/considering-surrogacy/principles-and-standards/

SurrogacyUK. (2025). *About us*. https://surrogacyuk.org/surrogacyuk/

Tanderup, M., Pande, A., Schmidt, L., Nielsen, B. B., Humaidan, P., & Kroløkke, C. (2023). Impact of the war in Ukraine and the COVID-19 pandemic on transnational surrogacy: A qualitative study of Danish infertile couples' experiences of being in "exile. *Reproductive BioMedicine Online Open Access*, *6*(3). https://doi.org/10.1016/j.rbmo.2023.06.013

Tanderup, M., Schmidt, L., Pande, A., Nielsen, B. B., Kroløkke, C., & Humaidan, P. (2025). Mapping the path to domestic surrogacy: Identifying key facilitators and barriers in the Netherlands. *PLoS One*, *20*(7), Article e0328469. https://doi.org/10.1371/journal.pone.0328469

The Economist. (2023, June 15). Why the baby business is booming. *The Economist*. https://www.economist.com/films/2023/09/21/whats-driving-the-baby-business-boom

Thomas, N. (2007). Towards a theory of children's participation. *The International Journal of Children's Rights*, *15*(2), 199–218.

Tinson, J. S. (2009). *Conducting research with children and adolescents: Design, methods and toolkit*. Goodfellow Publishers.

Tisdall, E. K. M. (2014). Children should be seen and heard? Children and young people's participation in the UK. In E. K. M. Tisdall, A. M. Gadda, & U. M. Butler (Eds.), *Children and young people's participation and its transformative potential* (pp. 168–188). Palgrave Macmillan. https://doi.org/10.1057/9781137316547_10

Tisdall, E. K. M. (2015). Children's rights and children's wellbeing: Equivalent policy concepts? *Journal of Social Policy*, *44*(4), 807–823.

Tisdall, E. K. M. (2017). Conceptualising children and young people's participation: Examining vulnerability, social accountability and co-production. *International Journal of Human Rights*, *21*(1), 59–75.

Tisdall, E. K. M. (2021). Meaningful, effective and sustainable? Challenges for children and young people's participation. In M. Bruselius-Jensen, I. Pitti, & E. K. M. Tisdall (Eds.), *Young people's participation: Revisiting youth and inequalities in Europe* (pp. 217–234). Policy Press.

Tranfield-Thomas, S. (2024, November 25). Film review: Joy. *Progress Educational Trust*. https://www.progress.org.uk/film-review-joy/

Trimmings, K., Shakargy, S., & Achmad, C. (Eds.). (2025). *Research handbook on surrogacy and the law*. Edward Elgar.

Triseliotis, J. (1973). *In search of origins: The experiences of adopted people*. Routledge and Kegan Paul.

Turkmendag, I. (2012). The donor-conceived child's 'right to personal identity': The public debate on donor anonymity in the United Kingdom. *Journal of Law and Society*, *39*(1), 58–75.

UK Government Education Hub. (2025, July 15). *New RSHE guidance: What parents need to know*. https://educationhub.blog.gov.uk/2025/07/new-rshe-guidance-what-parents-need-to-know/

UK Research and Innovation. (2025). *Co-production in research*. https://www.ukri.org/manage-your-award/good-research-resource-hub/research-co-production/

United Nations Special Rapporteur on the sale and sexual exploitation of children. (2019). *Sale and sexual exploitation of children, including child prostitution, child pornography and other child sexual abuse material (A/74/162)*. United Nations.

United Nations Special Rapporteur on violence against women and girls, its causes and consequences. (2025). *The different manifestations of violence against women and girls in the context of surrogacy (A/80/150)*. United Nations.

United Nations. (1989). *Convention on the rights of the child* (General Assembly Resolution 44/25). https://www.ohchr.org/en/instruments-mechanisms/instruments/convention-rights-child

Uprichard, E. (2008). Children as "being and becomings": Children, childhood and temporality. *Children & Society*, *22*(4), 303–313.

Uprichard, E. (2010). Questioning research with children: Discrepancy between theory and practice? *Children & Society*, *24*(1), 3–13.

Valc, J. (2025). Towards an international consensus on cross-border surrogacy: The role of the European Court of Human Rights? *Medical Law Review*, *33*(3), 1–18. https://doi.org/10.1093/medlaw/fwaf029

Van den Akker, O. (2003). Genetic and gestational surrogate mothers' experience of surrogacy. *Journal of Reproductive and Infant Psychology*, *21*(2), 145–161. https://doi.org/10.1080/0264683031000124091

Velleman, J. D. (2005). Family history. *Philosophical Papers*, *34*(3), 357–378.

Verrier, N. (1993). *The primal wound: Understanding the adopted child*. Gateway Press.

Vertommen, S., & Barbagallo, C. (2021). The in/visible wombs of the market: The dialectics of waged and unwaged reproductive labour in the global surrogacy industry. *Review of International Political Economy*, *29*(6), 1945–1966. https://doi.org/10.1080/09692290.2020.1866642

Vidalis, T., & Kriari, I. (Eds.). (2026). *Surrogacy today: A European legal overview*. Trivent Publishing.

Volkman, T. A. (2016). Seeking sisters: Twinship and kinship in an age of internet miracles and DNA technologies. In D. Marre & L. Briggs (Eds.), *International adoption: Global inequalities and the circulation of children* (pp. 276–297). NYU Press. https://doi.org/10.18574/nyu/9780814791011.003.0017

Wade, K., & Mills, C. (2025). Reforming surrogacy law: What can we learn from children's artwork? *Journal of Law and Society*, *52*(4), 677–704. https://doi.org/10.1111/jols.70028

Wade, K. (2020). Reconceptualising the interest in knowing one's origins: A case for mandatory disclosure. *Medical Law Review*, *28*(4), 731–752. https://doi.org/10.1093/medlaw/fwaa032

Wade, K. (2022). Hearing from children on surrogacy law: What are the important questions? *Surrogacy Awareness Week*. https://surrogacyweek.co.uk/2022/08/03/hearing-from-children-on-surrogacy-law-what-are-the-important-questions/

Wade, K. (2025). The creation of the surrogacy register: A new dawn for children's rights in relation to origin information? In K. Horsey, Z. Mahmoud, & K. Wade (Eds.), *Future directions in surrogacy law: Law and policy reform in the UK and beyond* (pp. 140–166). Bristol University Press. https://doi.org/10.2307/jj.18323798.13

Walker, R., & van Zyl, L. (2017a). *Towards a professional model for surrogate motherhood*. Palgrave Macmillan.

Walker, R., & van Zyl, L. (2017b). Towards a professional model for surrogate motherhood. *Bioethics*, *31*(8), 560–568. https://doi.org/10.1111/bioe.12378

Wallbank, J. (2004). The role of rights and utility in instituting a child's right to know her genetic history. *Social & Legal Studies*, *13*(2), 245–264. https://doi.org/10.1177/0964663904042553

Warnock, M. (1983). In vitro fertilization: The ethical issues. *The Philosophical Quarterly*, *33*(132), 238–249. https://doi.org/10.2307/2219223

Warnock, M. (1985). *A question of life: The Warnock Report on human fertilisation and embryology*. Basil Blackwell.

Warnock, M. (2016). Foreword: The need for full reform of the law on surrogacy. *Journal of Medical Law and Ethics*, *4*(3), 155–157.

Watkins, D., Law, E. L.-C., Barwick, J., & Kirk, E. (2018). Exploring children's understanding of law in their everyday lives. *Legal Studies*, *38*(1), 59–78. https://doi.org/10.1017/lst.2017.8

Watkins, D., Mills, C., & Wood, C. (2025). A framework for developing children's legal capability. *Legal Studies*, *45*(3), 432–445. https://doi.org/10.1017/lst.2025.10074

Watson-Smyth, K. (1997, November 2). Surrogate mother set for legal battle. *The Independent*. https://www.independent.co.uk/news/surrogate-mother-set-for-legal-battle-1291852.html

West Coast Surrogacy. (n.d.). *Surrogate mother compensation*. https://www.westcoastsurrogacy.com/for-surrogates/surrogate-mother-compensation

Westcott, H. L., & Littleton, K. S. (2005). Exploring meaning in interviews with children. In S. Greene & D. Hogan (Eds.), *Researching children's experience: Approaches and methods* (pp. 141–157). Sage Publications. https://doi.org/10.4135/9781849209823.n8

White, P. (2018). Commercialization, altruism, clinical practice: What explains similarities and differences in Californian and Canadian gestational surrogacy outcomes? *Women's Health Issues*, *28*(3), 239–250.

Wilkinson, S. (2016). Exploitation in international paid surrogacy arrangements. *Journal of Applied Philosophy*, *33*(2), 117–121. https://doi.org/10.1111/japp.12138

Wilson, D. (2011). Creating the 2ethics industry": Mary Warnock, in vitro fertilization and the history of bioethics in Britain. *BioSocieties*, *6*(2), 121–141. https://doi.org/10.1057/biosoc.2010.26

Women Deliver. (2025, September 16). *Surrogacy: A human rights-based approach* [Briefing]. https://womendeliver.org/wp-content/uploads/2025/09/A-Human-Rights-Based-Approach-to-Surrogacy.pdf

World Health Organization. (2018). *Engaging young people for health and sustainable development: Strategic opportunities for the World Health Organization and partners.* World Health Organization. [Online]. https://iris.who.int/handle/10665/274368. Accessed on April 22, 2026.

World Medical Association. (2024). Declaration of Helsinki: Ethical principles for medical research involving human participants. *Journal of the American Medical Association*, *333*(1), 71–74.

Wray, Z. (2025, July 3). *Voices of LGBTQ+ young people in family law matters.* Brodies LLP. https://brodies.com/insights/family-law/voices-of-lgbtq-young-people-in-family-law-matters

Yadav, V., Bakolia, P., Malhotra, N., Mahey, R., Singh, N., & Kriplani, A. (2018). Comparison of obstetric outcomes of pregnancies after donor-oocyte in vitro fertilization and self-oocyte in vitro fertilization: A retrospective cohort study. *Journal of Human Reproductive Sciences*, *11*(4), 370–375. https://doi.org/10.4103/jhrs.JHRS_115_17

Yee, S., Goodman, C. V., & Librach, C. L. (2019). Determinants of gestational surrogates' satisfaction in relation to the characteristics of surrogacy cases. *Reproductive BioMedicine Online*, *39*(2), 249–261.

Zadeh, S., Ilioi, E. C., Jadva, V., & Golombok, S. (2018). The perspectives of adolescents conceived using surrogacy, egg or sperm donation. *Human Reproduction*, *33*(6), 1099–1106. https://doi.org/10.1093/humrep/dey088

Zadeh, S. (2024). Direct-to-consumer DNA testing: The perspectives and experiences of donor conceived young adults in the UK. *Reproductive BioMedicine Online*, *49*(1), 103969. https://doi.org/10.1016/j.rbmo.2024.103969

Zelizer, V. A. (2011). *Economic lives: How culture shapes the economy.* Princeton University Press.

Cases

A & B v C & D [2026] EWHC 972 (Fam)

A (A Child) (Surrogacy: s 54 Criteria), Re [2020] EWHC 1426 (Fam)

A (A Child) [2015] *Re* EWHC 911 (Fam)

A (Parental Order: Domicile), Re [2013] EWHC 426 (Fam)

A and B (Children) (Surrogacy: Parental Orders: Time Limits), Re [2015] EWHC 911 (Fam)
A v B (No 1) [2015] EWHC 1059
A v P (Surrogacy: Parental Order: Death of Applicant) [2011] EWHC 1738 (Fam)
A v P [2011] EWHC 1738
A v X [2024] EWFC 304
A, B and C (UK surrogacy expenses), Re [2016] EWFC 33
AB (Foreign Surrogacy Children out of the Jurisdiction) [2019] EWFC 22
AB (Surrogacy: Consent), Re [2016] EWHC 2643 (Fam)
AB v CD [2019] EWHC 1695 (Fam)
AB v CT (Parental Order: Consent of Surrogate Mother) [2015] EWFC 12
AB v DE [2013] EWHC 2413
AB v XY [2023] CSOH 46
Adoption Application (Payment for Surrogacy), Re [1987] 2 FLR 291
AM v Norway, App no 30254/18
AY v ZX [2023] EWFC 39
B & C v D & H [2025] EWFC 366
B (Adoption: Surrogacy and Parental Responsibility) [2018] EWFC 86
B (Parentage), Re [1996] 2 FLR 15
B and C v D and H, Re [2025] EWFC 366
Briody v St Helen's and Knowsley Area Health Authority [2001] 2 FLR 1094
C (A Child) (Parental Order), Re [2013] EWHC 2408 (Fam)
C (A Minor) (Wardship: Surrogacy), Re [1985] FLR 846
C (Surrogacy: Consent), Re [2023] EWCA Civ 16
C (Surrogacy: Payments), Re [2002] EWHC 157 (Fam)
C v D [2025] EWFC 196
C v E [2025] EWFC 68
D and L (Surrogacy), Re [2012] EWHC 2631 (Fam)
D v ED (Parental Order: Time Limit) [2016] 2 FLR 530
F (Children) (Thai Surrogacy: Enduring Family Relationship), Re [2016] EWHC 1594 (Fam)
F (Paternity: Jurisdiction) Re [2007] EWCA Civ 873
G (Surrogacy: Foreign Domicile), Re [2007] EWHC 2814 (Fam)
G and M, Re [2014] EWHC 1561 (Fam)
Gillick v West Norfolk and Wisbech Area Health Authority [1986] AC 112
H (A Minor) (Blood Tests: Parental Rights) Re [1996] 3 FCR 201
H (Anonymous Surrogacy), Re [2025] EWHC 220 (Fam)
In re Baby M 537 A 2d 1227 (NJ 1988)
J v G [2013] EWHC 1432
JP v LP and Others (Surrogacy Arrangement: Wardship) [2014] EWHC 595 (Fam)
K v Z [2025] EWHC 927
L (A Minor) (Commercial Surrogacy), Re [2010] EWHC 3146 (Fam)
L (Adoption: securing legal parental relationship in surrogacy), Re [2021] EWFC 115
L (Re Adoption and Children Act 2002), Re [2021] EWFC 115
M v F & SM (Human Fertilisation and Embryology Act 2008) [2017] EWHC 2176 (Fam)
Mennesson v France App no 65192/11 (ECtHR, 26 June 2014)
Mother v Father [2024] EWFC 252.

MS v RS (Paternity) [2020] EWFC 30
MW (Adoption: Surrogacy), Re [1995] 2 FLR 759
N (Surrogacy: Enduring Family Relationship; Child's Home), Re [2019] EWFC 21
PQ v SSWP [2026] UKUT 1
Q (A Minor) (Parental Order), Re [1996] 1 FLR 369
QR (Parental Order: Dispensing with Consent: Proportionality), Re [2023] EWHC 3196 (Fam)
R & Anor v A (by her litigation friend, the Official Solicitor) & Anor [2024] EWFC 34
R (on the application of McConnell & Anor) v Registrar General for England and Wales [2020] EWCA Civ 559
R (on the application of Rose) v Secretary of State for Health & the HFEA [2002] EWHC 1593 (Admin)
R (Parental Responsibility) Re [2011] EWHC 1535 (Fam)
R and S v T (Surrogacy: Service, Consent and Payments) [2015] EWFC 22
S (Parental Order), Re [2009] EWHC 2977 (Fam)
S-H v Poland, App Nos 56,846/15 and 56,849/15
ST (A Child) (Surrogacy: Iran), Re [2018] EWHC 3439 (Fam)
T (Paternity: Ordering Blood Tests) Re [2001] 2 FLR 1190
W (Minors), Re (Surrogacy) [1991] 1 FLR 385.
W, Re [2013] EWHC 3570 (Fam)
Whittington Hospital NHS Trust v XX [2020] UKSC 14
WT, Re (A Child) [2014] EWHC 1303 (Fam)
X & Anor v B & Anor [2022] EWFC 129
X & Anor v Z & Anor [2023] EWFC 41
X (A Child) (Foreign Surrogacy), Re [2018] EWFC 15.
X (A Child) (Parental Order: Surrogacy arrangement), Re [2020] EWFC 39
X (A Child) (Parental Order: Time Limit) Re [2014] EWHC 3135 (Fam)
X and Y (Children), Re [2008] EWHC 3030 (Fam)
X v W [2025] EWFC 25
X v Z (Parental Order: Adult) [2022] EUFC 26
X v Z [2018] EWFC 86
X v Z [2025] EWFC 71
X, Re [2015] 1 FLR 349
XW (Parental Order: Death of an Applicant), Re [2024] EWHC 2082 (Fam)
XX v Whittington Hospital NHS Trust [2018] EWCA Civ 2832
Y and Others v V and Others [2022] EWFC 120
Z (A Child) (No 2), Re [2016] EWHC 1191 (Fam)
Z (Surrogacy: Step-parent Adoption), Re [2024] EWFC 20
Z (Unlawful Foreign Surrogacy: Adoption), Re [2025] EWHC 339 (Fam)

United Kingdom Primary and Secondary Legislation

Adoption Act 1976
Adults with Incapacity (Scotland) Act 2000
Births and Deaths Registration Act 1953
Children Act 1989
Children and Social Work Act 2017

Civil Partnerships Act 2004
Family Law Reform Act 1987
Human Fertilisation and Embryology (Parental Orders) Regulations 2010
Human Fertilisation and Embryology Act 1990
Human Fertilisation and Embryology Act 2008
Human Fertilisation and Embryology Act 2008 (Remedial) Order 2018
Human Fertilisation and Embryology Authority (Disclosure of Donor Information) Regulations 2004
Human Rights Act 1998
Mental Capacity Act 2005
Relationships Education, Relationships and Sex Education and Health Education (England) Regulations 2019
Rights of Children and Young Persons (Wales) Measure 2011
Surrogacy Arrangements Act 1985
United Nations Convention on the Rights of the Child (Incorporation) (Scotland) Act 2024

International Primary and Secondary Legislation

Assisted Reproductive Treatment Act, 2008 (Vic)
Children and Family Relationships Act 2015 (IE)

Treaties and Directives

Directive (EU) 2024/1712 of the European Parliament and of the Council of 13 June 2024 amending Directive 2011/36/EU on preventing and combating trafficking in human beings and protecting its victims [2024] OJ L1712.
UN Convention on the Rights of the Child (adopted 20 November 1989, entered into force 2 September 1990) 1577 UNTS 3.
Vienna Convention on the Law of Treaties (adopted 23 May 1969, entered into force 27 January 1980) 1155 UNTS 331.

Index

www.ingramcontent.com/pod-product-compliance
Lightning Source LLC
LaVergne TN
LVHW020829241026
850939LV00027B/377

* 9 7 8 1 8 3 5 4 9 6 4 5 9 *